WOMEN WITNESSING TERROR

ANNE CUBILIÉ

WOMEN WITNESSING
Terror

estimony and the
Cultural Politics
of Human Rights

FORDHAM UNIVERSITY PRESS

New York / 2005

Library of Congress Cataloging-in-Publication Data

Cubilié, Anne.
  Women witnessing terror : testimony and the cultural politics of human rights / Anne Cubilié.— 1st ed.
    p. cm.
  Includes bibliographical references and index.
    ISBN 0-8232-2434-1 (hardcover) — ISBN 0-8232-2435-X (pbk.)
    1. Reportage literature—Women authors—History and criticism. 2. Atrocities in literature. 3. Women and war. 4. State-sponsored terrorism. I. Title.
  PN3377.5.R45C83   2005
  303.48′5—dc22   2005006684

Printed in the United States of America
07 06 05   5 4 3 2 1
First edition

FOR MY FATHER
Jean-Jacques Alexandre Cubilié

CONTENTS

ACKNOWLEDGMENTS

I am grateful to the numerous colleagues, friends, and family who have provided me with encouragement, advice, criticism, and unending patience and support during the writing of this book. At Georgetown University I found a community of scholars and friends across the disciplines whose generosity in reading and commenting on various incarnations and drafts of this manuscript was immensely enriching. In particular, Lindsay Kaplan, Susanna Lee, Patricia O'Connor, Ricardo Ortiz, Jeffrey Peck, Henry Schwarz, Jim Slevin, Christine So, Alan Tansman, Matthew Tinkcom, Suzanna Walters, Kelley Wickham-Crowley, Steve Wurzler, and Alejandro Yarza all commented on and encouraged this project along the way. Michael Ragussis, Lalitha Gopalan, Mark McMorris, and Leona Fisher not only provided me with incisive critical commentary; their friendship and support have been crucial to the completion of this manuscript and to my own well-being over the years.

Georgetown University supported my work through numerous grants and course reductions as well as the leave that enabled me to spend a year in Pakistan and Afghanistan researching the book's final chapter. I also very much appreciate the enormously helpful editorial comments of Dominic Rainsford and Tim Woods, who published a version of chapter five in their edited collection, *Critical Ethics*. Ann Cvetkovich, Ann Pellegrini, and Janet Jakobson were equally careful and generous editors of a shortened version of chapter six, which appeared in their guest-edited "Public Sentiments" issue of the journal *The Scholarly Feminist*. In addition, I have benefited from a wide range of contacts with people outside the academy, and the encouragement I received from colleagues at the United Nations and throughout the nongovernmental organization community, who were always generous with their knowledge and always made time for discussion, added immeasurably to my understanding of the profound difficulties this book addresses. I would also like to thank my editor, Helen Tartar, for her strong support of this project.

Friends and colleagues who have added to my depth of understanding of the materials and concepts under consideration in this book are too numerous to mention. I would like to thank Itty Abraham, Abid Aslam, Rebecca Bach, David Bass, Clarissa Bencomo, Caroline Bernstein, Stephanie Bunker, Ezzedine Choukri-Fisher, Brenda Chrystie, Ann Cvetkovich, Judy Filc, Susan Garfinkle, Nathan Griffith, Yusef Hassan, Megan McLagan, Kerry Moore, Alene Moyer, Norah Niland, Tamara Paris, Vivian Patraka, Peggy Phelan, Susanna Price, and Amy Robinson, who have all provided me with invaluable encouragement, feedback, advice, and support from their various perspectives both from within and beyond the academy. Maria Reha, who undertook the challenging task of translating for me as we slogged through the mud of numerous internally displaced people's encampments, became a partner and friend as we worked together in ways neither of us had experienced before. I am much the richer for knowing her. I am also grateful to Peter Stallybrass for his friendship and support over the many years I have known him as a teacher, dissertation advisor, and friend.

I am particularly thankful for the love, friendship, critical engagement, and continuing presence in my life of Jennifer Brody, Joshua Dale, Lisa Freeman, Carl Good, Kim Hall, Sharon Holland, Nicole King, Chris Mills, Dominic Rainsford, and Paul Smith. In addition to my family of friends, I owe a debt to Marc Cubilié, Carol and Jacques Cubilié, Ro Kvarsten, and the rest of the Cubilié, Kvarsten, Boyer, Bara, and Largé clan for their guidance, support, and encouragement. Lynda Hart, Wes Kvarsten, and David Kadlec taught me a great deal about living a full life even through the time of one's death, and their memories are woven throughout the text of this book for me. Along with my father, Jacques Cubilié, Wes Kvarsten's fearless respect for life—while simultaneously challenging it—modeled for me how to live a life bravely and with love and trust. Lynda Hart taught me to embrace a life of the mind that was inseparable from all other aspects of my life, and her love and wisdom have greatly enriched me. My deepest thanks are reserved for Khaled Mansour, whose presence in my life made this endeavor all the more meaningful.

PREFACE

My project in this book arises, I have come to discover, from a set of concerns that revolve around silence: the silences of history and within families and the silences that mediate relations between individuals and states that shape and guide many of our cultural configurations. Arrayed against such silences are performative relationships of witness that challenge traditional structures of knowing, of power, of community, and of violence. Analysis of some of the ethical relations and engagements that such performative witness enacts is the overarching project of this book, as it addresses testimonials by survivors of war and human rights abuse. Placing various critical fields and analyses in dialogue with each other and with testimonial, the book attempts to open up new avenues for critical investigation of structures of violence, power, and identity as well as arguing for a much broader field of "testimonial" and a greater dialogue between critics, readers, witnesses, and citizens.

Much of critical studies is concerned with silences and silencing and their relation to structures of power, and the basis of much political organizing is directed toward or in the name of those who are silenced. The gap between critical theorists and practitioners and grassroots political organizers, however, seems as wide as ever, if not wider. Into this gap, I suggest, the voice of the survivor of human atrocity can intervene. Throughout the book, I seek to bring the voices of the silenced, the "everyday" survivors of mass atrocity who speak their experience into the silences of realpolitik, historical forgetting, and fear, into this gap between the theory and the practice of what I would call the politics of humanity.

As I will argue in the succeeding chapters, survivors of atrocity become deeply uncomfortable signifiers for the postatrocity societies within which they live, excessive to structures of normality that privilege forgetting, getting over and getting on with things through the denial of the terror of death, especially the possibility of mass death.[1] Survivors have come to be figured by us in the form of "ghosts" who haunt our cultural imaginary. Configured as the uncanny, visible only from the corner of one's eye or when one is not looking, and vested with a power and wisdom that have literally been brought back from the realm of the dead, they are valorized, memorialized, and heroized, but we cannot—will not—hear them. Such positioning strips survivors (once again) of their humanity, removing them from the quotidian realm of "us." Many survivors are quite articulate in their recognition that in order to "pass" for one of us, they must learn that we do not really want to hear their stories, what they have to say about their experiences of atrocity, or, at best, that we only want to hear "stock" stories, which are familiar and therefore already known.[2] From the testimony of the Holocaust survivor who does not understand why anybody would want to hear the stories of "ghosts" to the smug "politics" of *Ms.* magazine in referring to Afghan women in burqas as ghosts, we privilege voice and individuality in the face of death and repression, but only in the stories that we are prepared to hear, not necessarily the stories survivors would tell if we listened differently.[3]

To name a woman a "ghost" because we cannot see her face not only removes her (again) from the human but privileges her speech as that which comes from the realm of the dead or the uncanny. Survivors of atrocity come to function as ghosts, perhaps, through a similar sense that we do not see their faces. The faces we see are the same faces we might see on anybody, yet we know that they, too, speak from having survived "death." They do not show us their "true" faces. Again, speech is privileged, as we seek in their stories the key to their "impossible" survival. The gendered parallel that I have suggested here, between the "ghost" of the Afghan woman in her burqa and the ghostliness of the survivor is not accidental. The supposed connection of death to the feminine, of the feminine to "otherworldly" and extrarational knowledge, and of women to the borders of life and death has been widely acknowledged, excavated, and analyzed. This book, in primarily relying on the testimonies of women survivors, suggests that women, already familiar with the violences and pressures of difference, might bring to their testimonies a particularly acute concern with broad issues of ethics, justice, and the human that are themselves theoretically oriented interventions into the structures of power from which atrocities arise. I am not suggesting that there is a gendered hierarchy of suffering (although many acts of atrocity attack people through or because of their gender and sexuality) but that gender might be a lens through which we can interrogate some of our own formulations, and in doing so, perhaps, learn to listen to survivors differently, in ways that are more beneficial to us all.

The first chapter, the book's introduction, sets out some of the book's primary terms of consideration. It moves from a brief analysis of some current work on testimony and critical studies to a discussion of human rights as they are understood in the practical and theoretical arenas of international legal thought. The foundational document of current human rights practice and theory is the 1948 United Nations Universal Declaration of Human Rights (UDHR). Although much work, both legal and theoretical, has in many ways superseded the UDHR, it remains the foundational, visionary document shaping our global understandings of and arguments about human rights. My discussion of this document looks to a close reading of its articles and to some of the current critical discussions that surround it. I suggest a return to close consideration of its aims and ideals as the basis for a reconsideration of the ways survivors often understand themselves, in the most fundamental ways, to be humans who have the right to make basic ethical demands of the rest of us—for recognition, protection, and support.

Chapter two initiates an engagement between the juridical, the fictional, and the demands of performative witnessing by taking up an examination of two plays. Through analysis of Jean Genet's *The Balcony* and Marie Irene Fornes's *The Conduct of Life,* two plays that overtly consider the gendered relations of power and violence to the law, the state, and domesticity, I suggest that we pay more attention to the way identities are performatively enacted through structures of law and culture while also considering our own responsibilities as audiences and spectators. These plays, and the coercive structures of spectatorship that Genet and Fornes negotiate, bridge the difficulties of the juridical enactment of the universal human and the performance of difference that resists state violence within aesthetic, theatrical space. Survivor testimonial, which in prose and dramatic form must also negotiate aesthetics, often suggests the difficulties of witnessing from a position of difference—in regard to, for example, patriarchy, sexuality, ethnicity, language—but this is not its primary focus, which is witnessing. Genet and Fornes (who themselves have had to negotiate profound differences) stage such negotiations of difference and violence within theatrical confines—real bodies perform, but perform a "fictional" text.[4] The implications of resistance to and the maintenance of structures of power and domination within the texts of UN documents and such aesthetic productions help to set the terms of consideration for the testimony of atrocity, as both witnessed testimony and critical survivor intervention, that I consider in the remaining chapters.

The survivor texts I consider in this book employ various modes of intervention toward this end. Chapter three considers two texts by Holocaust survivors, a play by Charlotte Delbo and a memoir by Margarete Buber-Neumann, to parse out the ways Delbo and Neumann configure "the human" as an ethical category, employ generic forms to create gaps in the testimonial narrative where performative witnessing between the text/play and the reader/audience can occur, and examine the connections drawn by the authors between gender, resistance, and memory. Chapter four focuses on Alicia Partnoy's *The Little School* and Griselda Gambaro's play, *Information for Foreigners*, two texts from Argentina about torture, state violence, and the complicity of civil society in atrocity. This chapter reads these texts as testimonials that enact performative witnessing, while differentiating them from the rubric of *testimonio* as it has been developed by Latin-American studies. In the fifth chapter, testimony as a generic literary distinction is called into question even further through the readings of two prose texts about the war in former Yugoslavia. Slavenka Drakulič's *The Balkan Express* embodies the crisis of spectatorial guilt over performative witnessing, as Drakulič struggles throughout her text to mark an ethical position of witnessing that she herself cannot inhabit due to her inability to relinquish her role as "objective" journalist. Elma Softic's *Sarajevo Days, Sarajevo Nights,* conversely, is testimonial produced from within the atrocity event itself and highlights the differences that globalization and the infiltration of media into atrocity events makes to the witnessing project.

The final chapter of the book considers oral testimonials collected in northern Afghanistan in the fall of 2000. Highlighting the problems of translation that are inherent, yet secondary, within most written testimonial and studies of trauma, the chapter addresses the challenges facing efforts of intervention into both structures of power and human rights discourse through the use of testimonial materials. Throughout the book, I argue that these survivors make conscious ethical and critical interventions into the various fields of discourse within which their testimonies are imbricated through their demand for ethically engaged performative witnessing and the configuration of "human" as an ethical category.

For the literary testimonials under consideration here, the question of form becomes a vital element in considering the workings of the testimonial. I suggest in chapter four that one reason for differences of form between Holocaust and Argentinean testimonials may be the historical differences of the events themselves as survivors perceive them. Although the overwhelming nature of the "death events," which all involve extreme and ongoing pain, deprivation, violence, and death, can easily lead us to make sweeping comparisons based on a sense of shared, baseline, bodily and psychic experience, the testimonials themselves resist such comparisons, as does a consideration of the historical circumstances. While most Holocaust survivors were arrested, interned, and almost killed on no pretext other than that of state racism, Partnoy stresses the importance of political resistance in forming her community of friends and supporters both inside and outside the prison. And the events themselves do not "end" in the same ways. The death camps were abolished with the defeat of the Nazi government and the testimonials produced by survivors are written into a very different world—after the rise of a new government in Germany, massive movements of refugees and reshuffling of borders, and a growing public recognition of the atrocities. For many writers of Latin-American testimony, the government that tortured and abused them was still in power and the atrocities were ongoing at the time they wrote their testimonials. The question of how much such differences affect the form of testimonials is an open one but well worth bearing in mind if we hope to maintain complex distinctions that the authors themselves insist on in the face of the leveling effects of massive bodily atrocity.

Considering testimonials of atrocity as distinctive in particular ways from other forms of testimonial expression opens up new possibilities for reading survivor testimonials as critical texts that bridge theory and material experience. Testimonial of atrocity, which sometimes encompasses texts generally considered under the rubrics of, for example, slave narratives, *testimonio,* or Holocaust testimony, can also include oral interviews, therapeutic sessions, and other nonliterary witnessing forms.[5] As such, testimonial witnessing cuts across literary genres and disciplinary categories in its engagement with trauma as destabilizing narrative, memory, identity, and history, its performances of the fragmentation of identity effected by atrocity, its demand for a performative witnessing engagement with the survivor's interlocutor as witness, and its enactment of an ethical community of humans across difference, as those people who resist violence and their effacement from juridical and cultural fields.

WOMEN WITNESSING TERROR

1

Witness and Testimony:
Ethics, Trauma, Speech, and Paradox

Both critical studies and human rights discourse are grounded in post–World War II reactions to the massive atrocities of the first half of the twentieth century. The project of this chapter is to set up a productive engagement between these two discourses while insisting that both are missing an opportunity actually to engage with survivors of the atrocities themselves. Some of the most compelling philosophical engagements in this area are grounded in the idea of the impossibility of witnessing, but they do not, I contend, recognize the ethics that comes out of an actual engagement with the witnesses themselves. These apparently disjointed discourses, of ethics and of the United Nations Universal Declaration of Human Rights (UDHR), both of which have arisen in part from trying to think about and intervene in mass death, set up a contradictory hierarchy of sovereignty and universal humanity but are troubled by the ways that survivor testimonies and demands complicate tidy hierarchies and understandings.

In this book I seek to interrogate some of the various critical modes scholars have used to address questions of ethics, justice, responsibility, witnessing, and trauma in response to the testimonial expressions of survivors. Rather than challenging prevailing critical modes, I hope to bring some of the work of disparate critical communities together. While I have no wish to challenge the "narrow but deep" approach that is the hallmark of most academic inquiry, by bringing disparate fields and approaches together with the critical interventions that survivor testimony itself attempts, we can begin to open up new avenues for material as well as theoretical interventions into the ongoing violences whose ripples and fissures threaten our human communities. We badly need more inter- and transdisciplinary dialogue between academics and philosophers in various fields and between academics, legal theorists, and practitioners of human rights and humanitarianism. Throughout this book—which places testimonials by survivors in dialogue with various critical approaches and then, in its final two chapters, subjects the critical territories investigated in earlier chapters to the actual act of witnessing—I suggest that the building of human communities is an ongoing ethical and emotional struggle in which we all should be consciously participating.

Doing Justice to the Impossible

Giorgio Agamben, in *Remnants of Auschwitz,* delimits a "new ethics" whose threshold begins at the "specific ethical aporia of Auschwitz," a move that is similar to that made by many theorists, from Theodor Adorno to Jean François Lyotard.[1] I begin with Agamben as somebody whose work is increasingly taken up by scholars in several fields, from literary studies and philosophy to political science, and whose work embodies some of the most difficult challenges testimony poses to the philosophic consideration of atrocity. Beginning with a reading of the term "witness" and the meanings it takes on in the discourse of survivors such as Primo Levi, Agamben marks the Muselman (that inmate who was so starved and otherwise destroyed that he or she no longer exhibited basic elements of consciousness despite continuing a physical existence of some sort) as the physical marker of what he, in Levi's terms, calls a "grey zone" between the human and the nonhuman and between life and death. The importance of the Muselman for Agamben is his or her position as the impossible witness, the site of the lacuna of testimony that is that of witnessing for somebody who cannot bear witness for themselves. In noting that "not even the survivor can bear witness completely, can speak his own lacuna," Agamben follows the testimony of many survivors. Yet he goes beyond it when he writes that

> The language of testimony is a language that no longer signifies and that, in not signifying, advances into what is without language, to the point of taking on a different insignificance—that of the complete witness, that of he who by definition cannot bear witness. To bear witness . . . it is necessary that this senseless sound be, in turn, the voice of something or someone that, for entirely other reasons, cannot bear witness. It is thus necessary

that the impossibility of bearing witness, the "lacuna" that constitutes human language, collapses, giving way to a different impossibility to bearing witness—that which does not have language.[2]

This is an example of the sort of formulation at the heart of many theories of atrocity. It addresses itself to the limits of representation, but it does not allow for a witnessing that witnesses even from within language while in the midst of this impossibility. Testimony and the responsibilities of justice and ethics are not just about an impossibility; they are also about what we are willing to do as witnesses to the witnesses. This passage addresses the paradox at the heart of the testimony of atrocity, but as Agamben himself testifies through the act of writing his book in response to this call, testimony is more than the witness of this impossibility. Testimony is also, profoundly, a performative act between the mute witnesses (or the Muselman, in Agamben's terms), the dead, the survivor witness, and the witness to the survivor. This is more than a progressive giving language (testimony) to that which does not have language; it is a formulation of voice and identity within paradox. To become witness in this way to mass death and overwhelming atrocity is to acknowledge the formulation of voice from within this "grey zone" between human and nonhuman, life and death. Testimony, as I employ the term for the purposes of this book, is more than a "language that no longer signifies." It exists in a performative relationship of language and action, between the survivor-witness, the witness to the testimony, and what Jacques Derrida has called "the respect for those others who are no longer or for those others who are not yet *there*."[3] Agamben, in calling for a recognition of testimony's move from "the 'lacuna' that constitutes human language" to "that which does not have language" as the site of the impossibility of bearing witness, suggests an ethical move on our part, the witnesses to such testimony, to accept this "impossibility of bearing witness" as a site of absolute truth that cannot be challenged. His desire to find a site from which revisionists cannot challenge the event at least partially drives his formulations of testimony, but for the Muselman to be outside language so completely—marking the site of the border between life and death—risks completing the dehumanization the camps sought to enforce.

While writers such as Agamben and Edith Wyschogrod have used such testimonial to build analyses of, among other things, the radical break with individual death marked by Auschwitz, and its ramifications for contemporary philosophy and culture, they have not taken up the interventions into the cultural and political field that much testimonial itself seeks. Testimonial is more than a witnessing of the impossible witness and experience; it is also a profoundly political act that demands a performative engagement with the witnessing by the spectator witness and in this way and others works to intervene in the culturally violent reconfigurations that the experience of mass death founds and marks.

Agamben suggests that in discussions of the death camps, "one of the most common mistakes . . . is the tacit confusion of ethical categories and juridical categories," since almost all of these discussions use moral and religious judgments that are contaminated by the law—such as responsibility. Arguing that law is solely about judgment rather than justice or truth, he suggests that juridically contaminated categories might actually inhibit the project of his analysis: searching out the path to a witness to the Holocaust that cannot be denied or refuted. He finds this witness in the lacuna of testimony, as articulated by Levi as an impossibility of witnessing for the Muselman. "Insofar as it defines testimony solely through the *Muselman,* Levi's paradox contains the only possible refutation of every denial of the existence of the extermination camps," he writes in his conclusion. "If the witness bears witness for the *Muselman,* if he succeeds in bringing to speech an impossibility of speech—if the *Muselman* is thus constituted as the whole witness— then the denial of Auschwitz is refuted in its very foundation . . . [as these witnessings] articulate a possibility of speech solely through an impossibility and, in this way, mark the taking place of a language as the event of a subjectivity."[4]

But while Agamben seeks to remove ethics entirely from the overlap of the juridical, noting that the trials of perpetrators may have lead to the misperception that the Holocaust had been overcome, Lyotard opens his consideration with a term, *différend,* that operates within the realm of the juridical. Denoting a case of conflict where the absolute difference between the parties involved means that there can be no equitable resolution, where damages cannot be assessed and it is a case of wrong that cannot be resolved, Lyotard notes that "a universal rule of judgment between heterogeneous genres is lacking in general."[5] Are human rights excessive to the juridical category through which they find definition? If human rights are foundationally bound up with the violence of the law and with sovereignty, then perhaps it is the *différend* that survivor testimony repeatedly addresses. Derrida argues that "Law is the element of calculation, and it is just that there be law, but justice is incalculable, it requires us to calculate with the incalculable; and aporetic experiences are the experiences, as improbable as they are necessary, of justice, that is to say of moments in which the decision between just and unjust is never assured by a rule."[6]

Agamben argues that repetition, the trope Nietzsche evokes to formulate an ethics for the twentieth century as an overcoming of resentment, is no longer operative after Auschwitz. This is not because one cannot contemplate the possibility of the continual repetition of it, searching for difference, but because the event itself "has never ceased to take place; it is always already repeating itself." In evoking the sense of the event in such a way, he relies on Levi's recounting of dreamtime, in which the event of the death camp continues to infect his life in every way. As such, Agamben recalls work on trauma without referencing it, although trauma is itself defined at least partly through its relationship to repetition. His attempt to detail a new ethics arising from the witnessing of the death camps relies on an analysis of what he terms "Levi's paradox," the paradox of this impossible witnessing, which is exemplified by the figure of the Muselman.

The Muselman, not yet a ghost in Derrida's use of the term, marks the site of the abject, of boundaries from which physical and psychic life recoil in horror yet which necessarily structure and mark the boundaries of life.[7] This use of the Muselman and the figure's relationship to testimony continues Agamben's project of interrogating the relationships between power, sovereignty, states, and individual actors in the modern world. While his work is more concerned with the theoretical structures that can be built using concepts such as the Muselman to interrogate the conceptual paradigms of modern political power and less with the material conditions of and interventions into violence as it occurs today, his work is of great use in understanding the larger movements that structure violent events. Although the testimonies under consideration in this book do not directly address issues such as citizenship, sovereignty, the nation-state, and the uses of power that are of great concern to political philosophy, they do remind us that such concerns must always be at the forefront of our minds when we consider testimonials of atrocity and the ethical call to witnessing and responsibility that they enact.

While Agamben seeks to remove ethics from the realm of the juridical, Derrida notes the impossibility of removing ethics from the realm of law and of politics, which arises, he argues, in response to the singular demand of the other. Noting that "the act of justice must always concern singularity, individuals, irreplaceable groups and lives," Derrida goes on to state that "To address oneself to the other in the language of the other is . . . the condition of all possible justice, but apparently, in all rigor, it is not only impossible . . . but even excluded by justice as law (*droit*), inasmuch as justice as right seems to imply an element of universality."[8] The infinite ethical demand of deconstruction arises not just in response to the singular demand of the other and to the impossibility or incommensurability of justice, but even more in response to memory, to "those others who are no longer or . . . who are not yet there." If it is the "order of representation" that is so violently opposed to *différance* and has caused the deaths of millions, then it is also the order of the law that is so implicated. And the testimonials of the survivors of this violence both speak from within the logocentrism of this violent order and from *différance* itself, from the position of the infinite ethical demand for justice which is also the "responsibility toward memory . . . that regulates the justice and appropriateness of our behavior, of our theoretical, practical, ethico-political decisions."[9]

Although Derrida argues that "every juridical contract is founded on violence" and that, therefore, "an effective critique [of violence] must lay the blame on the body of *droit* itself," he does not claim that resistance, politics, or ethics can take place separately from and uncontaminated by the juridical.[10] Instead, he argues for a constantly monitored state of engagement with these impossibly balancing concepts and with what is excessive to them, the performative relationship of the infinite demand of justice to and for the dead of memory and those yet to come. He muses that before one can begin to think of and about "the final solution," one has to show a "readiness to welcome the law of the phantom, the spectral experience and the memory of the phantom, of that which is neither dead nor living, more than dead and more than living, only surviving, the law of the most commanding memory, even though it is the most effaced and the most effaceable, but for that very reason the most demanding."[11]

Like Agamben, Derrida and Lyotard are concerned with testimony and with the impossibility of justice as commensurate to the violence of the law, but despite their differences, neither seeks to ground an ethics outside the juridical, when it is the juridical within which testimony itself is produced (along with, perhaps, the individual and most definitely with the human). Derrida, through the linked concepts of *différance* and of what he terms *la démocratie à venir* (democracy to come), suggests a form of politics that would occur outside the nation-state model and would have the character of an ethical demand. As Simon Critchley states it, "The experience of justice as the maintaining-now (*le maintenant*) of the relation to an absolute singularity *is* the *à venir* of democracy."[12] He goes on to argue that "It is therefore a matter of thinking the ethical imperative of *la démocratie à venir* together with a form or forms of democratic action that move outside, beyond and against the state, as the *national* form of democratic government or indeed against any restriction of democracy to territory."[13] As an attempt to engage an ethics and politics beyond the nation-state and sovereignty, this is a much more material and immediate intervention than Agamben's concept of "whatever being," and one that resonates much more directly with the ethical demand of testimony. Throughout his work, Derrida is concerned with the performative—of ethics, of justice, of *différance*, of democracy to come—of the address to the other, and with the materiality as well as the philosophy of the address.

Anne Caldwell, in a thoughtful analysis, has provided a provocative account of human rights and humanitarian aid organizations' close ties to certain structures of violence and power in part by developing Agamben's work on the concepts of sovereignty and *Homo sacer*.[14] The term *Homo sacer*, as Agamben develops it, refers to a liminal figure marking the boundary between the categories of natural life and political life, of which the Muselman serves as exemplar. The *Homo sacer*, then, is foundationally linked to the emergent form of biosovereignty that Agamben interrogates. Caldwell's article meticulously traces Agamben's important contribution in situating sovereignty as outside the paradigms of traditional liberalism, and its resulting relationship to the category of "humanity" as it has emerged in the twentieth century. She notes:

> bio-sovereignty, structured by the exception rather than the law, is of a different order than liberal power. It is grounded not in a life or set of rights outside of itself, which it is compelled to respect and protect, but in the incorporation of life within its field of power. . . . The rights of humanity are as contingent as the rights the people of the nation-state were once ascribed. Human life, like the life of the nation-state citizen, "is kept safe and protected only to the degree to which it submits itself to the sovereign's (or the law's) right of life and death."[15]

Arguing that the power of such sovereignty, which exceeds the boundaries of the nation-state to encompass humanity, is visible in the increasing number of military interventions that resemble police actions more than traditional wars, Caldwell notes the complicity of humanitarian intervention with biosovereignty. She writes that "human rights . . . is the discourse of life in a state of permanent crisis. Moreover, human rights and sovereignty share the same referent: an indeterminate and precarious bare life. . . . Humanitarianism, speaking for the very life sovereignty grounds itself in, provides the justification for the "exceptional" measures of sovereign powers." Leaving aside the question of whether human rights are fully defined by "the discourse of life in a state of permanent crisis," of which I am not wholly convinced, Caldwell's parsing of the mutually enhancing connection between human rights and emergent biosovereignty is very compelling. Caldwell, following Agamben, provides an important explanation of the current, often confusing, relations of power to sovereignty, nation-states, and individuals, but she does not go far enough in offering possible avenues by which such categories and their attendant violences can be resisted. Such work, however, provides us with a generative formula for considering the larger structural issues that impede the prevention of and intervention in atrocity and inequity that documents such as the UDHR seek to enact.

As the women's testimonies under consideration in this book suggest, survivors themselves can provide important interventions into these current debates through their insistence on the importance of maintaining categories both of humanity and of difference—on a value that is always locatable within human relations of recognition of the other, of ethical relations, yet is always also impermanent, mobile, and contingent. By employing the Muselman as the ground through which the emergence of biosovereignty and *Homo sacer* become apparent, Agamben reproduces the Muselman as her- or himself nothing more than *Homo sacer*. Andrew Norris notes that Agamben follows Jean-Luc Nancy "in attempting to 'think' community without unity,"[16] a process Caldwell traces as Agamben's development of "whatever being," which is "a-metaphysical" and operates completely outside the traditions of sovereignty, as it "lacks the features permitting the sovereign capture and regulation of life in our tradition."[17] Unfortunately, compelling as such a theoretical concept is, it seems completely unworkable when asked to address the very material issues of violence that both humanitarian aid and survivor discourse seek to address. While neither this book nor the survivor testimonies it considers offer a concrete solution to such dilemmas, I do suggest that survivors themselves (*Homo sacer*, in Agamben's terms) provide theoretical interventions that help to structure frameworks for community that help to resist such violence.

The "complete witness," as Agamben terms the Muselman, need not be a person. He states that the "something or someone" who makes this "senseless sound" must have been rendered unable to bear witness for reasons other than the dehumanizing co-optation of their witness that Agamben's formulation of testimony implies. The figure of the Muselman exists largely, if not entirely, through survivor accounts, and I am skeptical of a theoretical strategy that is so utilitarian in its use of a figure that represents the abject horror of a form of living death. Part of my difficulty with Agamben's admirable attempt to formulate an ethic of testimony based on an impossible witness is that it does not sufficiently consider the role of the aesthetic response to this witness. Survivors themselves have created and maintained the person we term the Muselman through their numerous testimonies. An ethic of witnessing, if we can call it such in response to the testimonial demand, begins from the survivors' recognition of the impossibility of their own testimony even while performing it. It is both a speaking for the dead and from the lacuna—their own as well, since as survivors they cannot claim to speak from within the event—and a necessarily aestheticized project to make themselves understood by whatever audience is witnessing their testimony.

Derrida, in an essay that among other things addresses the problem of reconciling justice with law, writes:

> one cannot think the uniqueness of an event like the final solution . . . within its *own* system. One must try to think it beginning with its other . . . starting from what it tried to exclude and to destroy, to exterminate radically. . . . One must try to think it starting from the possibility of singularity, the singularity of the signature and of the name, because what the order of representation tried to exterminate was not only human lives by the millions, natural lives, but also a demand for justice; and also names: and first of all the possibility of giving, inscribing, calling and recalling the name.[18]

The witness to the mythic violence to which Derrida refers, which attempts the elimination of *différance*, speaks from an always already compromised position—as a survivor of the "unsurvivable," within logocentrism, without understanding of the mechanisms of her or his survival. Such witnessing, which must always attempt to speak from within the "lacuna" or "aporias" of language, despite its failure to do so, bridges these impossibilities through the performative enactment of testimony.

Trauma, Aesthetics, and the Witness

As Dori Laub, a Holocaust survivor and psychoanalyst, continually stresses in his work on testimony, the witness cannot be alone in the testimonial act.[19] Laub, in fact, writes of the clinical therapeutic process of witnessing such testimony in terms of a "password" that must be acknowledged by the therapist before "the hidden voice [can] emerge and be released," that he must "make [him]self known [to the patient] as one who knows."[20] This hidden voice is akin to the impossible language of which Agamben writes, and akin to the silence that structures the testimony of so many survivors. And the "reciprocal identification" that must occur before the patient can "really speak" is the recognition of speaking the language of this impossible witnessing. Laub writes that he must "hear it first, acknowledge that I spoke its language, identify myself to it, acknowledge both to myself and to my patient, who I really was" before the patient can "really speak." Trauma, as a term that describes a psychic state of memory/experience not easily accessible to the conscious mind of daily-life memory and narrative, is a conceptual tool that works to bridge this logocentric/performative divide through its definition by physical symptoms (material acts) and disruption of narrative memory and speech. Thus the acknowledgment of trauma, of sharing "the knowledge of what facing it and living in its shadow are really all about" is integral to the therapeutic work with the trauma survivor about which Laub writes.

Written testimonials by survivors require a similar move on the part of the reader—a willingness to engage openly with the witness's text and to acknowledge the aporias of the text as sites of witnessing that are bounded by but not articulated within language. They are not a one-way discourse, open to critical analysis but requiring no "reciprocal identification" on the part of the reader. While readers of texts are very diverse (one of the strengths of the dissemination of written expression), and many readers could choose to ignore this engagement, for those that do attempt an openness to such textual aporias, the traumatic markers of the text are the ground for a witnessing dynamic between reader and text—and, as such, between author, text, and reader.

However, written testimonial, especially in the forms under consideration in this book or that by authors like Primo Levi and Elie Wiesel, which is particularly literary, must also be considered aesthetic as well as documentary production. The aesthetic forms engaged by the survivors in their written works are integral to the testimonial as it is produced.[21] For an author with a stated project such as Agamben's to ignore as he does the literary elements of Levi's testimony in furtherance of his own critical agenda is to ignore a crucial element of witnessing and testimony: that of the performative enactment, through the text, of a witnessing dynamic with the reader. The testimonials under consideration in the following chapters exemplify specific methods by which some survivors configure experience, community, resistance, ethics, gender, and sexuality following their experience of mass death and atrocity. Our ethical engagement as witnesses to this survivor witnessing is a crucial element of the forms that state violence takes in relation to human rights discourse, and these survivors all testify to the importance of an engaged, ethical witnessing of atrocity that opposes the disengaged, guilt-ridden viewing of atrocity-as-spectacle that many forms of spectatorship take.

In discussing the ways in which extreme atrocity constructs forms of witnessing through the necessary negotiation of the "unknowability" inherent in such experiences, Laub writes:

> as a site which marks, and is marked, by a massive trauma I would suggest, then that the figure of "the concentration" is . . . a black hole. Concentrating at once life and death, the black hole in effect collapses, in this way, both the gaping hole of the genocide and the gaping hole of silence. The impossibility of speaking and, in fact of listening, otherwise than through this silence, otherwise than through this black hole both of knowledge and of words, corresponds to the impossibility of remembering and of forgetting, otherwise than through the genocide, otherwise than through this "hole of memory."[22]

Laub, who later goes on to argue that the Holocaust was an event that could produce no witnesses from within the event itself, writes these words in the context of an analysis of the ways that "the silenced memory of genocide" can be a structuring force in generational relations that, through the unrecognized memory of trauma, can lead to "an uncanny repetition of events that duplicate . . . the traumatic past."[23] One can, however, read these formulations more broadly to

11

suggest movements between silence, witnessing, trauma, memory, and repetition that not only perform testimonial but are crucial to the survivor call for an ethical witnessing that can open up the possibility of justice and perhaps of generational reconciliation.[24]

In Laub's often-referenced example of the woman who testifies that she witnessed four crematoria chimneys dynamited by the underground at Auschwitz, rather than the historically factual single chimney that was destroyed, Laub reads the woman as testifying "to the very secret of survival and of resistance to extermination."[25] Writing that one must hear the silences that bound her speech as well as the speaking itself to understand the most crucial element of her testimony, Laub illustrates that her resistance is intimately bound up with the processes of memory. She remembers four chimneys blowing up, and she remembers the people she helped by giving them items stolen from her job, although she does not remember that her assignment within Auschwitz was to remove the belongings of the people who had been murdered in the gas chambers. Laub argues that this silence that bounds her memories of her "job" is integral to our understanding of her testimony, which he reads as "breaking the frame" of the atrocity event itself through its witnessing of resistance, survival, and "the breakage of the frame of death" that her testimony reenacts. Trauma, that which is outside the frame, offstage, structures not just her memory and witness and our understanding of it but also our ethical relationship to her as survivor and to the witness she bears.[26]

Gender and Shame

That the survivor Laub discusses is a woman is not entirely coincidental to this formulation of witnessing and testimony. Gender norms do influence people's behaviors and memories, and while the death camps have often been discussed (largely by male scholars) as a gender-neutral site of universal devastation, scholars such as Joan Ringleheim, among others, have noted that it is scholarship itself that has tended toward this leveling of differences within testimony, and that women faced not only specific gender-targeted threats and attacks but also often emphasize different events (such as mutual support) as important within their memories. The women's testimonies I consider in this book locate difference as a site of resistance, witnessing, and identity while still claiming a form of universal humanity.

As Martha Minow observes in the context of South Africa's Truth and Reconciliation Commission (TRC) testimony, "There may be a systematic bias in who is willing to testify, who thinks his or her suffering is worthy, who is willing to come forward as a victim, and who is willing to accept responsibility as a perpetrator."[27] Noting that the number of women coming forward to testify was disproportionately large and that they tended not to speak of themselves but of "men who were brutalized, killed, made to disappear," the TRC created hearings specifically focused on women's issues, where women reported abuses that had happened to them that they had not included in their written statements. Minow attributes this to various cultural factors, especially shame and the women's sense that their own suffering is not as important as that of other people, especially men.[28]

John Keane, in *Reflections on Violence,* argues that shame compels actions through a sense of responsibility, while guilt focuses on the individual and does not necessarily compel action in any way.[29] The women whose testimonials are under consideration here make a dual move—emphasizing both responsibility (the juridical realm, as Agamben and Lyotard argue) and shame, which is connected with the imperative to witness.[30] Complicating this are the different reactions that survivors and their various witnesses may have to feelings and expressions of shame based on their gender, social positioning, and relationship to difference. Ullaliina Lehtinen, writing of the relationship of gender to shame, notes that shame is closely related to one's social position in relation to privilege or subordination.[31] She also notes that "women and other socially subordinate groups are more shame-prone than men (or otherwise socially privileged people)." Might shame, then, play a role in the strong configurations of witnessing and its ties to the enactment of "ethical human behavior" in the women's testimonials under consideration in this book? Shame, cultural norms related to women's gender roles, and the sexualized nature of violence and atrocity often, for example, lead women to silence themselves when testifying to sexual abuse such as rape.

Lehtinen's work suggests that shame might play a more complicated role for these women survivors than is suggested by Keane. She writes that shame, for the more privileged individual, can "form an occasion for moral reaffirmation . . . [and] mark a recommitment to principles," but for the socially subordinate individual, feelings of shame "often breed a stagnant self-obsession; they are unconstructive and self destructive; and they function as confirmations of what the agent knew all along—that she or he was a person of lesser worth." Thus she argues that women, "by force of their experiences of subordination," can have a much more conflicted relationship to shame and shaming. Speaking of women in an audience viewing a picture of a woman being violently publicly shamed, Lehtinen argues that "The women in the audience could . . . empathically recognize and understand—that is, know—that what happened to this particular woman could, in principle, happen to any woman, anytime, anywhere." She suggests, therefore, that the sight of the woman being shamed recalls for these women in the audience an empathic response in relation to their own personal safety. Because they experience themselves as subordinate and experience shame in a more fraught, unsafe, and sometimes self-destructive way, they link their own well-being and safety with the well-being of the woman in the photograph. Whether this can compel them toward action (intervention) and the building of witnessing relationships would depend on more than the presentation of the testimony (here, photograph) of the event; it also depends on their own subjective positions in relation to difference, perceptions of safety, and possibilities for action, and the negotiation of this is an element crucial to the testimonial attempt to build a performative witnessing relationship.

I want to suggest that we consider these complexities of audience subjectivity when exploring the ways that testimony might work to build ethical relationships between survivor and audience. Performance, that space of "the real" that is not mimesis—the lacuna of sight, narrative, testimony, action—is also the dynamic of witnessing, of the impossible position of speaking the unspeakable in a dynamic relationship with an other.[32] The performance of shame and its relationship to trauma as well as public expressions of community play a destabilizing role in the relationship of the survivor to her experience, her memory and telling of the experience, and her audience's engagement with the testimony. Shame and its connection to gender and other differences help to make testimonial witnessing of atrocity a zone that is unstable and unsafe but from which these witnesses seek to build forms of ethics that can negotiate such issues while also acknowledging difference.

More than "repetition with a difference," performance, closely tied to trauma, also seeks this "witnessing" from the impossible lacuna. And while both trauma and performance are bound up with and defined by repetition in certain important ways, they are also not limited to the play between repetition and mimesis. Cathy Caruth writes that "traumatic experience, beyond the psychological dimension of suffering it involves, suggests a certain paradox: that the most direct seeing of a violent event may occur as an absolute inability to know it." Using Freud's study of the father's dream of the burning child as an example, Caruth argues that traumatic repetition and nightmares are symptomatic of the way in which the very identity of the traumatized subject "is bound up with, or founded in, the death that he survives [and that] the shock of traumatic sight reveals at the heart of human subjectivity not so much an epistemological, but rather what can be defined as an *ethical* relation to the real."[33] And as Dori Laub notes, speaking of his therapeutic work with Holocaust survivors, trauma is more than "the return of the repressed" related to Freud's delineation of hysterical symptoms. While trauma involves elements of repetition and return that can be very dangerous to the consciousness involved, which Laub cautions could be marked by the number of suicides by prominent witnesses, he notes a dual movement both of the actual return of the trauma and its inadvertent repetition. As Laub states, speaking of generational trauma (that which is passed on from survivors to children), "through its uncanny reoccurrence, the trauma of the second holocaust bears witness not just to a history that has not ended, but, specifically, to the historical occurrence of an event that, in effect, *does not end*."[34]

What are we to do, then, with this traumatic experience that "does not end" in its material as well as psychic repetitions across generations? Minow cautions against too great a reliance on discourses of trauma, stating that "when it comes to the goal of national healing, it is simply unclear whether theories and evidence of individual recovery from violence have much bearing. The language of healing casts the consequences of collective violence in terms of trauma; the paradigm is health, rather than justice."[35] However, she also acknowledges that "Living after genocide, mass atrocity, totalitarian terror, . . . makes remembering and forgetting not just about dealing with the past. The treatment of the past through remembering and forgetting crucially shapes the present and future for individuals and entire societies."[36]

Testimony of atrocity negotiates these crucial questions of individual trauma and healing versus national (cultural) healing, ethics and epistemology, performance and mimesis, the juridical and the personal through some survivors' insistence on the space of difference (and perhaps *différance*) as the space from which both the ethical and the individual demands for justice emanate. Witnessing, from this position, becomes an ongoing process rather than a narrative and demands from us, the audience to the witnessing, an equally ongoing, often failing, fraught witnessing to the witnessing. These witness survivors figure the human as an ethical category that maintains difference while laying claim to the universal, and as such, they give us a new critical and theoretical language for negotiating these various concerns of legal, theoretical, and aesthetic thought.

Body of Atrocity: Body of Humanity

Elaine Scarry, in her groundbreaking *The Body in Pain,* undertook an ambitious project to intervene broadly, through critical analysis, into one of the most pervasive, hidden, and destructive forms of state violence—that of torture. Her book, which utilizes testimonial accounts by torture survivors, documents by Amnesty International (AI), literary and philosophical approaches to language, consciousness, and pain, and medical studies, is a broad and detailed analysis of the role pain plays in the development of cultures and societies. Through a painstaking analysis of the specific damage that torture does to human bodies and psyches as well as the power dynamic that necessarily develops between the torturer and the person being tortured, Scarry delivers a searing indictment of the tremendous damage torture does to human structures of culture and community as well as to individuals. She argues that because pain happens so profoundly within a single body, it is never communicable from the person suffering it to other people, and that profound pain actually destroys language because it is so heavily embodied that it breaks the conscious ability to articulate anything beyond unintelligible sounds. As such, she argues that the very invisibility of pain allows us largely to divorce ourselves from responsibility for those suffering from it.

The ramifications of her work for the study of survivor testimony are profound. The "impossible witnessing" with which thinkers as diverse as Agamben, Laub, Derrida, and Levi grapple is, her work suggests, due not just to the impossibility of logocentrism to bear the weight of witnessing events that defy metaphoric description but to the language-destroying physiological effects of pain, its literal incommunicability, and the powerful benefits this incommunicability holds for those who exercise the power of pain—the torturers and the regimes for which they are working. Her work on the very individual experience of deliberately inflicted coercive pain, when extrapolated more broadly to encompass the group experience of mass atrocity, echoes Laub's assertion that there could be no witnesses to the Holocaust from within the event itself—that it was an event which occurred with no witnesses.

Unlike the use of trauma to describe the incommunicability of extreme experience, which can be critiqued as overemphasizing the therapeutic model of individual subjectivity at the expense of collective political and social action and accountability, Scarry's model suggests that the pain of the individual can never be communicated in language, but that networks of communities can be built that seek to alleviate and avoid the pain of others, and that this is the ground of culture and civilization. Unlike the survivor testimonies under consideration in this book, however, Scarry's project is firmly grounded in the concept of the universal human body as it is elaborated in the UDHR and does not recognize or consider distinctions of gender, ethnicity, culture, and so on. While her work is uncritical of its own liberal and humanist foundations, it offers complex readings of our ethical relationships—to the unfelt pain of others, to the structures of power and coercion that justify and apply pain, and to the cultures and societies we participate in building.

By claiming the paradox of the unbelievability of the events they experienced while still insisting on their actuality, these authors build texts that enact a witnessing based on a traumatic instability of experience even while they resist it. These authors offer us as readers an alternative to a distanced and "safer" spectatorship of atrocity through the invitation to engage in performative relationships of witnessing. We must make conscious choices about our relationship as audience for these testimonial texts and, whether we choose to engage with the witnessing project or not, we must acknowledge the ethical demand of the text to witness to the dead and to the survivors. Although it is frightening to acknowledge the myriad ways that massive violence, inflicted by states and by individuals, disrupts boundaries between public and private and the safety of the cultural and juridical fields within which we live, it is through such recognition that we contribute to the building of ties to the "human."

Rather than the "body of atrocity" we have seen so many times in news photography and other media portrayals—which seems to threaten us with its very undifferentiated appearance, with the fear that "this body could be me"—these survivors' bodies become people with histories, voices, and communities. Such an engagement—with the modern concept of "human" and with complicated terms such as universal, individual, and community—marks these testimonial texts as im-

17

mediately politically engaged in the ongoing international struggle over these paradigms as they impact upon the law, civil society, and public spaces.

Performing Antiviolence Intervention: Testimonial Literature and the United Nations Universal Declaration of Human Rights

So far I have discussed the main currents in theoretical thought on testimony, witnessing, and trauma as they have been elaborated in the twentieth century. I turn now to a close reading of the key document of the period and to an examination of its rhetoric, which founds so much of our current discourse on rights but is rarely directly considered when we engage theories of human rights. Although I have space here only for a brief consideration of the UDHR and some of the contemporary scholarship that addresses it, I would highlight the most important aspect of the UDHR as the way that it performatively enacts, through rhetoric, an international "human" with internationally recognized rights and responsibilities who exists prior to entrance into any other structure of identity and regulation—national, ethnic, religious, gender, and so on.

Discourses of human rights, especially as they have been elaborated through the 1948 UDHR, attempt juridically to regulate and prevent the violences of states (which hold disproportionate power through control of military, police, and legal structures) against individual citizens or subjects of those states. Although the Declaration is essentially a nonbinding document, it has become a powerful force for the elaboration of both international law and unenforceable commitments by states to respect and further individual rights. Despite the ever-growing international attention that is being paid to issues of global human rights, however, abuses by states against individuals, both singly and in groups, seem to continue unabated, if they are not increasing.

Speaking as a spectator from within a powerful global player like the United States, I fear that the frustration level that is apparent in the news media over our inability to resolve very visible moments of abuse—such as Rwanda, Somalia, Sudan, and the former Yugoslavia, not to mention our own problems of violent military and police brutality and the violence within major urban centers—is dangerous to a continuing commitment by the United States to addressing issues of global human rights. The recent history of the United States's involvement in Afghanistan is an example of the competing interests and theories within (several) U.S. administrations in regard to support for human rights as it relates to the United States's perceived interests.

Following the Soviet withdrawal from Afghanistan, U.S. investment in the region dropped precipitously as the country degenerated into protracted civil warfare that eventually let to the victory of the Taliban Islamic Movement over most of Afghanistan. Despite the Taliban's ongoing, widespread, and well-publicized human rights abuses, especially against women, very little attention was paid to the horrifically degenerating situation of basic rights and safety in the country for the majority of its population until the terrorist attacks against the United States in September 2001 brought the country again to the forefront of U.S. attention. However, almost immediately following the end of the U.S. military campaign in Afghanistan, the issue of human rights and humanitarian aid to Afghanistan "dropped off the radar" for the United States and the international community to the extent that not even 50 percent of the year's donor commitments to the United Nations (UN) for humanitarian aid to the country had been met by July 2002.[37]

The U.S. invasion of Iraq has crystallized the most disturbing conflicts between the rule of international law and human rights and the various state and extrastate forces deployed against the ideal of global humanity protected from state and cultural depredations. The ongoing attacks against human rights and humanitarian aid workers in Iraq as well as in conflict zones around the world threatens the very ability of the UN and nongovernmental organizations (NGOs) to deliver aid and intervene in situations of atrocity and abuse. Without access to conflict zones and threatened populations and without security for their personal, aid agencies will be unable to function, and millions of people who depend upon them for some measure of protection will die. However, the extent to which aid organizations are complicit with the very structures of power responsible for the violence goes largely unremarked-upon by aid workers.

Norah Niland, speaking of current practitioner debates, notes that while some humanitarian aid workers are aware of and vocally concerned by the increasingly visible collusion between human rights and the imposition of sovereign power, most human rights workers seem unwilling to acknowledge it.[38] The increasing jeopardy of humanitarian workers in the field (kidnappings, murders, etc.) stems at least partly from the recent, very public, alignments of human rights workers with military interventions in the name of humanitarianism. Such violence against humanitarian and human rights workers, who are no longer

perceived as neutral actors, seems to evidence the material manifestation of Agamben's theory of biosovereignty. Human rights theorists
and practitioners need to begin interrogating the reasons behind their
perceived lack of neutrality, repudiating their collusion with armed
force and actively and publicly working to reaffirm their absolute neutrality.

Frustrated by the lack of a quick resolution to complex issues of
difference that have exploded into violence, the seeming failure of the
UN and its members to resolve such well-reported problems could
quickly turn to a repudiation by many people of human rights as an
important site of resistance to cultural violence. Jerome Shestack, in his
monograph *Understanding International Human Rights: A Primer,* in
a more hopeful tone states that "Archibald McLeish once predicted
that human rights, rather than Marxism, would be the true revolutionary movement of the twentieth century. That prophecy has come
home."[39] However, whether human rights are truly a "revolutionary
movement" or instead are an easy and unthreatening bandwagon for
most nations to follow, regardless of the violence of their domestic policy, is less clear to me. This question is made more pressing by the way
in which some states that are recognizably violent and repressive against
their citizens, such as China and Burma, use the language of respect for
cultural difference and the right to self-determination to deflect the
attempts of international bodies to intervene in their internal affairs.[40]
To address these issues best, the overlapping fields of law, politics, and
literature must be seen as engendering and in constant dialogue with
each other, not as separate pursuits, and the issues of nationalism, gender, and the body raised both by human rights discourse and by the
experience of state terror must be a focus of critical attention.

The major questions to be addressed in this section are related to
the way that the Declaration sets forth the rights that humans are to be
universally accorded, what the term "rights" means in such contexts,
and what some reasons are that this terminology is not laying a strong-
enough groundwork for the Declaration to function as a preventative
document. The role of the body as it is defined within the Declaration
is crucial to the document's legal and cultural project of human rights.
In order to lay claim to the right of governance over all bodies anywhere on the Earth, the Declaration must first construct an international subject that exists prior to its incorporation as subject/citizen
within state and cultural systems. Such a subject is not just granted
rights to which he or she is entitled regardless of national and cultural

circumstance, but is also proscribed from behaving in certain ways toward the other members of the transnational community. The crucial problem for the Declaration and the international subject, however, lies in the tension created by the dual existence of the subject as both internationally and nationally obligated; as well as the foundational nature of the state for human rights language and intervention/prevention. Are rights available for the stateless subject within a juridical structure that uses the nation and sovereignty both as foundation and as the legitimizing ground for visibility within its juridical field? The performative enactments and unravelings of identity staged by Genet and Fornes and the survivor demand for an ethical witness defined by mutual recognition of the unbridgeable incommunicability of the experience, under consideration in the subsequent chapters, directly challenge the assumptions of the UDHR that the law is not foundationally bound to the very violence against which the UDHR seeks to protect.

The next section examines the way in which bodies can be made nonvisible within the juridical ground of rights-based discourses that rely on an always-already rights-bearing universal subject. Introducing the work of the following chapters, I explore the necessity of subjecthood as a priority for preventative human rights documents, considering the role that testimonial literature by survivors plays in providing evidence both that torture or abuse has happened and of the effort to write oneself back into the juridical structure from which one has been "disappeared." The tensions created by the pressures of international versus national subjecthood, of visibility and voice versus state attempts at erasure and of universalizing discourses as a ground of both resistance to and perpetration of violence are the crucible within which subject of human rights is necessarily being formed.

The survivors of human rights abuse play a strong role in the elaboration and implementation of human rights as an evolving international discourse.[41] In the next section, I begin a consideration that will continue throughout the book: how to bring together an analysis of the opaque and universal language of the international documents with the political interventions that analysis of survivor testimony and literature suggests, to explore ways that the recognition of differences—of gender, culture, ethnicity, and so on—can be and often is a source for alternative forms of community that resist state violences.

Human Rights and State Sovereignty

A central problem of human rights discourse is that it always already presumes a body that has rights and can be protected—a body that

21

is visible within such a juridical system. The UN UDHR states that "recognition of the inherent dignity and of the equal and inalienable rights of all members of the human family is the foundation of freedom, justice and peace in the world," that "disregard and contempt for human rights have resulted in barbarous acts which have outraged the conscience of mankind," and that "the advent of a world in which human beings shall enjoy freedom of speech and belief and freedom from fear and want has been proclaimed as the highest aspiration of the common people." The Declaration's terminology (e.g., "conscience of mankind," "common people," and even "human beings") implies that discourse can effect change and that to give the appearance of unity and consensus is to enable their creation. In fact the Declaration has gone from a visionary document of suggested goals for its signatories to a document whose articles, it has been argued, set out certain binding agreements even for nonsignatories.[42] Louis Henkin, one of the most prominent theorists of international human rights law, argues that the Covenants on Civil and Political Rights and on Economic, Social and Cultural Rights have obviated many of the well-founded concerns about the dominance of "Western" (capitalist) universalisms by addressing the material conditions and welfare of the individuals addressed by the Declaration. They also, in some instances, qualify as well as elaborate the rights spelled out in the Declaration and contain an article that permits derogation of many, but not all, rights when a public emergency that threatens the life of the nation is proclaimed.[43]

Henkin has referred to the Universal Declaration and the two covenants as the International Bill of Rights, and notes that the Covenant on Civil and Political Rights, unlike the Declaration, creates legal obligations and begins to provide measures for their enforcement. However, as he states, "the enforcement machinery of the Covenant on Civil and Political Rights is, by standards of developed legal systems, primitive. Unilateral reporting [through the Human Rights Committee, the principle monitoring body] tends to be incomplete and self-serving. . . . The Committee cannot issue judgments but only make "general comments" and the degree of specificity of such general comments is also sometimes a subject of controversy."[44] This debate has become more concrete with the establishment of the International Criminal Court (ICC) in 2002, the first legal body that is capable of prosecuting on behalf of individuals who have allegedly suffered human rights abuses, if the states in which they were committed fail to perform that function. Though dependant on the goodwill of sovereign states, the

ICC remains a dramatic shift for the judicial world concerning the heretofore unchallenged position of state sovereignty in the human rights domain. This is due in large part, as many people have pointed out, to the long-standing struggle over the understanding that human rights are a matter of domestic rather than transnational concern.

The resistance of states to having their sovereignty "questioned" by an outside entity that wants to comment upon, much less interfere into, their "domestic" relations with their own citizenry is expressed in Article 2(7) of the United Nations Charter, which prohibits interference in domestic affairs. It states: "Nothing contained in the present Charter shall authorize the United Nations to intervene in matters which are essentially within the domestic jurisdiction of any state or shall require the Members to submit such matters to settlement under the present Charter; but this principle shall not prejudice the application of enforcement measures under Chapter VII." As Nigel Rodley points out,[45] the notion contained in Article 2(7) has deep antecedents in international law, which, as it evolved in Europe, "was that body of rules applicable to the relations of sovereigns with each other. Those relations did not traditionally encompass the relationship of the sovereign with his (or occasionally her) subjects."[46] Although he notes that there was some precedent for external humanitarian involvement in pre-twentieth-century Europe, he states that it "was more a response triggered by a humanitarian impulse to alleviate a human disaster than an attempt to uphold individual *rights* as against the oppressive state authorities."[47]

While the League of Nations, in Article 15(8) of its covenant, placed human rights "solely within the domestic jurisdiction" of states, Article 2(7) of the UN Charter prohibits the UN from intervening into or states from having to submit to settlement under the Charter "matters which are essentially within [their] domestic jurisdiction." This shift in language from "solely" to "essentially" seems to point toward a broadening of the sovereign domain of the state. Rodley points out that "the early practice of the United Nations clearly veered towards a broad interpretation of the 'domestic jurisdiction' rule and a narrow interpretation of the human rights promotions clauses. Thus, the first two decades of the organization were characterized by a strict practice by which private complaints could not be formally debated, much less acted upon, even by the UN Commission on Human Rights."[48]

Rodley notes that the changes in the UN's growing concern with human rights is probably due to several factors: the manifestation of intergovernmental concern for human rights in more local transnational organizations such as the Council of Europe and the Organization of American States (OAS); the UN Commission on Human Rights' obtaining authorization in 1967 to consider "consistent patterns of gross violations of human rights" and setting up ad hoc working groups of experts and mechanisms to study human rights violations (although it can still only visit relevant countries with their consent); and the coming into force in 1970 of the International Covenants on Human Rights, which have been adhered to by more than a hundred countries. For the nations that have ratified the Optional Protocol to the Covenant on Civil and Political Rights (about half, excluding the United States), the Human Rights Committee can consider individual complaints of violations committed by states that are party to the protocol. Rodley also notes "that (at least serious) human rights violations have simply become over the years matters of international concern and no longer ones 'essentially within the domestic jurisdiction' of states."[49]

For a combination of reasons, then, over the past thirty or so years the structural ability of the UN to intervene in various ways into human rights situations contained within particular nations has changed. This change has come about through the changing political climate of the UN (the end of the Cold War and the collapse of the Soviet bloc), the adoption of the Covenants, the growing concern with human rights as a transnational issue (even if the violations themselves do not necessarily "threaten international peace and security"), and the growing role that regional transnational organizations, such as the OAS, the African Union (formerly the Organization of African Unity), and the European Union (EU), play in taking up cases and situations of human rights violations.

Pointing toward the UN Security Council interventions in Yugoslavia in 1991 and Somalia in 1992, Rodley notes that both were possible because these states supported and requested such action. In both cases also, the Security Council referenced its concern "that the continuation of this situation constitutes . . . a threat to international peace and security," largely through the possible flow of refugees across borders into neighboring states.[50] In other words, as with regional interventions where the target state was a member of the organization (the Arab League–authorized Syrian intervention into Lebanon, the Economic Community of West African States [ECOWAS] intervention into Liberia, etc.), these interventions were permitted largely because the national government was in almost total collapse, causing chaos, violence, and nonprotection of national and foreign rights. However, should an

internal situation have collapsed to such an extent that there is no recognized government representative to request such intervention, Rodley speculates, at the present time the Security Council would be unable
to act.

The final section of Rodley's article is a consideration of UN Security
Council Resolution 688 (1991), a response to the Iraqi campaign
against its Kurdish and Shiite populations that sent refugees fleeing
across the borders into Turkey and Iran. This resolution states that the
Security Council:

> *Condemns* the repression of the Iraqi civilian population in many
> parts of Iraq, including most recently in Kurdish populated areas,
> the consequences of which threaten international peace and se-
> curity in the region.

> *Demands* that Iraq, as a contribution to removing the threat to
> international peace and security in the region, immediately end
> this repression and expresses the hope in the same context that an
> open dialogue will take place to ensure that the human and politi-
> cal rights of all Iraqi citizens are respected.

and

> *Insists* that Iraq allow immediate access by international humani-
> tarian organisations to all those in need of assistance in all parts of
> Iraq and to make available all necessary facilities for their opera-
> tions.

Rodley's article discusses at length the dissension that took place
during the Security Council meeting over the possible precedent-set-
ting nature of the resolution, noting that nearly all the statements made
at the meeting directly addressed the topic. Iraq, as well as the three
members voting against the resolution, Cuba, Yemen, and Zimbabwe,
argued that its human rights and humanitarian concerns were beyond
the purview of the Security Council and that even discussing them was
incompatible with the Charter's Article 2(7).[51] Rodley notes that China
and India, which abstained, also expressed such reservations, and that
Romania, which voted in favor, felt this was "a special case in the aftermath of the Gulf War." The other states voting in favor argued that the
situation, with its mass refugee problem, was a threat to international
peace and security, especially affecting Turkey and Iran.

Rodley notes that some states also underlined the human rights aspect of the problem, but that only the United Kingdom stated that

Article 2(7), "an essential part of the Charter, does not apply to matters which, under the Charter, are not essentially domestic, and we have often seen human rights—for example in South Africa—defined in that category."[52] Here, the United Kingdom took the step of using the Security Council's concerns over apartheid in South Africa as a precedent for defining human rights abuse as a nondomestic situation which is therefore not liable to Article 2(7) regulation. Although this language did not make its way into the resolution, Rodley suggests that it underlay it, noting that the first paragraph emphasizes internal repression rather than its external consequences. He states that "effectively then, an internal human rights problem, from the geographic point of view, albeit with external consequences, is being considered a threat to international peace and security, the pre-condition for action under Chapter VII of the Charter."[53] He goes on to note that the word "demands" of paragraph two connotes decision-taking over recommendation-making and "applies to the ending of (internal) repression," and that paragraph three "can be understood as requiring Iraq to cede the normal right of a state to refuse access to the country to any foreign individual or organisation."[54]

The extent to which this article traces the development of a juridical basis for a more interventionist stance by the UN regarding situations of massive human rights abuse is both encouraging and alarming, although, obviously, the fact that Iraq was the target of a regionally supported U.S.-led offensive over the invasion of Kuwait made Iraq's regime more vulnerable and its sovereignty less sacrosanct. Nevertheless, the way the Security Council resolutions evolved highlights the ways in which the UN, while it is not supposed to function in any way like a world government, can work to temper and refine the actions of various governments toward their citizens through the collective force of international dialogue and censure. By creating a framework through which individual states are answerable to a larger community of states—with which they must carry on economic and diplomatic relations—by a series of agreements that they themselves are party to, the UN has saved countless lives. This is not something to lose sight of in the frustration we feel over the massive loss of life that is occurring in many places around the globe where the UN is not intervening, or is not doing "enough," or has "failed" in its mission. Considering the major changes that have happened around the globe in the last thirty years and which are reflected by the UN, as well as the extent to which the UN is still an evolving body, there has been a lot of progress toward a

UN that reflects and acts upon the growing concern of transnational communities for human rights. The ICC is a step in that direction.

However, by its careful reading of the slowly evolving groundwork being laid in the UN as a forum for considering human rights abuses, Rodley's article also highlights the extent to which the UN is a largely ineffective entity for intervention into all but the most gross and massive violations, and maybe not even then. While it is true that international concern over human rights abuses is growing and that this is marked by a changing attitude toward defining human rights as intrinsically part of the domestic province of a nation, the interventions examined by Rodley are largely the product of the political maneuvering within the UN and the Security Council of a few powerful nations. These nations, for example the United States, France, and Britain, do not have an unself-interested concern with global human rights abuse. Their responses to particular situations are shaped by past history (such as colonial responsibility), economic interest, domestic concerns, and media pressures. Thus they cannot be counted upon either consistently to push a human rights agenda in the Security Council or to promote human rights within their own borders.[55]

In a less optimistic tone, scholars Mahmood Monshipouri and Claude Welch argue for an incremental approach to human rights universalism.[56] Emphasizing the importance of incorporating international norms into domestic law, they state:

The promoters of the notion of "justice backed by power" maintain that if or when "power is used to do justice [as in the case of humanitarian military intervention], law will follow." This rationale is adamantly opposed by many states reluctant to join in a global legal order with strong moral overtones. . . . Ultimately, the most effective way to protect human rights in transitional political contexts is to facilitate the creation of a culture of law—that is, strengthening local and national mechanisms of legal accountability.[57]

This grassroots approach to human rights, encouraging them at the local and national level, should work in tandem with the very visible transnational rhetoric of the UN and the incremental development of juridical norms and precedent that Rodley details.

While it is encouraging that the UN is increasingly able to be directly concerned with human rights, a glance at AI reports reveals such massive numbers of abuses around the world that the UN's actions appear to be a drop in the bucket. Because of its cumbersome nature and because it is not in the mission of the UN to be either a world government or a world police force, probably the most important outcome of the UN's changing interest in human rights is in the realm of rhetoric. Despite their own human rights records, most countries are very concerned with their reputation within the international body and will sometimes alter their oppression of individuals or groups rather than face negative publicity. For this reason, the more the UN, through its rhetoric and actions, supports human rights as belonging to the domain of international concern, the stronger will be the ability of regional, grassroots, and nongovernmental human rights organizations to intervene into particular situations.

The equivocation of the UN over Taliban human rights violations in Afghanistan, as far as they are related to the UN's massive humanitarian efforts in Afghanistan from 1995 to 2001, is a case in which rhetoric, usually produced by UN organs in New York and European capitals, was not always backed by concrete actions on the ground. The innovative concept of rights-based programming led to certain positions in defense of human rights (for example, the World Food Programme [WFP] threat to close down subsidized bakeries if Afghan women were not allowed to operate them), but the use of humanitarian (sometimes lifesaving) programs as a tool of pressure remained controversial at best. The current UN-backed, U.S.-led effort for the political and economic restructuring of Afghanistan has largely compromised the many efforts of human rights groups there by expediently accommodating warlords who have allegedly committed massive human rights abuses and giving short shrift to efforts to establish a human rights commission. The UN has functioned at best as a registry of abuses, without any large-scale operation or intervention to address or prevent such acts.

The Universal Declaration and "Human" Bodies

Louis Henkin states:

> Together the Declaration and the two Covenants are the International Bill of Rights. They have established human rights as the political idea of our time, perhaps the only idea which is universally accepted. They have ended the traditional dogma that how a state treats its own inhabitants is its own business and made the condition of human rights everywhere the concern of all. They

have launched a new field of international law which includes some binding obligations for all states, whether pursuant to the UN Charter or as customary law, and comprehensive additional obligations for the many states that are parties to the covenants.[58]

Henkin's model of human rights as the "political idea of our time" marks the necessity of a continuing critique and elaboration of its rhetoric. What does it mean to say that human rights are "universally accepted" when we live in a world where the murder, torture, and repression of people by their respective states seems almost commonplace?

Human rights provides us simultaneously with a groundwork for despair and for intervention. For those murdered and wounded during the dictatorship in Argentina, for example, the existence of the UDHR provided no discernable protection. At the same time, however, it provided a rhetorical and juridical ground from which survivors such as Alicia Partnoy could formulate possibilities for resistance and intervention. Although the Universal Declaration has made "the condition of human rights everywhere the concern of all" in its first article, there is no binding juridical power to enforce this rhetorical enactment. In fact, the document's emphasis on universal individuality is based on the following analogy: that the groundwork it lays for the enactment of a world government is to the state what the state is to the family, that is, regulatory and mutually reinforcing. This analogy is as important as the basis the Declaration establishes for a performative speech act that empowers citizens to undertake grassroots organization against state abuse.

Henkin's emphasis in the quoted paragraph is on the legal framework that is constructed through these documents—the growth of customary law as well as signatory obligations that signal a new field of international law and the formulation of conventions on specific rights. However, it begs the question of how effective the growth of specific conventions is in elaborating the protection of the "international citizen." Does the articulation of specific differences that make individuals subject to the rights laid forth in the "International Bill of Rights" not risk undermining the very ideal of universal rights?—not because universality cannot accommodate difference, but because if all individuals are always already, by virtue of being born, granted certain universal rights, then why must some be granted the same rights again? I ask this question rhetorically because, while it is clear that these conventions

29

are necessary due to the disenfranchisement of certain groups for cultural or economic reasons, it seems that to reenfranchise them in this way is to support the same set of cultural standards that accepts their disenfranchisement.

In all of these documents, the question remains as to how to interpret the problematic nature of their sweeping and assumption-laden language. Are we simply to agree, as some critics have suggested, that "now that the sterile debates over drafting are long past, the texts have been agreed, the code is in full force, and the UN General Assembly has said ever since 1950 . . . that all human rights are 'interdependent and indivisible,' it is far better to leave all these scholastic disputations behind"?[59] Can we afford to rank or even discard rights in order to concentrate on the rights that seem less contentious?[60] Or can we find a way to maintain both the integrity and the spirit of the UDHR while criticizing its inherent weaknesses?

To assume that there is a single "conscience of mankind" or a unified "common people" throughout the globe, as the prelude to the Declaration states, is absurd. As a discursive construct meant to enact the assumption from which it proceeds, it sweepingly obviates the importance of differences as a source of strength and consensus as well as of weakness. The massive ideological, cultural, religious, and other differences that marked the creation and signing of the Declaration and its conventions are erased—and this erasure has led, perversely, to the very contentions that it was meant to preclude. James Nickel suggests that "to gather as much support for the movement as possible, the philosophical underpinnings for human rights were left unspecified [in the Declaration]."[61] But to leave them unstated does not erase them or even make them invisible. Although the Declaration was partly modeled on the U.S. Bill of Rights and France's Declaration of the Rights of Man and Citizen, the "Western" humanist underpinnings of the Declaration were not the only force behind its conception. Many nations besides those of the "West" were closely involved in the drafting of the document, and their concerns are also embodied within its discourse.[62] This is especially true since the coming into force of the two covenants.

Rather than continuing to question the validity of the entire Declaration, I believe we must proceed from the groundwork laid within the last fifteen years to make the enforcement of human rights a priority. However, this does not mean we cannot question some of the ways in which these rights are formulated, if their articulation leads to a reification of categories such as privacy or gender that in turn produces cultural violences that must be arbitrated.

A Priori "Human"

The Declaration, following its preamble, goes on to lay out in thirty articles just what constitutes the "inalienable rights of all members of the human family." In this section, I address several of the Declaration's articles to explore the ways in which they articulate an international subject who is then situated within national and international structures of private and public life.

How can abstract ideas such as rights, coming from the historical tradition of Western rationalism and "natural" rights, be applied to a universal category such as "man"? As Kenneth Minogue states, "The idea of natural rights involved appropriating ideas current in philosophy and religion in order to create, by philosophical fiat, a kind of universal status from which all other forms of status were thought ultimately to derive."[63] While I would argue that "universal status" does not necessarily lead directly to universal sameness within the theater of global politics, with its multiplicity of differences, I find it difficult to imagine a world where such universal status could be achieved without insisting upon certain universal commonalties. However, while commonalties per se are often positive, the commonalties as they have been elaborated as goals within the Universal Declaration are, I believe, highly problematic.

While Nickel argues that human rights standards allow for diversity through the broadness of their definitions, I believe that this abstractness often rests on assumptions that perpetuate cultural and state structures that are inherently violent. I agree with him that it is positive that because "they provide only minimal standards in a limited number of areas. . . . the terms used in formulating human rights are often broad or abstract enough to allow some latitude to local interpretation."[64] But while this allows for greater support for and enforcement of human rights across differing cultures and state systems, it does not begin to address issues such as the relationship between privacy and domestic violence and their formative role in the constitution of many modern states. Unfortunately, because privacy plays such a formative role in the structure of modern states, and women are inextricably associated with the "private" realm of the home and the family, presided over by a man as "head of household," women's rights have a very precarious relationship to human rights. Although "women's rights are human rights" is a long-standing feminist slogan, there is not yet an operative commitment on the part of the UN and major NGOs to recognize gender equity as a fundamental human rights issue.

For example, in Afghanistan, which I address at greater length in chapter six, there is neither a consensus on nor a strong commitment toward gender rights on the part of the international agencies operating in the country. The UN and NGOs generally have difficulty negotiating the difference between juridical and cultural norms, and in Afghanistan, where the cultural norms toward women are often extremely violent and disenfranchising, where women are routinely killed for alleged infractions against male honor and violence against women is a widespread method of social control, the UN has been largely paralyzed.[65] Although equality between women and men is enshrined in the preamble to the UN Charter, women's human rights programming in Afghanistan is largely nonexistent because of the difficulty the agencies have in articulating a strong juridical stand against traditional cultural practices of disenfranchisement.

Confining women to their homes or villages and not allowing or providing for their education and health care, for example, are cultural norms that are not sanctioned by Islamic law and contravene human rights and international law, yet the UN, many NGOs, and most recently, the U.S.-led occupation have put very little effort into programming that would lead to fundamental change. Rather than addressing this issue as a structural concern of programming and pressuring all actors to push for change at all levels while still ensuring access and aid delivery, the humanitarian agencies and other actors prefer to relegate it to a secondary concern addressed on a local, ad hoc basis. While one could suggest that this might be due in part to the unexamined biases of the agencies themselves, my concern here is to highlight the distinction between women's rights and human rights. As long as human rights are understood as a universal category associated with the male and public realms, and women's rights are seen as a corollary to rather than a fundamental aspect of the discourse, women will never have the benefit of the full range of human rights protections that men have. For the UN, a body made up of and dependant upon states that are themselves structured through patriarchy, women's human rights will always be uncomfortably and irreconcilably political in a way that (men's) human rights are not.

Article 1 of the UDHR states: "All human beings are born free and equal in dignity and rights. They are endowed with reason and conscience and should act toward one another in a spirit of brotherhood." The imperative behind this article—that there is a base level of commonalty shared by everyone that distinguishes them as human—is the foundation of the Declaration. In two sentences it erases struggles over what, if anything, differentiates one person from another from the moment they are born. According to this reading, a "natural" human is what emerges from the womb, only to be immediately encased in overlapping structures of class, gender, social code, and so on. Taking priority over all cultural and state systems of marking and classifying the body, however, is the Universal Declaration, which claims the right of juridical ownership over all bodies anywhere on the globe at all times. As most of the juridical base of the Declaration is designed to protect individuals from the state, the language of the Declaration itself lays claim to all bodies prior to their recognition by the state as subjects/citizens. Thus, before a body is subject to state regulation and protection, it is subject to international regulation and protection.

This internationally recognized and regulated body is then "endowed with reason and conscience" by the authors of the article. Endowing this a priori international subject with reason and conscience is the first step the document makes in the construction of the international subject. According to the order of the wording of the sentences, this international body is "born free and equal"—read uncontrolled by any state—and is then defined by the international union as a being with "reason and conscience." Thus, before international subjects become subjects or citizens of any state, they have a responsibility, beyond and before their positions as national subjects, to behave in very particular ways: to "act toward one another in a spirit of brotherhood." To declare, however, that all bodies, to be considered human, are endowed with reason *and* conscience is to enact a definition of human that is exclusive in its origin. The human being recognized by the Declaration must be thinking and moral in a way that leads "naturally" toward the compulsion to act in a "spirit of brotherhood" toward other humans. Prior to education within state and social systems, there should be a compulsion in the human to act in positive (and here I would suggest "spirit of brotherhood" implies nonviolent, socially constructive, and so on) ways toward other humans. This is both a "natural" tendency of the international human and a prescription toward certain behaviors by the international government. Not to behave in these ways is to commit a human rights violation and to be subject to the sanction of international government.

Article 2 is as follows:

Everyone is entitled to all the rights and freedoms set forth in this Declaration, without distinction of any kind, such as race, color, sex, language, religion, political or other opinion, national or social origin, property, birth or other status.

Furthermore, no distinction shall be made on the basis of the political, jurisdictional or international status of the country or territory to which a person belongs, whether it be independent, trust, non-self-governing or under any other limitation of sovereignty.

All the articles following Article 1 follow the general pattern of Article 2. Seeking to build on the work of the first article, the rest elaborate some of the specific rights to which the international human is entitled. Article 2 does not really stand alone as a separate idea or distinction as much as it reiterates the work of the first article, giving a reading of it that presents some specific examples of the kind of national and social distinctions over which "human rights," the rights of the international body, have priority. To declare that these rights and freedoms apply without distinction and then go on to elaborate a specific set of common distinctions between peoples implies, despite the "such as," that it is specifically these distinctions that are overridden by international fiat.

The second paragraph of this article also specifically addresses the issue of nationalism as it affects individuals living within contested geographic areas. While the paragraph clearly positions the nation-state as the pinnacle and very definition of sovereign achievement , it is careful to point out that all other kinds of state formation, regardless of their sovereignty over their own affairs (as in the case of colonial holdings), are equally bound by the Declaration. But this paragraph (and the rest of the Declaration) does not address stateless persons. As is made clear in this article, the Declaration addresses an international order structured through states and their holdings, and people who exist outside and between these formations of states—such as refugees or in areas of chaos where states no longer exist—*are not* specifically addressed by the Declaration. As such, the Declaration assumes that people cannot live outside of state structures. The detainees at the U.S. military complex at Guantánamo Bay, for example, appear to be even less protected than refugees and internally displaced people, who at least are governed by certain international regulations. While Article 6 of the Declaration grants everyone everywhere the right to recognition before the law, such inadvertent or deliberate "disappearance" of so many persons from protection provides easy evidence of massive lack of coverage of the articles.

Article 3 states: "Everyone has the right to life, liberty and the security of person." This article elaborates upon the basic rights that follow from the affirmation in the first article that all humans are born free and equal. Because of the contested nature of the second and third terms, however, and the dubious logic of liberty and security of person following directly from the right to life, despite the strong rhetorical history of such a linkage in documents such as the U.S. Bill of Rights, this article remains vague and largely unenforceable. While this article is the basis for UN condemnation of states that practice the death penalty, liberty, for example, is certainly culturally determined and specific, and to define what is meant by liberty without regard to cultural practice would be impossible, if not dictatorial. Organizations such as AI have used this article as the basis for their work to free political prisoners and prisoners of conscience, but their scope is extremely narrow. Liberty, according to AI definition, is improperly abridged by unjust imprisonment, being imprisonment based not on the prisoner's tangible harm to his or her surrounding community according to the laws of the state but on the state's perception of him or her as a potential threat to its order and stability.

Article 6 states: "Everyone has the right to recognition everywhere as a person before the law." But whose law? While this article clearly springs in part from the imperative in Article 4 prohibiting slavery and enforced servitude, "law" is an abstract but powerful force that is not the same everywhere and is always contingent. Not only is law not at all the same in all states, but there is no guarantee that each state makes internal laws that are most beneficial to its own subjects. While granting every individual personhood before the law might help to make extreme brutality against them less likely, it does not in any way protect them from other forms of abuse, such as indefinite imprisonment because of differences with the state. This is particularly the case because the right of the individual to petition the UN as an international arbiter was removed, partly at the request of the United States, from the Declaration prior to its ratification. What this article does do is attempt to enact both the personhood of all international citizens, as they are articulated in the previous articles, and a law to which they are visible. If the law does not operate "properly" at the level of state or local government—in recognizing this personhood—then it will at the level of the international through its construction in the Declaration and corollary documents.

Article 7 states: "All are equal before the law and are entitled without any discrimination to equal protection of the law. All are entitled to equal protection against any discrimination in violation of this Declaration and against incitement to such discrimination." Keeping in mind that the "all" to which this article refers are the international bodies elaborated in Article 1, then the term "the law" before which all are accorded equal protection is in a state of constant and deliberate slippage. The law, according to Merriam-Webster's dictionary, is defined as: "a binding custom or practice of a community : a rule of conduct or action prescribed or formally recognized as binding or enforced by a controlling authority." The "law" accordingly acts as an ultimate arbiter and leveling force; since "everyone has the right to recognition everywhere as a person before the law," then "the law" is all law—civil, federal, international—regardless of cultural context or state formation. This formulation constructs the law as a single entity that subsumes all of its parts in a linear motion; the law becomes the dominant force of social regulation across the entire globe to which all bodies are subject by virtue of their existence. As Article 1 states, one is not a body at all without this regulation. The equal protection clause, which states that all bodies, despite differences, are entitled to the same "blind" justice, enacts yet another level of this universal "law" that the Declaration articulates.[66]

Article 12 states: "No one shall be subjected to arbitrary interference with his privacy, family, home, or correspondence, nor to attacks upon his honor and reputation. Everyone has the right to protection of the law against such interference or attacks." This article, in its explicit statement conflating privacy with the family, highlights one of the problems with the conceptual groundwork of the Declaration's enactment of the "international citizen." Because the domestic family, in a variety of forms that it takes in many cultures, is both a protected private space and a space of considerable—and I would argue formative—violence, the grounds by which it is constituted as private space need serious consideration. Just as the internal domain of the state is protected through the UN Charter from incursions, even in the case of incredible violence, the family is often granted such protection by state and local governments. To the extent, then, that the Declaration upholds and protects the space of the family as private space without a consideration of the formations this space takes, it upholds a tradition of cultural formations founded on patriarchy, institutionalized inequality, and violence. Although the Declaration, in its formation of human rights, tries to enact systems of equity between men and women, it does so without a critique of the basic cultural formation that confirms their inequality. This issue is addressed again in Article 16, which concerns the right to freedom of marriage and divorce.

Article 16 is as follows:

(1) Men and women of full age, without any limitation due to race, nationality, or religion, have the right to marry and to found a family. They are entitled to equal rights as to marriage, during marriage and at its dissolution.

(2) Marriage shall be entered into only with the free and full consent of the intending spouses.

(3) The family is the natural and fundamental group unit of society and is entitled to protection by society and the State.

What definition of the family is used here depends both upon interpretation and the prevailing cultural norms of the interpreters. I have no doubt, however, that the family unit in mind here is the traditional model of two (differently sexed) parents with their children and possibly grandparents. Different kinds of family structures, such as communal families, single-parent families, gay and lesbian families, and so on, are not explicitly left out of this article, since it does not specify the sex or number of partners that the men and women who are granted freedom of marriage must have (although it does provide grounds to regulate age of consent, arranged marriages, etc.). By singling out marriage as a protected category, however, the article continues the work of Article 12, which constitutes the family as a private space protected from state interference. Given the pervasiveness of state structures founded on the family as the private space against which they find definition, alternative family models are not protected and are in fact threatened and controlled by terminology that states that "the family is the natural and fundamental group unit of society and is entitled to protection by society and the State."

Article 17 states: "(1) Everyone has the right to own property alone as well as in association with others. (2) No one shall be arbitrarily deprived of his property." This is one of the articles that has been identified with the capitalist countries of Western Europe and America and has caused friction with countries whose economic and social systems do not hold private property to be a right. The two covenants that follow the Declaration, however, do not mention this clause and are more inclusive of other social and economic systems.

Articles 18 through 25 state rights to freedom of thought, expression, assembly, participation in government, social and economic security, work, rest, and leisure, and adequate standards of living. Social rights such as these are also addressed more directly and at length in the two covenants, which focus on communities much more than does the Declaration. In this way, many of the problems of supposed "Western" bias of which the Declaration has been accused are addressed.

Article 26 is as follows:

(1) Everyone has the right to education. Education shall be free, at least in the elementary and fundamental stages. Elementary education shall be compulsory. Technical and professional education shall be made generally available and higher education shall be equally accessible to all on the basis of merit.

(2) Education shall be directed to the full development of the human personality and to the strengthening of respect for human rights and fundamental freedoms. It shall promote understanding, tolerance, and friendship among all nations, racial or religious groups, and shall further the activities of the United Nations for the maintenance of peace.

(3) Parents have a prior right to choose the kind of education that shall be given to their children.

The emphasis on education is the hallmark of the rational belief that enlightenment proceeds through education and will lead to a less violent and more just society. This is one of the grounding beliefs from which the Declaration was produced. This, along with the other provisions for social well-being are the "unenforceable" rights that authors such as James Nickel suggest should be discarded. However, these are also the rights that the Covenant on Economic, Social and Cultural Rights addresses at length. Rather than stating these rights as individual entitlements, however, the covenant makes it the obligation of the state to recognize these rights and progressively to take steps, to the "maximum of available resources," to achieve them.

Articles 27 and 28 guarantee the freedom to participate in the cultural life of the community, as well as the protection of the "interests" resulting from scientific, literary, or artistic authorship, and state that all are entitled to "a social and international order in which the rights and freedoms set forth in this Declaration can be fully realized." Articles 29 and 30 state the individual's duties to his or her community so that these freedoms can be possible and state that nothing in the Declaration can be interpreted as implying any right to engage in activities that destroy any of the rights and freedoms it elaborates.

Although its ability as an interventionist force is very limited, the discourse of human rights developed through the UN remains extremely important for its rhetorical and symbolic force. NGOs such as AI rely on the rhetoric of the Universal Declaration for their own mandates, and the individual members of the UN do try to present as respectable a face as possible to the transnational community. For this reason especially, it is imperative to the project of human rights to address the underlying causes and assumptions of violence. When a document such as the Declaration hides some problems behind the veil of privacy, this supports the fundamental roots of certain violent state structures.

Because of the severely limited role that the UN can play, practically, as an interventionist body (i.e., many people have to die before it can or will intervene and even then, if it wants to intervene, which is not at all constant, it must find a loophole to do it) regional human rights bodies and NGOs are vital. Regional bodies such as the European Union, the Organisation of American States, and the African Union (AU) can intervene earlier to preempt situations of human rights abuse through diplomacy and regional pressure. I agree with Anthony Parsons, who notes that regional organizations should have closer, more organized ties to the UN; he states that "it would make it easier for the more reserved members of the Security Council if notionally domestic questions were brought to the Council's attention either by a regional organisation or after all efforts by that regional organisation had failed."[67] In this way the UN and the Security Council would not have to be seen so much as the fist of international governance (and those nations that control the Security Council) as they are court of last resort for regional bodies trying to maintain order within their own constituencies.

Among NGOs, AI is one of the most effective international agencies at stopping state abuse against individuals exactly because it disrupts the disembodying practices of the state by coordinating the sending of individual letters about individual prisoners. By forcing states to recognize that people they have illegally detained are not "disappeared" but are in fact visible and recognized by transnational organizations, AI has found that such states will sometimes exercise more accountability toward their prisoners. Within the transnational arena, NGOs as "private" bodies must do much of the human rights (and humanitarian) work because public-, that is, state-affiliated agencies are too "political." In this formulation, the "private" NGOs must work for the protection of individuals whose abuse is "hidden" in the private spaces of the state—torture chambers, illegal (not supported through the structures of a fair trial) imprisonment where the state often will not admit to knowledge of the detention, and so on—while the UN human rights bodies must wait for situations of abuse to become "public" before they can intervene. They must wait for the abuse to affect neighboring states or for the invitation of the government involved in the situation. This does not mean that the local UN human rights officers in the field do not work closely with human rights NGOs; they often do, but they are more constrained in their actions and public statements.

Although AI and Human Rights Watch have been criticized for employing too narrow a focus on human rights abuses, such human rights NGOs cannot be expected to play all roles within the international theater. Harry Scoble and Laurie Wiseberg state that "the central focus of the organization [AI] has remained both clear and narrowly restricted . . . [and can] be likened to a US First Amendment approach to the problem of operationalizing the concept of political repression."[68] Although AI has widened the definition of political prisoner over the years to include, for example, disappeared persons and homosexuals, it is effective in its work largely because of the narrowness of its focus and the fact that it can target specific individuals—not allowing them to be disappeared from the juridical field to which they should have recourse. Thus AI focuses intently on the constitution of the individual within state culture and on attacks against the integrity of this individuality.

As Wiseberg and Scoble point out, however, because of the visible status AI enjoys around the world and the narrow field of human rights it addresses, the rhetoric about what human rights are and how they are violated could become equally narrowly restricted in public imagination, with the equal importance of social and cultural rights forgotten. Such a narrow understanding of human rights could also contribute to undermining the critique of privacy as a site of violence. This is neither AI's fault nor its goal, but it is the responsibility of other human rights bodies, perhaps the regional governmental bodies, to continue to address and be concerned with the wide range of human rights.

"Prisoners of conscience," defined as "individuals who have been wrongfully imprisoned because their *thoughts* and *attempts to communicate* those thoughts have been judged dangerously deviant by national political elites" are AI's main focus.[69] As such, AI attempts to intervene behind the veils of privacy, but only through maintaining its structures. As a "private" (nonstate, objective) agency, AI attempts to protect private citizens from the illegal intrusion of the state into their lives. Torture is also seen as an illegal (nonconsensual) incursion by the state into the private body of an individual. However, by insisting upon the right to privacy of the individual without a parallel (and public) critique of the role privacy plays in supporting the institutions of state violence and the epidemic violence of social structures linked to the state through the family, AI maintains the distinctions between private/family/female and civil/political/public/male that support such violence.

The universal "individuals" that AI and other human rights organizations seek to protect are, within this discourse, always already male, since, as Carol Pateman notes, "The creation of the 'individual' presupposes the division of rational civil order from the disorder of womanly nature."[70] The women's testimonials under consideration in subsequent chapters evince a strong awareness of the multiple roles the women must occupy as they shift between gendered cultural positions and the extreme leveling force of state terror and violence. For human rights to make the same move, albeit in the opposite direction, as state terror, is to enact rhetorically a violence that both Genet and Fornes explore in meticulous detail in their plays. Although "gender violence," "gender mainstreaming," and "gender-based programming" are very popular jargon terms with most large, donor-funded NGOs and UN agencies, programming initiatives and policy papers that seek to address gender inequities in human rights and humanitarian aid work have made very little headway against institutional structures founded on a profoundly unexamined faith in the (always already male) "universal human."

"The Erotics of Violence": Performing Violence in *The Balcony* and *The Conduct of Life*

This chapter examines the body staged in order to focus specifically on the ways in which identity is formed in violence and the ways such violence can be aestheticized in theatrical representation. While the chapter considers to some extent the role that eroticism, especially in the discourse of perpetrators, plays within violence, the plays upon which I focus, Jean Genet's *The Balcony* and Maria Irene Fornes's *The Conduct of Life*, are concerned with issues of unraveling and resisting such cultural violences rather than presenting them as pleasurable spectacles.[1] Both plays undertake an examination of cultural and domestic acts of violence as they are utilized and played out on the "public" stage of "political" relations and the "private" stage of sexual/domestic relations. While Genet's drama uses the structures of sadomasochistic play within which to build a satire of theatricality, culture, and political structures, Fornes's play uses state torture as the rubric through which to read the violence of patriarchal domesticity.

I concentrate on Genet's exploration of (always eroticized) violence as foundational of Euro-American configurations of the State and on *The Conduct of Life*'s resistance to such foundations. How do these plays posit eroticism and violence as constituting elements of social identity and culture, and what role does the feminization of those perceived as "others" play within these violences? How do political and legal structures constrain bodies within different representational systems? What is the role of performance within such cultural/representational systems? What is the relationship between mimesis and violence? And what is the relationship between performance, spectatorship, witnessing, and violence as these plays address it?

Genet's *The Balcony* is a play that examines both the representational facades upon which society is constituted and the mechanisms of power that underlie them. The economic system of the play is founded on a nexus of violence and desire where the constant representational reinscription of the excess inherent within eroticism is in continual tension with the systemic disruption that eroticism, occupying the break between the body and language, promises. As in Marie Irene Fornes's play *The Conduct of Life*, however, this attempt to inscribe the disruption of eroticism into rigid structures of power results both in horrific yet legally sanctioned violence through the attempt to maintain these structures and in the constant destabilization and even destruction of these very systems. Just as *The Balcony* reveals the dynamic of a false oppositional binary—that repression on the "fringe" of culture often simply conceals the existence of such "corruption" at the cultural center (as the brothel is revealed as a cornerstone of cultural hierarchy)—Fornes's play brings this center home to the family. The domestic space in *The Conduct of Life* is revealed as a site of violence and torture, and Orlando's murder at the end of the play does not promise a shift to a less violent and hierarchical structure any more than does the revolution in *The Balcony*, as no avenue of escape from the cultural system is posited. In both plays, it is not eroticism itself that is a license for violence and the imposition of the law, but rather the fear of its disruptive and undifferentiated excesses which do not obey laws and the drive to fix such erotic energies into frameworks that channel their power.

Both plays address violence from a cultural and structural perspective. *The Balcony* is in large part a work that explores a foundational (and of course fictional) cultural binarism—that recognition of violence and eroticism as existing on the fringes of society only serves to hide their constitutive relationship to the cultural center. The brothel that is the centerpiece for the action of the play is the present/space that in the schematics of the play represents the boundary between the two opposing forces of law and revolution. As the Judge says to the thief, "My being a judge is an emanation of your being a thief. You need only refuse—but you'd better not!—need only refuse to be who your are—what you are therefore who you are—for me to cease to be . . . to vanish, evaporated."[2] Portrayed by the law as a marginal space of social transgression—perversion, violence, fantasy—the brothel is recognized by the revolution as a strongly conservative space of cultural and political reification. The fantasy being acted by the Judge would literally cease were the prostitute to refuse to continue acting her role as thief, just as on the symbolic level the enforcers of the law would have no reason for existence if there were not transgressions they could punish. Thus the sexual fantasies of heterosexual sadomasochistic power that are enacted in the brothel called The Balcony performatively enact the unconscious of cultural disciplinary structures and the flows of capital that support them.[3]

Although Mme. Irma controls the brothel as the queen controls the state, both depend for their positions on the patronage of men. The women's bodies as ground of the violence on which state power rests must, as the Bishop notes, be used with the women's "willing" participation in their subjection. From Chantal's murder to the prostitutes' participation in The Balcony's sadomasochistic scenarios in exchange for money, the coercive nature of the exchange is masked by the seeming "free will" exercised by all of the "actors." For the play's spectators, no demand is made to intervene or participate differently in the structures of power within which they operate in their lives beyond the theatrical space. The performative gaps toward which the play gestures (the "hangnail," the chaotic violence of the revolution, the denial of the equivalence between signifier and signified that Una Chaudhuri notes, etc.) do not in themselves compel a more engaged response from the audience. Instead they suggest closed, cyclical structures of power in which one participates, willingly or not and despite one's critical awareness of *difference*. This inscription of order, through a seemingly erotic language of violence and sex, onto other "feminized" bodies is the ground upon which the law builds its death-defying edifice, denying the dissolution and end to discontinuity that the erotics of the revolution promises. Roger's castration of himself as he kills himself to solidify the Chief of Police as a figurehead in the pantheon of state authority both acknowledges the feminized position of the bodies that are subject to such patriarchal violence and resists the facade of free will through which he participates in the violence.

Using sadomasochism as a trope for the relationships that the institutional branches of state power have with their subjects, the play posits mimesis as the "unconscious" of the law. The sadomasochistic dynamic of the play critiques and satirizes patriarchy and heterosexuality as forming the "private" spaces, the site of the family, as the foundational ground for "public" disciplinary structures. The "law" in *The Balcony* is both the disciplinary structure that enforces social codes through the use of judicial proceedings, the police and penal institutions, and the regulatory structure of social consciousness (in the Lacanian sense).

Performativity becomes the mediating space between the subject and the structures of power through which she or he is defined. Or as Una Chaudhuri argues, "Whereas the mimetic theater strives to blur the distinction between the realms of theater and reality, Genet insists on maintaining—indeed, foregrounding—that distinction. He will admit only those signs which can be made to look *like signs.*"[4]

In the world of *The Balcony*, then, mimesis is/seems to be the opposite of the law, because in the mimetic (fantasy) world there are no prohibitions—all is play, performance, and everything is allowed. This is not the fantasy of Genet's play *The Balcony*, but the fantasy world of The Balcony brothel itself. As the play goes to great lengths to explore, however, it is exactly this binary (mimesis vs. law) that forms and enables the structures of institutional power. Because the revolution is also dependant upon such a mimetic relationship for its own power (the romance between Chantal and Roger, her positioning as a Marianne-type figurehead, etc.), it cannot occupy a radical position in relationship to the institutionalized hierarchies it fights. The revolution is doomed to failure as merely another section of the circular power structure of mimesis and the law because it cannot envision an outside to this relationship.

The setting of Genet's play, a brothel, displays what seems at first to be a strict division between the private and the public world. Outside the brothel, the world is involved in a bloodbath of violence, a revolution that murders randomly and in excess and that during the course of the play comes to surround the brothel, causing the brothel to stand, absurdly, as the monumental edifice of conservative social construction upon which the revolution is finally broken. The brothel, realm of fantasy and a sexual economy based on hard currency, becomes the fortress that protects the four cornerstones of society: the law, the clergy, the military, and the police.

The Balcony is a brothel whose proprietor, Mme. Irma, prides herself on being able to stage any fantasy a customer could desire for the right price. The fantasies performed during the course of the play are all sadomasochistic fantasies of power, where middle-class workers act out their fantasies of being a judge, general, bishop, or beggar. Outside the brothel the monarchy is on the verge of collapse, as a revolution slowly takes more and more sections of the city during the course of the play. Because the revolution is gaining such control over the rest of the city, The Balcony slowly becomes one of the last refuges for members of the threatened social order. The Chief of Police is not only the coordinator of the city's antirevolutionary forces; he is Mme. Irma's lover, and under the pressure of the revolution the link between state power and organized "vice" has become visible, represented by the convenient relationship between Mme. Irma and the Chief of Police. On the other side, however, Chantal, a former employee of Irma's, has become the symbol of the revolution personified, and her lover, one of the leaders of the revolution, is The Balcony's former plumber.

The fantasy scenarios of The Balcony that we see acted out in the play are all fantasies of ordinary middle-class men assuming symbolic roles of authority. When they become the bishop, the judge, or the general, they do not become a specific bishop, or judge, or general, but the one of their fantasy; they perform this piece from the symbolic order. As the Bishop-performer says "The majesty, the dignity that light me up come from . . . the fact that the bishop precedes me." As the play progresses and the revolution topples the state and forces the queen into hiding, it becomes clear that what is important for the maintenance of state power and the symbolic is the ability to perform these roles that manifest symbolic power and authority. Thus the workers who paid to play the bishop, judge, and general in the brothel are pressed into service to become them on a permanent (public) basis by the bureaucrats/queen's emissaries, who are setting up a new (same as the old) state.

Most of the scenes of *The Balcony* take place in either Irma's office or one of the fantasy rooms of the brothel. The play opens with the four fantasy scenes that introduce us both to the function of the brothel and to the Bishop, Judge, and General acting out their roles. Immediately following these scenes, we are introduced to Mme. Irma, her assistant Carmen, and the Chief of Police. Scene 6 is the only scene to occur outside the brothel and is the pivotal scene in the struggle between the revolution and state order in the play, as Roger and Chantal part so that Chantal can enter the symbolic of the revolution. As the new queen (Mme. Irma), judge, bishop, and general display themselves on the balcony of The Balcony in public view to mark the end of the revolution, Chantal is shot when she enters the balcony to join them. The play ends as Roger pays to enter The Balcony to impersonate the Chief of Police, thus ensuring his role's entry into the panoply of state figureheads. Although he must die to assume fully the "immortality" of the role, he castrates himself first, in an act of despair and resistance. The play ends as the queen and the figureheads exit the stage and the revolution begins again.

The play itself is antimimetic in structure. It privileges facades and clearly absurdist moments over a more conventional fourth-wall realism and audience identification. Mimicking the structure of sadomasochism, the play emphasizes the erotics of the tension of waiting for something to happen as well as the one element in a scenario (what I term the "hangnail," the intrusive element) that reassures the actors/partners that it is not "real" and that consent is involved. Chaudhuri argues that Genet

> affirm[s] the theatrical by denying the dramatic. By endlessly refusing to grant theatrical preeminence to the fictional level of his play, by repeatedly rendering it as unstable and artificial at the theatrical level, he combats the idea of a play as a re-presentation, an afterimage reflecting some prior meaning emanating from some absent creative consciousness. In so doing he creates a theater of presence, in the present, a theatrical message in a theatrical code instead of a literary message translated into theater.[5]

However, the literariness of *The Balcony* is quite striking, and as Richard Schechner has noted, in order to be able to stage the play effectively Genet "deconstructed a literary text and reconstructed it as a performance text."[6] Laura Mulvey writes that "sadism demands a story, depends on making something happen, forcing a change in another person . . . all occurring in a linear time with a beginning and an end," and Genet uses the trope of sadism to performatively enact facades of power and identity that masquerade as difference under the guise of erotic play.[7] The "theater of presence and process" he creates is, Chaudhuri argues, an "experience of theater, as well as [an] experience of self, [which] resides in the vast space of nothing between desire and its fulfillment, self and other, actor and character . . . the denial of this powerful space, this *"difference,"* transforms experience into slavery."[8] Sadism, which makes a spectacle of play as absolute power, is related not just to narrative but to mimesis and the denial of difference (in *The Balcony*, sameness that masquerades as difference).

Chaudhuri notes that by the end of *The Balcony* the play has constituted the audience as spectacle, seeking to eliminate the boundary between play and audience.[9] This performative elimination of boundaries, and of the antimimetic theater of signs Genet has produced, invites the audience to acknowledge this *difference,* this "vast space of nothing between desire and its fulfillment" as an antitotalitarian space that opposes sadism and slavery. The space of difference, what Chaudhuri calls "that terrifying abyss between self and other which is the only space of self-realization," is also the space Derrida suggests is site of the possibility of justice.[10] Genet's play, while not addressing the ethical possibilities inherent within acts of witnessing, does suggest the possibility of ethical relationships through the recognition of the space of *difference* as a site for the resistance of authoritarian violence.

The "human," performatively and juridically enacted as a category in the Universal Declaration of Human Rights, is elaborated in the Declaration's articles as dependant on these same private/public distinctions and foundational formations of identity to the state that *The Balcony* satirizes. The "human," as either the a priori universal category of the Universal Declaration or the ethical category enacted in the survivor testimonials under consideration in this book, is the absent category of *The Balcony*. While the characters' identities are articulated through a nexus of erotic drives, monetary exchange, aesthetic representation, and power in their relations with other characters, they do not articulate any relationship between identity and death—the bodies of the dead—until the ending of the play, when the characters' attempt to ground legal and historical authority in death goes awry through Roger's act of castration. Derrida's space of difference, which opens up the possibility for justice, is also the space of the ethical relation to the dead and thus a gap wherein the material body must be acknowledged and negotiated. The "authenticity" of the material body that testimony must negotiate—the belief and experience of the body as ground and truth of authentic experience that "authorizes" torture and authoritarian violence and that we conversely demand to authenticate the testimony of the survivor—is absent from *The Balcony*. Instead, Genet's characters exist within the simulacrum of role play and facade, destabilizing categories of authenticity and humanity as the law figures them. In the play, when the role-playing brothel patrons become the representatives of the law to quell the chaos of the revolution, the authenticity of the body is completely denaturalized as a ground of authority, but the negotiation of the materiality of the body that is necessary within the survivors' demand for ethical witnessing and Derrida's formulation of justice remains absent from the erotic *difference* that Genet marks as the site of resistance.

In *The Balcony*, it is precisely because the brothel remains the one edifice that is as yet untouched by the revolution and yet could fall at any moment that it becomes the nexus of action for the characters of the play. The erotic investment in power that gives stature to the various figures of the play is made possible by the threat of the revolution. Without the revolution against which to define them, the various institutions would be empty of the representational resonance that their representatives so crave.

The play of this erotics of power is felt most/made most visible when the relationship between the law and mimesis comes closest to being revealed. At moments of violence or death, and mimicked by the brothel patrons in their sadomasochistic scenarios, the world of mimesis erupts into that of the law. As Carmen tells Roger prior to his entrance into the tomb to become the Chief of Police, all of The Balcony's scenarios are reducible to the single theme of death. The mimetic world— one of mimicry, facades, in essence different from the world of the law yet (like the world of the stage) bearing a surface resemblance to it—is always recognizable for the characters of the play by the one "hangnail" that marks it as mimicry, as not the real. In the world represented by the brothel and the law, then, the "hangnail" is the reminder of violence that could threaten the representatives of the law, and it is within this possibility that the erotic investment of the law in the mimetic world lies.

The great "mistake" that the brothel patrons make in *The Balcony* is their belief in the freedom of the world of mimesis as a space within which everything is allowed. They maintain a claim to the "real" through eroticism, and the play itself seems to toy with the notion that some sort of "fundamental" truths about cultural hierarchies can be revealed and disrupted by the violence of erotic play. Playing both on Shakespeare's adage "All the world's a stage" and on the utopian possibilities of (sexual) revolution, *The Balcony* posits a cynic's view of the possibility for any "true" freedom from the disciplinary structures of culture and representation.

This in itself mimics the play's staging and structure, which work to disrupt realist theatrical conventions not by denying them but by constantly pushing them over the top into parody or the absurd. Thus it is that on one level the entire drama plays like an in-joke, poking fun at anyone and everyone. Topics like revolution, law enforcement, and sadomasochism play as an attempt to make bourgeois audiences uncomfortable through their centrality to the narrative, yet the scenes and characters of *The Balcony* parody those very same roles in their portrayal. Mme. Irma is on one level a shrewd, manipulative business woman who knows how best to make her way in the world (and provide employment to quite a few workers as well), yet she is also a caricature of the "whore with a heart of gold" who truly does care for Carmen and who in the end loves and is tragically abandoned by her suitor, the Chief of Police. Chantal and Roger are caricatures of revolutionaries precisely because they are so passionate about both each other and their cause, just as the Bishop, Judge and General are not just caricatures of the symbolic personages themselves but are also parodies of the man who must act his fantasies in paid sadomasochistic scenes, sneaking in and out of the brothel to go back home to his work and family.

Limitations of Reason

Rather than being a site of disruption, the brothel is revealed as a site of inscription, where fantasies of power are institutionalized and reified through mimicry. As the Bishop states, "The majesty, the dignity, that light up my person, do not emanate from the attributions of my function.—No more, . . . than from my personal merits.—The majesty, the dignity that light me up come from a more mysterious brilliance: the fact that the bishop precedes me."[11] He wishes to be bishop "in solitude, in appearance alone," reassured that somewhere there is an original, "real" bishop preceding all representations. In this way, the power of the social order becomes reified through mimesis, a constant reinscription of the power of the symbolic realm into that of the actual. Because the Bishop believes that he only impersonates a bishop, wearing the "attributions of [his] function," he is free to explore the ways in which the power of the bishop is founded on a fascination with and corresponding fear of transgression and evil. He states that ". . . our holiness lies only in our being able to forgive you your sins. Even if they're only make-believe."[12] Fascination with the shifting realm that lies beyond the boundaries of the law and order of the Church is the foundation upon which the rhetoric of the Church rests, and the Bishop, in his "solitude" within the brothel, can explore these boundaries without fear of instigating any "real" disorder.

As Georges Bataille has stated, "the domain of eroticism is the domain of violence, of violation. . . . Eroticism always entails a breaking down of established patterns, the patterns, . . . of the regulated social order basic to our discontinuous mode of existence as defined and separate individuals."[13] These are the patterns that in Genet's play are represented by the figureheads of the law: the Queen, the Chief of Police, the Judge, and so on against which the revolution is waging its unending battle. As becomes clear during the course of the play, these figureheads are not only replaceable, they become replaced by the very workers and petit bourgeois who impersonate them inside the rooms of the brothel.

In this way, the brothel is a tightly controlled staging ground for the exploration of fantasy. Firmly grounded in patriarchal and heterosexist law, the brothel provides a "safe" space for this theater, assuring the customer that every appearance of reality will be maintained to facilitate the fantasy, up to and always including the one "hangnail" that proves its "truly" theatrical and therefore unreal nature. The screams must sound real, but Mme. Irma must also always be able to persuade the customer that they are not. The Bishop reassures himself that in the brothel, "there's no possibility of doing evil," because it is all theater and therefore all "evil" since the world of mimesis is a world without remorse.

The Balcony tacitly claims that a world that is wholly mimetic is one that does not by necessity make moral or ethical claims because it exists, in the same way that Bataille argues literature exists, "independently of the necessity to create order."[14] The fantasy of erotic disorder that this theater promises, however, is undermined by the fear of its actors, who insist always on its containment. The "hangnail" that provides the link to the reality of social order may be hidden, but it must always be present to be recalled as a barrier against the dissolution that would occur in the event of a complete rupture between the world of mimesis and the world of the "actual." Thus the Bishop must be reassured that the woman's sins are not real, because, as he says, "If your sins were real, they would be crimes, and I'd be in a fine mess."[15] All "realness" can be discursively disclaimed within a mimetic realm that claims no ethical imperatives.

The fantasies of the Bishop, the Judge, and the General all depend for their existence on the body of a woman as the other/actor of the fantasy. The Bishop's urge to "destroy all function" and "cause a scandal" is revealed as a fraud. It is not the longing of true evil, but the longing of good for the disorder of evil.[16] The Bishop, like all of The Balcony's actors, fears death, and his fear of death, despite his longing for the dissolution it brings, is what causes both his entrenchment in the realm of social order/good and the necessity of his fantasy's fixity on the body of Woman. These three representatives of the state link their erotic desire and the partial dissolution of being that this desire brings to the function of "power" as a force that denies death. Linking themselves representationally to the monolithic figures of their chosen law, they deny through the rigidity of their chosen forms the dissolution that sex and violence threaten.[17] They use violence only to conquer its threat.

Eroticism, for Bataille, is always a movement toward death and dissolution of being, a longing for the end of this "discontinuous" existence which is our state of being as isolated, living individuals. In *The Balcony*, Genet has staged the tension between the realm of reason/reality/good and eroticism/fantasy/evil. To make use of definitions provided by Bataille, "Good is based on common interest which entails consideration of the future," while evil, when "seen in the light of a disinterested attraction towards death," and "represented by violence, [is a] revolt against the real world, dominated as it is by reason and based on the will to survive."[18] Thus, "Though the being is not doomed to Evil, he must try to avoid becoming enclosed within the limitations of reason."[19] Schematically, in the play, the world of reason/good exists in islands or pockets of space, surrounded by the violence of the revolution. As the revolution waxes and wanes, these pockets have a fluctuating ability to communicate, so that when the violence is at its height, envoys (such as Arthur) must risk their lives to travel from one pocket to the other with information. The brothel pretends toward the space occupied by eroticism and fantasy, but ultimately it is revealed as a space ruled by order and the fear of death.

Thus no hint of the orgiastic (and perhaps "real," offstage) violence of the revolution outside the brothel can be allowed to enter the insulated world of the brothel itself. When the sound of gunshots or screams sneaks past the insulating barriers of the brothel, it is disruptive to the play inside and must immediately be contained. The only "legal" means for the revolution to be present within the brothel is through language, as a subject of discussion. Locked safely within the boundaries of a linguistic code (and representational codes), the disruptive excess of the revolution (bullets flying through windows, random death, etc.) is "safely" contained. As with all of the economies that operate within the play, however, slippage not only constantly threatens but actually occurs. Sounds do find their way through to the staging rooms of the brothel, and Arthur is shot dead by a stray bullet that comes through a window.

Genet's play takes great relish in uncovering the way in which brothels and the sex trade, traditionally stigmatized in cultural rhetoric, are actually a cornerstone of society. The Balcony, through its institutionalization of fantasy and its reliance on a capitalist model of exchange, spectaclizes and contains erotic excess rather than reveling in it. This perhaps hints at possibilities for other sexual practices and relationships that, like the violence of the revolution, occur "offstage" and beyond regulatory culture and political authority.

The private world of the brothel is the bedrock of the entire public world that has been constructed around it, and as much as it may try to separate its private world of fantasy from the public world of reality—with the one small hangnail that proves it is not real—there is a constant slippage between the two worlds. The sound of gunfire and finally the bullets pierce the world of the brothel, reminding the actors that their fantasies exist synonymously with the world of the revolution outside and are not separate from it, in the same way that the woman's intermittent scream pierces from one room of the brothel to another. It is through this constant slippage between representation, fantasy, and reality that *The Balcony* exposes the foundations of society.

This representational framework of society that Genet explores has built its foundations upon the channeling of eroticism into fixed structures. Fear of the eroticism occurring in the split between the body and language serves as the motivating force behind the construction of hierarchy. The revolution will always be doomed to failure as long as it fails to recognize the ways in which it serves the very system it opposes by positioning itself in an oppositional binary against which the hierarchy of the law, the Church, and the "social order" can be constituted. Spectators are perhaps asked to make this critical move as well, but the mechanisms whereby change might be effected are not suggested. Instead, the play falls back on a circular model of critique of the violences under consideration, which calls more for ironic distance and play than engaged and ethical witnessing from the space of *difference* in the gap created by the detaching of signifier and signified.

The Conduct of Life: Staging Torture's Stages

> Her specific attempt to tell her story by the very conduct of her life led to an unavoidable dead end, in which the fight against the obliteration of the story could only be at the cost of the obliteration of the audience.[20]

The violence that Genet is fascinated with as it weaves its way between the realms of fantasy and reality is the focus of Maria Fornes's play *The Conduct of Life*, which examines the moments of violence, both spontaneous and premeditated, that occur within society as the locus both of its constant reinscription of its own power and of the possibilities for disruption that are always contained within it. The very specific act of torture against the physical body, which Fornes takes as her subject, is one of the most blatant manifestations of the way in which the violence in the realm of "fantasy" that Genet explores spills over into the realm of lived experience.

The play is performed entirely within privately controlled space—the home—rather than public space—the space controlled by the state. The subtext of torture, however, causes this private space to become conflated with that of the public. Through this conflation, the set becomes a representation of the torture room itself.

The visual construction of the stage is tightly controlled by the stage directions, which tell us exactly what is contained by each room and the positions the various pieces of furniture must occupy. This attention to detail is important to the play's self-consciousness regarding the theatricality that is always present during acts of violence and torture. It is a way of tightly controlling the play itself when dealing with this subject that is inherently theatrical and that contains such potentially disruptive and dangerous forces, not least of which is possible pleasure for the audience from portrayals of violence. The play moves, through the story of Nena, a young woman kidnapped by Orlando, a state torturer, from the warehouse to the basement to the living room, closer and closer to the heart of "civilization." This is also the progression of torture, which, through the experience of physical pain, moves from the public to the private constructions of civilization, deconstructing them as it progresses, until finally they are indistinguishable, and the body becomes the totality of the experienced world.[21] In the play, this progression also marks the reclamation of Nena's relationship to culture (from which she has been disenfranchised by Orlando's torture) as the other women reclaim her from Orlando's world.

Nena epitomizes the ultimate victim within the play's spectrum of representation. She is not just a woman but a child, homeless, and without even the last vestige of her family, the senile grandfather who has lost control of his body's functions. Her world has been shrunken, as in the case of the torture victim, to the smallest possible circumference, that of her body. Orlando, in the role of torturer, from his first scene with Nena begins to deconstruct her final link between her body and her self by destroying her relationship to language. He accuses her of having called him a "snake," which she first denies completely and then qualifies by saying she was "kidding." This is the betrayal, the act of complicity on the part of the victim, that is so important to the process of torture in Elaine Scarry's analysis in *The Body in Pain*.[22] Nena's attempt to defend herself through a verbal attack on Orlando has become the reason for her "punishment"—rape. It does not even matter whether she actually said this to Orlando; he is the author of her words, and—her world constricting steadily—language itself (her voice) becomes party to the torture.

Rape in *The Conduct of Life* becomes synonymous with torture through this act of bodily colonialism, where the world of the self of the rapist/torturer expands to fill the area left by the contraction of the victim's world into the space occupied only by the physical sensations—pain—of the body, where the self has been annihilated. Anthony Wilden, in his article "In the Penal Colony: The Body as the Discourse of the Other," equates rape, as a crime of power, with the mark of fascism, the complete breakdown of a democratic ideal.[23] The axiom that underlies the act of rape within society is, according to Wilden, that "sex is an act of violence."[24] From this, he goes on to quote Sade, who writes that "The sexual act has a close affinity with murder. . . . Murderer and victim are in the same sort of relation as the male penetrating the female."[25]

This conflation of the relationship of heterosexual sex to murder is integral to the construction of rape as a form of violence which mimics the sexual act—it is the acting out of a power relationship, where the murderer/rapist inscribes his name/discourse/self upon the body of the victim through the violence of penetration, negating the self of the victim and leaving only the body. Wilden goes on to state that "(t)orture is gang rape taken to its pathological conclusion. The torturers are competing with each other over who has control of the victims' bodies and what they do to them."[26] The power of the torturer is directly related to the disempowerment, in the most physical way possible, of the victim. Orlando is not just a torturer in his public role as the arm of the state and the traditional patriarch of his private world, as his wife Léticia has believed him to be. Instead, he creates his own private world as torturer by kidnapping Nena. His repeated rape of her is a reenactment of his role as torturer, but without the competition of the state in the form of other torturers or of men such as Alejo, who hold the authority of the state over him.

In his role as torturer, Orlando displays a pathological need for control that must continually expand outward to occupy all space and that is finally achieved through the inscription of his power onto the bodies of other people. However, simultaneous with his constant expansion of power and control is his overwhelming fear that he will become out of control or will be controlled. He states that he "will not spend time feeling sorry for (him)self," that his goal is to "achieve maximum power." Underlying this boundless drive to "achieve maximum power" is his fear that he will be "overwhelmed by sexual passion . . . degraded beyond hope of recovery." He is introduced to us through the physical action of doing jumping jacks until, the stage directions note, "it can no longer be endured."

Stage directions that request an action until "it can no longer be endured" suggest that the relationship between Orlando and the audience is one of spectacle, competition, and physicality. Who is it that can no longer endure the jumping jacks? Is it Orlando, who will eventually become physically tired? Or is it the audience, who will become perhaps bored, tired, irritated, or uncomfortable as Orlando repeats this strongly physical action over and over again? The audience is reminded that they are trapped in their seats at the mercy of the play, despite their discomfort; and as the play progresses, the audience will be forced to consider their relationship to the violent actions taking place on the stage—for them, as it were. Orlando, on the other hand, is performing the identity he will inhabit throughout the play—as a man whose need for control over himself and others is always expressed through the lens of patriarchal masculinity and profound embodied violence. While *The Balcony* suggests that the detaching of signifier from signified might lead to a profound pleasure in the gap of *difference* which such a move creates, *The Conduct of Life* stages the physical and psychological intimacies of profound violence—which through intense coercive pain attempts to eradicate all spaces of *difference*. Through conventional staging and identification, Fornes's play positions the audience as spectators whose own voyeuristic pleasures must become a site of discomfort if we are to identify with any character other than Orlando.

Integrally connected to Orlando's need for power and fear of being overwhelmed is his production of violence through the desiring-production of his unconscious, which equates femaleness with the unconscious and desires nothing more, as he expresses it, than to "break out . . . in an edenic freedom from responsibility."[27] Fornes positions Orlando as a fascist and torturer who tortures both from a profound pleasure in his own absolute control over (feminized) others and from a fear that, equating femininity with the unconscious and lack of control, he will himself lose his power and position if he does not exercise violent control over himself—and therefore others—at all times. Bataille has marked such a personality as a discontinuous being who is in search of the dissolution that is always present in eroticism and that finds its final expression in death.

The link between the "private" erotic search for dissolution and death, which is commonly presented as the heterosexual norm of patriarchy which always positions the person being penetrated as feminine, finds its link to violence against others in the conflation of sexual control with violence and containment of the feminine. Klaus Theweleit, examining the diaries and writings of pre–World War II German fascists, states: "In patriarchy, where the work of domination has consisted in subjugating, damming in and transforming the 'natural energy' in society, (the) desiring-production of the unconscious has been encoded as the subjugated gender, or femaleness. . . . What fascism allows the masses to express are suppressed drives, imprisoned desires."[28]

Orlando, speaking to Nena, does not express himself as torturing out of a need to maintain state order or to survive but out of "pleasure. It is quiet and it pierces my insides in the most internal way. It is my most private self. And this I give to you."[29] The "gift" of his "most private self" is the pain that he inflicts on Nena (and his other victims); here he turns the language of threat into that of a gift, divesting himself (once again) of the responsibility for any negative results of their interaction and making her, even more than she already is, into a victim without recourse (to recall Lyotard). He stages—acts out—what he does not know—his private, secret self—his unconscious, and these stagings take place in the basement—the "hidden" area of the house. Léticia may know what is happening but remains complicit through her silence, taking action only through trying to get another man to notice her.

As torturer, Orlando absolves himself of his responsibility for violence through the act of his violence. Through the fiction that has been created by the use of the interrogation—Nena's having called him a "snake"—she is positioned as responsible for her own abuse. He also absolves himself of the equation of sex with violence, which posits pleasure/orgasm as an act of violent penetration and destruction. His desire to torture is "a desire to destroy and to see things destroyed and to see the inside of them." His desire is not just destruction but the curiosity of transgression, crossing borders to see what is hidden behind them. Theweleit, in his discussion of fascist literature, examines the "pleasurable perception of women in the condition of 'bloody masses'" and states:

It's as if two male compulsions were tearing at the women with equal strength. One is trying to push them away, to keep them at arm's length (defense); the other wants to penetrate them, to have them very near. Both compulsions seem to find satisfaction in the act of killing, where the man pushes the woman far away (takes her life), and gets very close to her (penetrates her with a bullet, stab wound, club, etc.). The closeness is made possible by robbing the woman of her identity as an object with concrete dimensions and a unique name. Once she has lost all that and is reduced to a pulp, a shapeless, bloody mass, the man can breathe a sigh of relief. . . . What we are dealing with here is the dissolution of the body itself, and of the woman as bodily entity as well as love object.[30]

Orlando has conflated love with this desire to destroy as well as to "see the inside" of things. The "shapeless, bloody mass" of the torture victim becomes synonymous with sexual climax, or his sexuality itself. Orlando constantly discusses violence and torture, as well as the body of the victim, in blatantly sexual terms. In scene 6 he describes his relationship to a victim he is torturing. "He was pouring liquid from everywhere, his mouth, his nose, his eyes. He was . . . a sexual organ.—Helpless. A viscera.—Screaming. Making strange sounds. He collapsed on top of her. She wanted him off but he collapsed on top of her. Like gum." Orlando has released the hidden flows from the confines of his victim's body—blood, urine, vomit, bile, and so on. He has made the inside visible, destroying the person's personhood, language, and identity. And with this act he has made visible the hidden sexuality of his victim's body as he conceives it. The body of the victim is in the realm of noncivilization, a spectacle, pre-"human" and therefore without rights and the markers of society.

And Orlando has created this—the deconstruction of the civilization and language of the victim and his own expansion into their place—by the pain and abuse he has inflicted on the victim's body. This sexual, flowing, screaming organ then collapses on a "her," a woman's body, which is repulsed by it but cannot escape it because of its fluid, sticky consistency, like "gum." Finally, through her indifference, the woman is freed of his body, which lifts itself off her. Orlando's violence is a fantasy of dismemberment and rememberment, destruction and reconstruction, a theatrical acting-out upon another body his own desiring production and absolute power.

However, as Orlando seeks through Nena to merge his worlds of private and public, torturer and husband, which is a way of consolidating his power, he also opens the door to the reconstruction of civilization and his own destruction. By moving Nena into the domestic realm of his house (the basement), he also moves her into the proximity of other women, and the reconstruction of her world and self begins. Although she has not talked since her first appearance onstage, when Orlando destroyed her relationship to language, in scene 11, when we first see her with another person besides Orlando she is playing patty-cake with Olympia. The reconstruction of her world and language has begun, although in a preverbal form, through the mediation of Olympia, who herself suffers from a speech impediment and therefore occupies a position on the threshold between nonverbal communication and language. Already Orlando's power over Nena (and therefore over his expanded world) has begun to slip, and he retreats from Olympia's violent threat to dismember him, rather than acting against her in some way.

It is directly following this scene that Orlando begins to attempt to curtail Léticia's world by forbidding her to invite her friend Mona to visit. However, even as he is trying to break down Léticia's communication with her friend and shrink her world so that his may expand into it, Nena completely reenters the world of language. She not only expands her world beyond her body into the immediate area occupied by herself and Olympia, but she gains a history and a family/grandfather, as well as the story of how Orlando has brutalized her. She has not somehow miraculously recovered, but recovery has begun. She still believes the lie that she deserves Orlando's abuse because it is she who is dirty. She also gives us the elaboration of the title of the play by telling the story of how she wants to "conduct each day of her life." In direct opposition to Orlando's violent enactment of his desires, she sees in herself an image of the mutilated body of Christ killed and eaten by the raging, all-consuming violence of society. She wishes to receive her victimizers kindly, recognizing their pain as greater than her own. She eschews violence by giving in to it and she is still trapped within Orlando's construction of violence perpetrated out of love. By remaining within this role of the forgiving victim, however, she is denied any chance of direct action as a way to remove herself from the cycle of abuse.

By using the dining-room table to shell beans, Olympia and Nena are reclaiming it as a marker of civilization (in Scarry's terms) and are using it to perform a domestic chore of the most basic kind—the preparation of food. It no longer belongs to the realm of the disappearing suitcase strap, which Orlando has presumably stolen from the house and whose basic civilizing function has been perverted by Orlando into an instrument of pain to assist in the destruction of civilization (torture). It is immediately following this scene that Orlando has his nightmare. He has been sleeping upon the dining-room table, and as his power as torturer is being deconstructed in the same way that the table has been reclaimed, he dreams that he has lost control and that it is his body, rather than the woman's body, that the bloody, shapeless mass of the tortured body falls upon. In the first account of this tortured body, Orlando controlled the representation of it through language, but here it is out of control because the event occurs unconsciously in his dream. His body is in the same position as the woman's body from the first account, triggering Orlando's violent fear of being feminized in any way. It is here that the overwhelming fear of the tortured body and correspondingly the fear of his own death—and thus the need to control it through torture—become evident, and it is after this dream that Orlando begins his last final push to regain control through his role as torturer, which results finally in his murder.

Although it is Léticia who shoots Orlando, the final action of the play is her placement of the gun in Nena's hand. While this could be read as an empowering moment of solidarity between the women and return of control to Nena, I believe it is more easily read as an ambiguous and threatening ending. Léticia, the upper-class woman, places the "smoking gun" in the hands of the person—a brutalized, impoverished orphan—who is both least able to defend herself and already willing to take the blame for any action. Nena will take upon herself the guilt for Orlando's death, believing that it was his "gift" to her, the rape and torture, that has caused his murder. Ending with violence in this way, the play does not suggest a solution to the problem of the violence that has occurred either in the home (private realm) or the state (public realm). Orlando has been stopped from his further abuse of the women in his home and of the people he tortures for the state. Yet the violence of this act will have repercussions for the women involved—both psychically and legal—while leaving the institutions of patriarchy and the totalitarian state untouched.

Although Fornes herself, through the staging of the play in the domestic/private space of the home, points toward the conflation of public with private that happens in totalitarian violence, both in the structures of state rhetoric and in the "individual" relations of torture, the women in the play make no larger political connection to their situation. The violence that occurs at the end is a violence that contains within it the seeds of the continuation of violence. Orlando, through the action of his murder, is figured as an intrusive figure of violence that has entered and defiled the private space of the home. Once he is dead, the home can once again revert to "private" space, existing (in the women's fantasy) as separate from the "public" world of violence and state terror. Just as the revolution in *The Balcony* must fail because it does not understand that it is an integral part of the system it is supposedly fighting against, Olympia, Léticia, and Nena have formed a private solidarity among themselves, perhaps, but they, too, are doomed to fail because their actions do not embody any larger critique of or resistance to the fiction of public/private space that supports the cultural systems through which Orlando operated.[31]

The Bishop, the Judge, the General, and finally the Chief of Police in *The Balcony* all seek to deny death and dissolution through the inscription of themselves into monolithic representations, and Orlando also betrays his fear of death and dissolution through his driving need continually to reinscribe himself into his role as torturer. He uses violence and the representation of sex through rape to deny his own fear of death by enacting this dissolution upon the bodies of other humans. He confirms his own boundaries and control by destroying the boundaries of others. Just as the fantasies acted out within the walls of The Balcony are constantly reinscribed into the social order to deny disorder (the revolution's wish to destroy all social patterns randomly and completely) while simultaneously this (patriarchal, heterosexist) process is revealed as a cornerstone of and constitutive of "domestic order," in the same way Orlando's actions as a torturer are supported by the "law." Through the fiction of the interrogation—in Nena's case, her having called Orlando a "snake"—the torturer is placed on the side of order and given the authority to "interrogate" or "punish."

While *The Balcony* appears to be a play that is all about violence and sex, it is so much focused on play and facades that there is little "actual" violence or sex in the play itself. *The Conduct of Life*, however, is a play completely about violence that very tightly controls all of its representations. The "realist" structure of the play is a way of controlling a subject that Fornes is invested in presenting in a particular fashion. Torture and the issues of complicity, pain, and denial that surround it are issues fraught with such anxiety that even the issue of control over its representation is a possible subject for anxiety. Since Orlando, the patriarch, torturer, and rapist of the play, is introduced to us as a character for whom control over himself and his environment is all-consuming, all attempts of ours and of spectators (in the world of the play) at exerting control over things must therefore be suspect. Perhaps because of the fictionalizing nature of mimesis, however, the play represents violence (through the rape scenes) much more directly than *The Balcony*. And while *The Balcony* presents a dialogic between eroticism and rhetoric, *The Conduct of Life* is much more focused on the body itself, not just as an object defined by the disciplinary forces brought to bear on it but as an actor with and between different cultural apparatuses.

In *For they know not what they do*, Slavoj Žižek states:

> in the words of Lacan against Dostoevsky, against his famous position "If there is no God, all is permitted": if there is no God—the Name-of-the-Father as an instance of the law/prohibition—everything is forbidden. And is it too much to suggest that this is precisely the logic of "totalitarian" political discourse? The "impediment" of the subject, produced by this discourse, results from a similar absence, suspension, of the law/prohibition.[32]

Without the law, there is no possibility for transgression (as Genet, Bataille, and Foucault have all demonstrated), and we are left then with precisely nothing but the law.[33] In *The Balcony*, the characters mistake the mimetic world as a world separate from the law where everything is allowed. But they do not recognize that the "hangnail" that they need always to be able to find to reassure themselves that they are within the mimetic world is reassuring precisely because it represents the law—there would be no transgression were it not there. In *The Conduct of Life*, however, Orlando is completely within the logic of just such a totalitarian political discourse marked by the absence of the law. In his role as a torturer, he enacts this "absence" over and over again on the bodies of other people.

Violence in these plays functions as "evidence" of the mimetic relationship—proof of embodiment and therefore of nonarbitrariness. Performativity, both for Orlando and for the actors of *The Balcony*, mediates between the world of mimesis and of the law. The violence in the plays, however, is not the purview only of the representatives of the law. Both plays end with a violent death acted as a form of resistance, yet even in the moment of their enactment, these actions are recuperated again into the world of disciplinary structures. While this order can be momentarily subverted and replaced, as *The Conduct of Life* clearly illustrates, it is not clear that what it will be replaced by will not just be a slightly different state of the same order that authorized Orlando. In other words, as *The Balcony* traces the waxing and waning influence of revolution upon the forces of "rational" order, ultimately the order remains unchanged at its root, and the brothel stays in business.

"Private" Violence, "Public" Blindness

The testimonial literature I discuss in the following chapters directly addresses this concern of the gendered split between public and private and the role of individuals in relation to state violence. Although the women writing these texts were victims of the most vicious and murderous sort of attacks by the State, they discuss their experiences not as individuals operating within a universal field of standards but as members of distinct and various communities that both overlap and require constant efforts of communication. In texts such as *Who Will Carry the Word?* and *The Little School,* the systems of oppression that have combined to do violent damage to people such as Charlotte Delbo and Alicia Partnoy cannot be separated and ranked as to their viciousness. In other words, the (hysterical) sexism that constituted part of the rhetoric of both the Nazi and Argentinean fascist regimes was as important an element in those governments' murderous actions as was racism or nationalism.

Given the advent of sophisticated technology and the increasing involvement of members of the medical establishment in torture, the traces of torture that are left on a body can be largely nonexistent. This is not to say that many people are not seriously and permanently wounded and debilitated by torture, but that now especially, the attack does not have to leave people visibly wounded in a lasting way. Through the use of electricity, selective beatings, immersion, and many other methods, extreme pain can be inflicted on a person without ever leaving a visible trace. Thus torture more than ever can become a privatized experience that has no language beyond the specific sensation and memory of the pain itself. For this reason, as a method of resistance to torture, other members of the medical establishment work to find more and more sophisticated methods of tracing the markers that the experience of pain leave physiologically, so as to give it public voice. Also for this reason, survivor testimony about the experience of torture is both increasingly necessary and increasingly fraught with the danger that monolithic State discourses can deny its occurrence.

Along with the possible "invisibility" of its process, torture has increasingly moved away from the realm of the public disciplinary spectacle into the realm of the "private."[34] Thus the growing trend toward "disappearances" in the 1970s and 1980s as a method of state terror worked to confine torture within the realm of the "private" spaces of the state, hidden from public view. In similar fashion, the Nazi concentration and death camps as well as many other sites of mass murder were "hidden" from public view, thereby both juridically disappearing their victims and "containing" them according to the viral model of discourse employed to describe them. This move to make subjects of abuse invisible presents an immediate difficulty for juridical discourses of human rights that rely on visibility and recognition of all bodies within national and transnational systems, as Article 6 of the Universal Declaration asserts when it states that "everyone has the right to recognition everywhere as a person before the law."

To recuperate bodies that have gone from being full citizens of civil and political life to being illegally removed from it, as difficult as this might be, is easier than granting such full citizenship to bodies that for specific structural reasons, such as the relationships of power and domination inherent between different sexes and races, have never fully enjoyed it. As is clear from the Declaration, human rights as they are constituted today, although always in a process of change, have dealt with this inequity by rhetorically enacting the universal individual and then attempting to provide some guidelines on the structure of social and cultural life through which the playing field will be made more equal. This is only half a solution, however, as the obfuscating veils of privacy serve the same function in supporting the State through terror as they did during the recent military dictatorships in Latin America and as they do in supporting the vast structures of economic and social power that oppositionally constitute themselves against women as the space of privacy and family.

Women usually do not enjoy the same protection by the law in their daily lives as do men, and as victims of state oppression, they often encounter violence aimed directly at their gender and sex. As Ximena Bunster-Burotto painstakingly illustrates in her article "Surviving beyond Fear: Women and Torture in Latin America," military regimes have increasingly attacked women through patterns of punishment that attempt to coerce and dominate them through their gender and position as women.[35] That this is not simply a Latin-American phenomenon has recently been made very public through the systematic campaign of rape and torture carried out against Bosnian women in the former Yugoslavia and Rwandan women during the genocide. Although patriarchy as a violent social order is not addressed in the Declaration and the systems that produce it are protected, it lays at the root of much of the both random and systematized human rights abuses perpetrated against the "international citizens" whom the Declaration and covenants seek to protect. Simply to designate all people as universal individuals is not enough. Charlotte Bunch notes:

> Few governments exhibit more than token commitment to women's equality as a basic human right in domestic or foreign policy. No government determines its policies toward other countries on the basis of their treatment of women, even when some aid and trade decisions are said to be based on a country's human rights record. . . . the assumption that states are not responsible for most violations of women's rights ignores the fact that such abuses, although committed perhaps by private citizens, are often condoned or even sanctioned by states.[36]

Bunch goes on to cite a few representative statistics of abuse against women in various cultures—such as wife battery, rape, dowry deaths, genital mutilation, and female sexual slavery—that confirm that violence against women is both pervasive and far greater than anything reported by Amnesty International and other major human rights organizations. These are not private acts defined by cultural heritage, they are "structural relationships of power, domination, and privilege between men and women in society. Violence against women is central to maintaining those political relations at home, at work and in all public spheres."[37] Therefore, as Bunch and others have argued, nongovernmental organizations (NGOs) and regional bodies need to incorporate women's rights and a critique of privacy into their practices of monitoring and intervention.

Recently there has been a rise in the creation of "gender advisor" positions in UN agencies and NGOs, partly in response to donor demand for addressing gender as a central concern both within organizations and in programming. However, the institutional will to recognize gender as a crucial foundational issue to be addressed in situations of conflict, humanitarian aid, human rights, and capacity-building as well as in the organizations undertaking such programming is largely lacking. Gender advisors are often women with no particular training in gender who are appointed from within the ranks of the organization by managers who feel that a woman, regardless of qualifications, fulfills the mandate for hiring. Trying at best to mainstream gender concerns into existing programs without a serious effort to address very real and dramatic gender imbalances is very harmful, presenting the appearance of a problem having been solved without even beginning to truly address the depth of the crisis.

The state abuse suffered by concentration camp survivors such as Charlotte Delbo and Alicia Partnoy is not so far removed in its structural dynamics from that suffered by Nena in *The Conduct of Life*. Just as Nena is tortured through rape and abuse within the confines of Orlando's private domain (his house), his job as a state torturer serves to conflate the "private" space of abuse between men and women with the "public" abuse of individuals by the state. But this structural relationship is itself confused through the way in which torture and the torture room come to be constituted as "private" space. Not only is torture itself usually a hidden act by the perpetrators, but the relationship between the perpetrator and the person being tortured comes to be constructed as a gendered relationship between men and women, with the victim occupying the position of the woman whose body is controlled, penetrated, emasculated, and immobilized.[38] The extent to which the extreme pain of torture destroys language, as Scarry painstakingly illustrates, contributes to its positioning as private, unspeakable, and unrepresentable. By giving identities and public recognition to the individuals it is working to save, Amnesty International "reappears" them from this intensely private, hidden space within the State and is a powerful force for intervention. But as the testimonial literature by survivors recounts, only by an engagement with the complex relationships between language and silence, history and forgetting, public and private constructions of community can the systemic foundations of the violence to which they have been subjected be resisted.

Torture within the legal discourses of corporal punishment must obey three principle criteria, according to Foucault. First, it must "produce a certain degree of pain, which may be measured exactly, . . . compared and hierarchized"; second, the "production of pain is regulated" according to a legal code regulating its infliction; and third, "from the point of view of the law that imposes it, public torture and execution must be spectacular, it must be seen by all almost as its triumph."[39] Foucault states that one of the primary intentions and effects of torture is to inscribe upon the body of the victim the signs of the crime, and therefore, "the very excess of the violence employed is one of the elements of its glory [the spectacle]: the fact that the guilty man should moan and cry out under the blows is not a shameful side-effect, it is the very ceremonial of justice being expressed in all its force."[40] With the move away from corporal punishment and public spectacle, however, the mechanisms of punishment become hidden. Prisoners are hidden from the public, and executions take place privately within the walls of the prison. The violent public inscription of justice upon the body becomes the privatized pressure of reform upon the soul and the removal of the "property" of freedom. All bodies within this system are subject to the panoptical gaze of the cultural system, which will restrict their freedom for transgressing the system.

Just as prisons have become more "private" and less "public," so has torture. This does not remove the spectacle from torture, it privatizes it. Torture is still a "private" spectacle of power and domination for the torturers, and the theatrical discourse used to describe the mechanisms and dynamics surrounding torture reflects this. However, since torture is no longer a public, judicial "spectacle," the function it fulfills now is largely one of terror. As we have seen enacted in many countries, including Argentina during the dictatorship, the fear of arbitrary arrest, imprisonment, and torture are used to enforce the rule of the State. The invisibility of torture therefore becomes an important element of its function. Because torture is more concerned with pain than with leaving permanent traces, the visible marking of torture upon the body of the victim is not the Foucauldian spectacle of the brutalized body but is instead the marking Scarry discusses, which may not outlast the pain itself or the imprisonment. For this reason, survivor testimony and bearing witness to abuse become vital.

To move these questions into a context closer to "home," consider why, if we have moved into the panopticon and torture and imprisonment have become private rather than public spectacles, do we have public spectacles of torture or abuse happening in the United States and many other countries with such daily regularity? Perhaps because the people who are subject to them, such as Rodney King, Amadou Diallo, and Abner Louima, urban, working-class, African and African-American men, are not recognized as subjects/bodies to the extent that they must be to be fully recognizable either to the American disciplinary (juridical) structure or to its agents (the police).[41] Such very visible incidents of police brutality have something in common with the public spectacle of torture that Foucault implies has become submerged with modern culture's movement toward a panoptical method of control. Because these abuses usually happen within very specific contexts, such as African-American inner-city neighborhoods, they occur within subcultural, semiprivatized zones that are not completely visible within the larger field of American culture.

These privatized zones are subject to state control through spectacles of terror and violence that are no longer permitted within the larger public arena. The video camera, such as the one that made King's brutalization more public, consequently occupies the dual position both of a method of resistance and of increasing panoptical control. By serving as the means by which the "public" eye has access, behind the veil of privacy, to the violence of this zone, the video ensures that the perpetrators can be arrested and brought to trial. At the same time, however, through the broadcast of the violent spectacle of abuse throughout the country, the video increases terror both of the State and of the racist stereotype of the violent, excessive black man. In this way, the video itself serves a reifying function, proving Foucault's contention of the spectacle's glory. The reason such visible brutality can exist is because it occurs largely in privatized spaces where the bodies that are subject to it are perceived as excessive to the panopticon. Similarly, the brutalized bodies that are often "dumped" in public places during regimes of terror that utilize torture serve to bring the private world of pain, torture, and state terror into the public view of civil and political life.

During the Holocaust, the language that the Nazis used to describe people whom the State was working to annihilate was not the language of people and humans and bodies but of bugs, vermin, and inanimate objects such as logs. By thus dehumanizing and disembodying people, the Nazi state was able to make its murders, illegal internments, and slave labor forces juridically justifiable within its own legal system as well as more palatable to its individual actors. Such rhetorical dehumanization also took place in Argentina during the dictatorship, as it has in many other places during massive attacks against selected groups of citizenry. For example, the Taliban edict making the wearing of the burqa state law for women, moving the wearing of the burqa from a cultural norm to the realm of the juridical, was a very public way of dehumanizing women and making them less "public" and hence even more eligible for private, "nameless" violence.

Alongside such state discourses of disembodiment, torture works to remove the consciousness from bodies. As Scarry points out, torture

69

and other experiences of extreme pain are moments of total embodiment, where the consciousness's relationship to language and other cultural institutions and markers is completely severed. It is in exactly this moment of embodiment, however, that the body—the visible juridically recognizable body—is lost, as the torturer takes control over the voice and space of the victim.

Given the importance of language to the maintenance of cultural violences, language itself becomes an important and difficult site of resistance to such violences. Much survivor literature deals with the issue of language disjunction and having to relearn or reenter language upon returning from the camps. For the survivor of extreme instances of abuse, the recounting of one's experience is often the beginning of the survivor's reintegration into a "normative" cultural frame. Testimony and memoir-writing are often said by their authors to be attempts to "come to terms" with the experience. Within prison or camp situations, retaining the ability to speak or communicate can become vital to survival.

In *Who Will Carry the Word?* the constant and seemingly futile resistance to the process of abuse within the world of the camps becomes the central struggle of Delbo's characters. The importance of language, of expressing the inexpressible, is the primary focus not just of Delbo's play but of most Holocaust literature. Unlike the experience of torture, which usually relies on the complete physical isolation of the victim, the camps forced this retreat of the consciousness into the world of the physical sensations of the body within a group context. Like fascism itself, a mass movement relying on the submersion of the identity of the individual into the consciousness of the group, the camps worked to make the individual internees into completely anonymous and interchangeable bodies. These texts, however, explore a variety of strategies of and meanings for resistance within the camps. Within these texts, the emphasis is not upon the loss of identity and retreat into the body exemplified by Agamben's Muselman, who no longer exhibited basic elements of consciousness, but upon the strong community that the women in the camp formed in response to this pressure.

Language itself, that final link with the world that is broken during torture and for the Muselman, becomes necessary for survival. The women talk to each other continually about the need to survive, about their histories and fears, even about food, continually reaffirming themselves as individuals and subjects who have some link, however tenuous, to a world outside that of their own physical pain. As Mounette says in

Who Will Carry the Word? when Françoise suggests that they should take advantage of their brief opportunity to sleep, "talking is as important as sleeping. It helps as much. If I did not talk, it would seem to me as if I was no longer alive. I say anything; we say anything." In *Milena: The Story of a Remarkable Friendship,* also, this resistant form of community-building serves as an important site of survival for Margarete and Milena. By telling each other the stories of their lives, they help each other to recover the ability to be a witness to her own life.

In these texts, it is the survival of history that will make the future possible. The irony of this situation, of course, is that the very humanist system against which fascism emerged is the culture these women must write themselves into in order to reconstitute themselves as subjects. They must write themselves back into the juridical system, reconstructing what the Nazis destroyed, preserving the "Word" with all of its implications of patriarchal law and public/private bifurcation, in order to regain a ground from which to speak and to act. In the very act of preserving the word, however, they disrupt the totalizing systems it implies.

The women—and other persons' bodies feminized by such totalitarian violence—must be deconstructed as juridical subjects in order to justify not the "random" outbreaks of violence against them but the systematic internment and murder of individuals who as universal humanist subjects have the right to human rights and considerations. Thus, by excluding certain bodies from the juridical discourse of human rights, such systems can maintain the facade of civilization while enacting mass murder.

It is in this tension between the assumption of the always already private and juridically recognizable body of humanism and the inability of humanist, rights-based discourses to protect so many bodies around the globe that one of the great problems of a rights-based juridical theory surfaces. Torture and abuse happen within the confines of private spaces of the home as well as of the state and in public spectacles involving actions by the police and the military, but in all instances they happen because the bodies that are being acted upon are not fully subjects and are therefore not bodies at all. They are not the (universal individual) body that is juridically recognizable.

The problem of the rights-based Universal Declaration and its relationship to visibly recognizable subjects has been addressed by the proliferation of conventions, charters, and other documents that have tried to bring more and more subjects/bodies into the representational spectrum. This has lead to a dangerous reliance on discourses of privacy and concomitantly of identity (such as the battles over race, gender, and sexuality in the United States as well as the global rise of violence based on ethnic identifications) that in the long run do not advance the goal of protecting bodies transnationally. The dangers of such reliance are especially obvious when one considers that state respect for privacy is often contingent upon whether or not the instruments of the state, for example the police and the military, perceive something to be a threat to their security.

Within state structures, torture and other forms of human rights abuse often take place in "private" spaces within the country, and the people subjected to them are juridically "disappeared" from the fields of cultural and state discourse. In this way, just as the UN cannot intervene into human rights abuse until it becomes "visible" outside the private domain of the State, human rights discourse cannot protect citizens that it cannot "see." What I have tried to suggest in this chapter is the way the construction of the private realm of the family versus the public realm of civil and political life serve at the most fundamental level to prevent the realization of truly universal ideals of human rights. As Charlotte Bunch has argued, the "universal" individual of human rights discourse will always be gendered male until the patriarchal formulations of human rights, based on this public/private bifurcation, are reenvisioned. Women will therefore never be protected from human rights abuse as long as the family remains a realm of privacy outside the discourse of human rights.

The "International Bill of Rights," as Henkin has referred to the Universal Declaration and the covenants, cannot function truly to protect bodies around the globe until NGOs and regional human rights organizations have revised their definitions of human rights to include a critique and revision of structures of privacy that disguise and support violence of epidemic proportions. Although many (especially national) NGOs now work under very difficult conditions specifically on domestic abuse in countries such as Egypt and Pakistan, the lack of a textual and legal support for this work and activism at the international level makes such intervention much more difficult and dangerous. As *The Balcony* and *The Conduct of Life* elucidate, however, with their refusal to suggest an "outside" to the foundational relationship between structures of public/state and private/family violence, such widespread structures of power and hierarchy are not easily revised.

Testimonial and the issues raised by the authors in the following chapters cut across the lines of difference, speaking in the voice of all survivors/members of the community and undercutting the traditional single author's voice. Through their insistence on formations of authorship and text that deny the unifying voice of humanism/juridical culture, these texts create grounds for broad cultural critique. Although they spring from instances of extreme bodily and psychic trauma, these texts are not caught in a language of private individuality. Instead, they stress the collectivity of experience and speak to a broad criticism of and call for revolution in cultures of racist, patriarchal, economic systems of oppression that allow (and are founded on) genocide, mass death, violence, and "human rights" abuse. As such, gender is an imperative category for analysis in emergent discourses of testimonial and their political exigency. In its very position of writing both with and against the assumptions of the Universal Declaration, gender provides a necessary critique of its underlying humanism.

3

Testimonial and Surviving: Gender and the Crisis of Witnessing

> The fear that fate will strike again is crucial to the memory of trauma, and to the inability to talk about it. On breaking the internal silence, the Holocaust from which one had been hiding, may come to life and once more be relived; only this time around, one might not be spared not have the power to endure. The act of telling might itself become severely traumatizing, if the price of speaking is *re-living;* not relief, but further retraumatization. Poets and writers who have broken their silence may have indeed paid with their life for that deed (Célan, Améry, Borowski, Levi, Bettelheim).[1]

> The light seared the eyes that dared to seek.
>
> Françoise, in Who Will Carry the Word?

Because the Holocaust happened before and was one of the primary motivations behind the adoption of the UN Universal Declaration of Human Rights in 1948, this chapter treats testimony by Holocaust survivors as a first step toward considering the ways in which such concepts as "the individual," "the universal," and "community" remain critical problems within contemporary human rights discourse. Increasingly, testimony is used as a preventative tool for intervention into situations of human rights abuse. But rather than understanding testimony as an always already flawed authenticating document used to support historical claims of mass death and atrocity, I read certain survivor testimonials as texts that can help to provide us with the theoretical tools better to understand and utilize these categories in positive (active interventionist) ways.[2]

More specifically, this chapter considers two published testimonial texts by women survivors that confront the reader/spectator with the ethical problems of telling and remembering the Holocaust. These testimonies are exemplary texts to the extent that they rehearse some of the central problems of Holocaust survivor testimony, but I do not mean for them to stand in for all, or even some, of the many other texts by survivors that have been written. My interest lies, instead, in the ways in which these texts posit a witnessing survivor voice that speaks *from* and acknowledges the space of fragmentation through which identity is constituted. Rather than returning to a belief in the necessary fiction of the unified and coherent speaking subject, these authors rebuild a post-Holocaust speaking voice through their acknowledgment of the always already sutured-together nature of identity—an identity that has been marked for them as such through the horrific rupture of their experiences in the death camps.[3] Far more than the notion of a posttraumatic return to the site of an identity not yet interrupted by the violences of the Holocaust, these testimonials acknowledge a survivor identity that is formed through recognition of the excess—to structures of memory, language, understanding, and knowledge—that sits beyond, haunts, and structures formations of identity.

Both Charlotte Delbo, in her play *Who Will Carry the Word?* and Margarete Buber-Neumann, in her testimonial *Milena: The Story of a Remarkable Friendship*, performatively enact through their texts and, in Delbo's play, on the stage itself, a testimonial dynamic with the reader/audience that builds a witnessing relationship.[4] The characters in and authors of these testimonial texts bear witness not just to the atrocities they have experienced and seen but to the ethical complexities of their positions within the camps and as survivors, to the reconfiguration of resistance as consisting acts of support and love for fellow prisoners, and to the redefinition of "human" as a category that distinguishes between ethical and unethical actors in and toward situations of atrocity. In addition, both of these authors provide a gendered witnessing that positions difference as an important category for resistance, memory, and constructions of the human.

As authors who have chosen to write their testimonies to be read or performed, these survivors also participate in a textual economy that is very different from testimony as it is enacted in the storytelling spaces of corporeal encounters: the therapeutic space, the interview, the classroom, or the family. These commodified testimonials are both written and published, circulating through and available to various economies such as the academy, the reading public, theatrical producers, and survivors. Not least because they are written accounts, they address problems of language and speaking as central to the identity of the survivor, for whom memory, history, and the performances of daily living have all become continuously and traumatically contested ground.[5] Charlotte Delbo's play *Who Will Carry the Word?* ends with a crisis of witnessing—the surviving characters confront the audience directly with the unbearable paradox of the imperative to tell of their experience and yet the inability ever to convey it adequately. Thus the play rehearses the central problematic of this chapter, since the crisis of witnessing, of telling the untellable, is emblematic of the crisis at the heart of the testimonial act. As a play, it performatively builds and enacts a witnessing dynamic over the course of its production, disrupting fourth-wall conventions and forcing audience members to confront their own role and decide between the positions of disengaged spectator and ethical witness.

Margarete Buber-Neumann's *Milena: The Story of a Remarkable Friendship* also rehearses this dynamic, as her testimonial combines witnessing and storytelling in a way that produces not a consistent or coherent narrative but an examination of differences through which community and memory can survive. The witnessing of each others' stories that occurs between Margarete and Milena and the love between the two women are resistant acts that rely on the exploration of difference as vital in rebuilding a world where, as Dori Laub formulates it, "the imagination of the Other is still possible."[6] Her testimonial provides and opens up the opportunity for a queer reading of same-sex relationships as complex sites of resistance to the ongoing atrocities of a concentration camp. Rather than claiming to excavate a "hidden truth," I discuss the possibilities such a reading provides us for better understanding the role of difference as crucial both to resistance and to an ethical formulation of "the human" that claims universality while maintaining particularity.

Both of these testimonials combine storytelling with searching analysis of the authors' and characters' own moral implication in the camp hierarchies to create fractured texts that raise destabilizing questions rather than seeking stable and easily accepted "truths"; they question the role of monolithic oppositional ideologies, such as communism and some religious groups, as sites of resistance in the camps. Adhering to a rigid ideology comes to be figured in these testimonials as at best undermining possibilities for survival and at worst complicit in the mass death of the camps. Terms such as resistance, therefore, come to be figured in new ways, as the characters of the testimonials locate survival as a complex nexus of ethical, political, humanist, and commodified exchanges. Acknowledging the resonance of trauma, these texts build new ways for us to understand the role that survivor testimony can play in the struggle against such totalitarian violences as those exemplified by the Nazi death camps.

Language, Testimony, and the Performance of Witnessing

Language, performances of contiguous identity, and modes of resistance are central foci of these accounts of survival and witnessing. To be one's own witness is an important site of resistance and is fundamental in perceiving oneself as a subject within the juridical field. The ability to speak and to act for oneself, which is so important and contested a position for the narrators of these testimonials, is a resistant act necessary to their survival both within the narratives of their time in the camps and afterwards as survivors. These moments are not constant, but as they punctuate the totalitarian concentrationary universe, they become important and remembered links in the attempt to rebuild a history and narrative within which the individual-as-subject—and therefore as person—can begin to exist again. From these kernels of memory comes the narrative of the testimonial, performed as oral or written event for the witness/survivor as well as the witness/audience—crucial to the rebuilding of the survivor's voice and therefore identity.

This performative act of memory—the placing of oneself inside historical narrative and the rebuilding of one's voice and identity as witness—does not construct a unified narrative of a historical event but instead functions as the truth of witnessing experiences whose truths can never be known. As James Young notes, "The Holocaust survivor who continues to testify in narrative seems to have intuited the paradoxical knowledge that even though his words are no longer traces of the Holocaust, without his words, the Holocaust takes no form at all."[7] But much more than "intuiting" a dilemma basic to representation, these authors consciously present the blurred ground between lived and representational experience. Writings about the Holocaust *are* traces of the event, as are the witnesses themselves. These testimonial texts perform witnessing as a paradoxical act, both insisting on the authenticity of the lived experience to which the texts bear witness and insisting on the inability of ever knowing or comprehending the events being re/membered. Survivors within our cultural imaginary function as corporeal ghosts, and just as their presence both disrupts and founds cultural forms as they are reconstituted after an event of mass atrocity, their witnessing also disrupts and confounds unified historical narrative. In addition, such witnessing resists their designation as "ghosts" of the atrocity event, demanding an ethical engagement with them as survivors. Rather than fearing the instability of historical memory and trying to stake a claim for the greater validity of their own narrative over all others, these author/survivors constitute an authorial voice from discontinuity.

To the extent that testimony as a personal and political act is commodified, it faces the same untenable paradox of survival as Françoise and Denise at the end of *Who Will Carry the Word?* By using language as the mode of entry and intervention into the social and juridical fields from which they have been excised, as survivors they must accept implication within the totalitarian cultural field responsible in part for their abuse. Thus to witness is not just to attempt to affirm the material reality of one's existence and history within the world, but to enter consciously into the uncertainty of structures of power where one is neither completely subjugated nor completely dominant. Testimony can never be an unproblematic political act of resistance, as the structure of language itself is a structure of power that is often utilized to enhance the domination of those in power over the less enfranchised. Published testimonial accounts of atrocity enter into the commodified field of discourse much more directly and widely than oral testimonial accounts, many of which might stay within a family, therapeutic, or community setting. But connections between the therapeutic work done with trauma survivors and the writings of survivors are vital. The ways in which trauma survivors in therapeutic settings articulate their experiences provide us with readings for the ways in which trauma operates behind and between written narratives. Dori Laub, Cathy Caruth, Peggy Phelan, and others build connections between individual experiences of trauma and cultural and social configurations that inform both the totalitarian violences of mass atrocity and the postatrocity culture into which survivors must integrate themselves.[8] Witnessing, trauma, and testimony are deeply interconnected, and the testimonies of atrocity under consideration here are textual examples of a form of testimonial witnessing that cuts across disciplinary categories and literary genres.

Dori Laub, referring to the Holocaust, states that "the perpetrators, in their attempt to rationalize the unprecedented scope of the destructiveness, brutally imposed upon their victims a delusional ideology whose grandiose coercive pressure totally excluded and eliminated the possibility of an unviolated, unencumbered, and thus sane, point of reference in the witness."[9] From this he concludes that there could be no witness to the Holocaust from within the event itself. Thus the attempt to rebuild the "internal witness" through testimony results in the doubled role of testimony as the political act of witnessing an event that has been radically denied and the "private" necessity to rebuild one's historical link to the experience by recounting one's memories of it in front of a witness—language and representation serve to give substance and "reality" to an experience that no longer exists or seems real.

The compulsion of some survivors to tell their stories over and over again—and Laub suggests, in the quote I have used as an epigraph to this chapter, that many of these survivors have ultimately not lived through this continual retelling—is an act of resistance against this "delusional ideology" that denies survivors' memories of their experience. As an act that functions far more as an exploration of difference than as a solidifying of identity, however, testimony is a continually shifting ground of memory and present experience that refuses easy categorization or assimilation. It is exactly here that its resistant possibilities are strongest, as it counters the totalitarian imaginary which denies atrocity with a fluid construct of performed memory. The paradox inherent in the act of using language to witness one's banishment from a juridical field comprised by this same language is overridden by the need for visibility and subjecthood.

Within the totalitarian imaginary of the Third Reich, the concentration camps were a "hidden" site of torture and mass death, but they were bounded by public roundups and deportations and the extensive documentation carried out by the bureaucratic apparatus of the death machinery.[10] The panoptical system of control utilized by the camps, where all prisoners were watched and controlled at all times, was punctuated by random and horrific violence that could strike any prisoner at any time, creating an atmosphere of oppressive terror. This contradictory and paradoxical "system" created the "delusional ideology" to which Dori Laub refers, and it was only under such conditions that the Nazis could fully create this "delusional" universe peopled by inmates who had been removed from the juridical field of personhood. Aside from the economic reasons for supporting the vast slave labor system of camps, they were also a psychic and representational necessity for the Nazi imaginary to support the project of genocide.

As Edith Wyschogrod argues, discussing the structure of the "death-world" exemplified by the Holocaust, "in the death-world, adversary lines are drawn between complex bureaucratic structures which control the technologies of man-made mass death and those who lack effective counterforce. Many who died in recent wars and almost all who died in the death-world never participated in the events which resulted in their own deaths. Victims, divested of personal identity, they enter the ranks of the numberless dead."[11] The spectacle of the tortured prisoner discussed by Foucault as necessary to the earlier (prepanoptical) penal system of control was translated by the Nazis into the spectacle of the degraded, emaciated, death camp inmate—no longer human— justifiably executed as a dangerously diseased and extraneous other. The fascist economies of fear, control, and sexuality that Klaus Theweleit documents in *Male Fantasies* culminate in the death camps and concentration camps that reached their fullest purpose only toward the end of the war, as the Nazi armies were already retreating.[12] The illogic of rerouting resources vital to the war effort to support the continuation of the Holocaust is symptomatic of the Holocaust's vital importance to the fascist imaginary of the Third Reich.

To oppose this imaginary and to replace its delusional history with the history and memories of one's own experience, it is necessary for survivors to reclaim for themselves the position of juridical subjects who have the right to speak, to be heard, and to be free from violence. To stay alive within the concentrationary universe is to support the project of the Nazi imaginary (as Françoise suggests in Delbo's play) but it is also an important site of resistance. Similarly, testimony must acknowledge the paradox of not defining oneself against the experience of the camps or refusing to speak while still maintaining the awareness of the essential inability to communicate the experience.

I suggest in following chapters that the testimonies of survivors of other experiences of human rights abuse are in some ways very similar in their difficulties with language, memory, and history to the testimonies of Holocaust survivors examined in this chapter. As Young notes:

> The aim of an inquiry into "literary testimony" is rather to determine how writers' experiences have been shaped both in and out of narrative. Once we recognize that the "facts" of history are not

distinct from their reflexive interpretation in narrative, and that the "facts" of the Holocaust and their interpretation may even have been fatally interdependent, we are able to look beyond both the facts and the poetics of literary testimony to their consequences.[13]

Young here suggests that the Holocaust was a diverse and ongoing event generated through constant interpretation and reinterpretation of events as they were occurring. In addition, the traumatic nature of the event suggests that the event is still ongoing in various forms, through myriad traces of cultural and individual memory and experience. While the consequences to which Young refers remain vague, beyond a stated hope for a self-reflexive criticism that seeks to understand "the ways our lives and these texts are inextricably bound together,"[14] Young concludes toward the end of his book that the criticism of such literature should be "life-affirming." That is, not only that we should read it as the (overdetermined) narrative of a traumatic event or as an (underdetermined) textual product, but that the criticism of such works should be synergistically connected with the larger project of furthering our understanding of our lives in the world.

Beyond the "postmodern" project that Young suggests—of recognizing the profound instability of our identities while maintaining an awareness of the constitutive nature of traditional cultural norms—is the possibility we have for altering our own responses to mass violence. I hope to suggest in the following chapters that there is value in reading the testimonies of Holocaust survivors alongside the testimonies of survivors of other moments of state-sponsored human rights abuse that have occurred more recently in this century. In doing this, I am not trying to suggest either a continuum of traumatic experience to be analyzed or a relativistic leveling of witnessing into universal norms, but I am suggesting that the genre of testimonial and the imperative to testify are culturally bound to a developing moment in which our understandings of bodies and subjects and their positions within juridical fields is deeply in flux. The positions of ethical witnessing that these texts performatively enact and their development of a definition of "human" as an ethical category that lays claim to the universal while preserving difference are crucial interventions into the human rights and humanitarian discourses being developed to alleviate and prevent atrocities around the globe. I believe that to understand "the ways our lives and these texts are inextricably bound together" and by extension to begin to understand our positions within the larger postcolonial cultural moment is to begin to understand ways that we might be better able to save lives—some of which might very well be our own.

Gendered Survival

When Young suggests that we read Holocaust writings partly through engaging a postmodern project that self-critically understands our own inability to perceive the cultural frames through which we project ourselves onto our objects of perception, he himself fails to recognize the crucial role that gender plays in all such analyses. That writers and survivors remember their experiences as men or as women is as crucial to their testimony—and for us to our reading of it—as is their Jewishness, their communism, or any other critical identification. For gender to be the unmarked term, as it is in so much Holocaust criticism, is symptomatic of our ongoing inability to reconcile an awareness of difference with the humanist and human rights imperative of universal equality. Only by acknowledging and recognizing our own investments in fundamental inequalities and differences can we begin to inhabit this paradoxical yet vital relationship between difference and universality.

Among the many testimonial works written by women survivors, none has achieved the prominence of the works of Des Pres, Levi, or Wiesel, among either readers or critics. This lack of attention is unfortunate to the extent that a lack of concern with issues of gender and sexuality precludes in many ways the examination of difference as a crucial element of witnessing.

While it is not within the scope of this project to attempt a sweeping analysis of gender differences within the experiences of Holocaust survivors, I would like to suggest some common themes found in these works. In two ways especially, works by women seem to differ from those of men. Women's texts often foreground issues of community and sharing as necessary for survival, while men's texts emphasize the radical individuation and vicious selfishness imposed by the camps. Also, the women's literature discusses specific problems faced by women in the camps—for example, pregnancy, menstruation, rape, abortion, and enforced prostitution—that the men's narratives often not only do not address, but also sometimes condemn as instances of promiscuity, collaboration, or amorality. Such male accounts of women's experiences are filtered through the men's often extreme anxieties over their own loss of control and loss of position as women's protectors and providers. The differences between men's and women's testimonies about their experiences stems, I believe, from cultural difference, the different structural relations of men and women, and the workings of memory and is not evidence of inherent gender differences between the sexes.[15]

A case in point is the essay Lawrence Langer has contributed to the volume *Women in the Holocaust*.[16] An author who has spent much of his extensive and important career documenting Holocaust literary testimony, Langer has been one of the founders and leaders of the field. His essay quite explicitly implies that if one considers gender as an important category of analysis, then by definition one relegates other aspects of experience to the background. He employs caricatured arguments about gender that come from unexamined stereotypes rather than from a detailed engagement with the intellectual projects of feminist analysis, and the essay itself takes the form of a competition with an unclear and reductive notion of such an analysis. Although I am singling out Langer's essay here, I am taking it as exemplary of a large trend in Holocaust studies that is now only slowly being overcome.[17]

In Langer's essay, gender is never defined and is often confused with biological sex and cultural stereotypes of women's roles, such as childbearing, motherhood, and so on. Rather than addressing the work of feminist Holocaust scholars such as Joan Ringleheim directly, Langer takes instead an oppositional and reductive stance toward feminism's perceived project to use gender as the trump card through which to filter all analysis of Holocaust experiences. This causes him to assume that considerations of gender are part of a project to elevate women's suffering and valorize it over that of men's. What this critique responds to most directly, however, are not any of the nuanced and detailed studies of women's Holocaust experience that have been written recently but remarks written by Primo Levi about Auschwitz-Birkenau following the war. In his brief foreword to Liana Millu's testimonial, *Smoke over Birkenau,* Levi writes, "For a variety of reasons, the women's situation was a good deal worse than that of the men: first, less physical endurance, coupled with work more arduous and degrading than the labors imposed on the men; the agonies of disrupted families; and above all the haunting presence of the crematoria, located right in the middle of the women's camp."[18]

The historical situation within which Levi made these remarks in 1947 was prior to, among other things, the Universal Declaration of

Human Rights (1948), the post-1968 development of gender and women's studies as academic fields, and the field of Holocaust studies itself. One could read these remarks as responding to the trauma for women inherent in the violation of their traditional cultural norms coupled with living in the physical presence of the crematoria, or as an inherent cultural sexism that found it hard to believe that women and children could be as abused as men in such a wartime situation in Europe, or as a form of misplaced chivalry on Levi's part. They do not, however, reflect a contemporary understanding of women's survivor writings.

Unfortunately, Langer enacts in his essay the very same reductive moves for which he criticizes feminists. Indeed, Langer's readings of these texts are not much more than a reading and iteration of his own biases and misapprehensions. More important than this critique for Langer, however, is the utopian urge to transcend gender that he posits as necessary for entrance into the "human" community. Within this rubric, men do not need to transcend gender; they are always already within this human community because they are the norm through which it is defined. Thus any consideration of women's experience as different from men's implies an excision of women from this "human community" upon which Langer insists. In line with the major trend of human rights discourse, Langer understands gendered identity as antithetical to "human" identity. He juxtaposes the two, for example, in the sentence that precedes his extensive quote from Holocaust survivor Edith P.'s testimony toward the conclusion of his essay, stating that "she accents for us the delicate balance between gender and human identity, and the tension between personal and cultural origins of the self."[19]

This "delicate balance between gender and human identity" is one of the major problems with which the human rights community is still struggling. But acceding to the notion that gender is a convenient fiction that belongs in the realm of the personal rather than the cultural, as Langer differentiates them, both creates a false dichotomy between the personal and cultural spheres and refuses to recognize the constitutive role of gender in the formation of identity and culture. Although discourses of privacy often serve to mask and sometimes to authorize violence against women (as I have discussed at greater length in the previous chapter), gender is constituted within and through cultural frameworks. As Joan Ringelheim has noted:

To the Nazis, Jewish women were not simply Jews; they were Jewish women, and they were treated accordingly in the system of annihilation. Research suggests that more Jewish women were deported than Jewish men, and more women than men were selected for death in the extermination camps. . . . For Jewish women the Holocaust produced a set of experiences, responses, and memories that do not always parallel those of Jewish men. . . . If in the gas chambers or before the firing squads all Jews seemed alike to the Nazis, the path to this end was not always the same for women and men. The end—namely, annihilation or death— does not describe or explain the process.[20]

As Ringelheim persuasively argues, to ignore or underemphasize the importance of gender in the study of the Holocaust is to enact a form of violence upon our understanding of its many different layers of meaning; instead it channels collective memory into certain avenues that are "comfortable" and acceptable rather than focused on a more whole accounting of experiences. Not only does this do a disservice to the women who have been victimized by such massive abuse in the Holocaust, but such unexamined positions, despite their frequent positioning within a well-intentioned humanist ideology, continue to do violence to women in the present, as women seek to escape violent situations from which they are unprotected by national and international laws regulating such categories as "asylum seeker" and "refugee."

There is no "balance" between gender and human identity to be achieved in these situations. To juxtapose these terms in such a way is to begin analysis from a faulty premise. Gender is integral, not secondary, to human identity and it is a complex and varied set of norms and performances in which all humans participate. Although human rights discourse posits the human as a category prior to the body's entrance into cultural structures such as gender, race, or nationality, this does not erase particularity. For Edith P. to highlight her comments as belonging to "a wife and a mother" at certain times in her testimony, to which Langer calls attention, does not imply that at other times she is speaking from a nongendered position. Instead it is a rhetorical device that calls attention to the way in which these are overdetermined roles that exceed her own individual identity and connect her to much larger structural frameworks.

Langer, speaking of Edith P., argues:

The curtailed potential of her stillborn life as a sister and a daughter, or her incomplete life as a wife and mother, because she is cut off together with her husband and children from the family she cannot share with them, leaves her a legacy of internal loneliness that nothing can reverse. But if we substitute for these gendered terms the more generic ones of parent and child, we move Edith P. and the other women I have been discussing into a human orbit that unites them through a kind of regret that cannot be sorted by sex.[21]

This quote is symptomatic of the way gender is considered in both Langer's work and that of many other Holocaust scholars. Gender here is both the most overdetermined factor guiding our reading of Edith P.'s experiences and the factor that, perhaps by nature of its excessiveness, must be completely erased.

Interestingly, Langer himself uses a childbirth metaphor—a gendered term, according to what I understand as his definition—to refer to what he calls Edith P.'s "stillborn life" as a sister and daughter. To call her identities as sister and daughter stillborn, however, is to imply that they were dead on arrival, that they had potential for life but never experienced it. Just as her siblings and parents continue to exist in Edith P.'s own history and memory, so her identities as sister and daughter continue to exist in some form. Edith P., like all of us, exists as a multitude of identities. The fact that her parents and siblings were murdered does not retroactively cause the psychic death of her identities as daughter and sister. These are some of the strongest identifications that we experience, and they are key to psychic formation. The death of the persons with whom those identities have been formed does not negate the identities; it might even make them stronger in particular ways. The "curtailed potential" to which Langer refers is not present within Edith P.'s own words but emerges in Langer's reading of them. Her parents and siblings continue to exist for her as the specters of memory, and she continues an identificatory relationship to them, although it is now a relationship of mourning and memory rather than material exchange with conscious beings.

This reading is followed by Langer's reference to "her incomplete life as a wife and mother" because she cannot share the experience of an extended family with her husband and children. But surely the experience of grief and loneliness that one might feel on holidays when remembering the dead does not lead automatically to a feeling of incompleteness regarding one's current roles as spouse and parent. Langer consistently reads Edith P.'s experience of grief and remembering as an experience of gendered lack, marking her twice as the symbol of lack—first as woman and second as survivor. This double signifying of lack is unbearable to Langer. Through a sleight of his critical hand, however, gendered terms can be replaced with more "neutral" terms, and Edith P.'s experiences reclaimed as universally human, as she and other women survivors are moved into a "*human orbit* that unites them through a kind of regret that cannot be sorted by sex" (emphasis added).

The implication that Edith P. is not a member of the "human" community until she is removed from the realm of gender and her experiences of grief changed to a "regret" that is beyond the markers of gender and sex is a form of transcendent utopian longing that wishes to assimilate women into the universal category of human. Not only does the category of human, as it is deployed by Langer, demand the erasure of all particularity, but it seems also to mitigate the incommensurate loss that is the legacy of her trauma into the very manageable emotion of regret. Although we might wish that trauma were so easily incorporated into the psyche, the testimonials themselves do not bear this out.

The quote by Edith P. to which Langer is referring reads:

> I just want to say, I've been liberated thirty-five years, going to be this month—April fourteenth [1980]. And as I get older, and my children are all self-sufficient and no longer at home, and I am not busy being a mother and a wife, and I can be myself—I have given a great deal of thought how I should conduct myself vis-à-vis the Germans, how I should feel. Should I hate them? Should I despise them? . . . I don't know; I never found the answer. . . . But sometimes I wish in my darkest hours that they would feel what we feel sometimes, when you are uprooted, and bring up children—I'm talking as a mother and a wife—and there is nobody to share your sorrow or your great happiness. Nobody to call up and say something good happened to me today: I have given birth to a beautiful daughter; or she got all "A"'s; she got into a good college. I mostly remember when holidays come, I have tried to preserve the holidays as I saw it at home, transfer it to my own children. We have beautiful Passovers like I saw it at home. But the spirit is not there. It's beautiful, my friends tell me,

when I invite them, that it's beautiful, it's very spiritual. But I
know it's not the same. I . . . I . . . there's something missing. I
want to share it with someone who knows me really.

Twice in the quote Langer utilizes, Edith P. uses the phrase "a
mother and a wife" to mark the identities from which she is speaking.
In the first instance, she states that "as I get older, and my children are
all self-sufficient and no longer at home, and I am not busy being a
mother and a wife, and I can be myself" to contextualize her explanation of the difficulties she faces in her present thoughts about the German people. Her statement clearly points toward a sense of herself that
is separate from the domestic gender roles she plays, but it does not
valorize or highlight any of these positions over the others. Interestingly, though, she must divest herself of these gender roles—mother
and wife—in order to make space for a consideration of how she feels
toward "the Germans."

This reflection is bookended by the second reference to herself as a
mother and a wife in the statement that ends this section: "But sometimes I wish in my darkest hours that they would feel what we feel
sometimes, when you are uprooted, and bring up children—I'm talking
as a mother and a wife—and there is nobody to share your sorrow or
your great happiness." The "we" of this sentence seems to refer to
herself as a member of a community of exiles, initially without emphasis
on gender but then recuperated by her reference to the positions of
mother and wife that she claims for herself as she makes this statement.
Why does she feel the need to emphasize her claim to the positions out
of which she has just previously, if momentarily, stepped? For Edith P.
her positions as a member of a human community and as a gendered
being are not antithetical. She participates as a gendered being in various roles, mother and wife, but not one or all of them are the totality
of her sense of being. She seems to move fluidly and without anxiety
among these positions, and it is the categories of national identity (the
Germans) and family that are naturalized and unremarked-upon in her
testimony.

Not just in the field of Holocaust studies but in all areas of study that
approach problems of atrocity, abuse, disenfranchisement, and human
rights, critics must recognize the importance of gender along with
other categories as legitimate sites from which to articulate experience.
Preserving and acknowledging particularity does not undermine human
rights; instead it helps us to understand the broad range of categories

that help to define the "human" and moves the definition from the arenas of the "natural" and the "cultural" to that of the ethical. If we cannot preserve differences of gender within the universal category of the human, we lose the very basis upon which universal human rights depends.

Gender, in its regulation through patriarchal cultural norms, is a category to which all women are subject, and our negotiation of its strictures and performances profoundly influences our lives. Thus the vantage of already inhabiting categories of gender difference may encourage some women to negotiate their positions as survivors in ways that more readily acknowledge difference, fragmentation, and the negotiation of multiple identity categories. Such gender difference does not uniformly suggest a "female" relationship to atrocity but it does suggest that some women approach their position as survivors from a certain critical location that is more open to the instability and flux that negotiations of difference suggest. In the following sections, then, I take up the testimonials of survivors themselves as important theoretical interventions into categories such as the ethical, the human, resistance, witnessing, and responsibility.

Performative Witnessing: *Who Will Carry the Word?*

Charlotte Delbo's *Who Will Carry the Word?* is a Holocaust play about the lives of a group of women interned in a death camp. The play is introduced by music and a prologue in which one character states what will be the central concern of the play: the paradox of surviving an experience to which one must serve as a witness while always knowing that one's experience will never be understood by the audience and that in fact the language through which the experience must be conveyed will always be completely inadequate to the task.

Suggesting ways that performance can function to overcome the difficulties of representing violent experience, "the word" for the characters of *Who Will Carry the Word?* becomes crucial for rebuilding their relationship to history and juridical culture. Delbo's use of the performative space of the theater—the play between actors and audience—as a space to stage the problematics of language as a tool both of oppression and of survival establishes witnessing as a performative dynamic between the actors and the audience that challenges yet maintains the "fourth wall" of the stage upon which the play is performed. This suggests the possibility for performative spaces as spaces that play out the problematics of the survivor's need to reconstruct her or his personal narrative within larger narratives of history through the ethical demand that the spectators become witnesses to the atrocities being recounted on stage. Maintaining yet disrupting the fourth wall becomes itself a performative enactment of the witnessing dynamic, which demands an engaged listener who recognizes the absolute incommensurability of her or his own experience with that being recounted by the survivor.[22]

In Delbo's play, the constant and seemingly futile resistance to the process of complete destruction within the world of the camps becomes the central struggle of her characters. The importance of language in attempting to express the inexpressible is the primary focus not just of Delbo's play but of much Holocaust literature. As Françoise and Denise say to the audience in the epilogue to the play:

> **Françoise:** We have come here to tell you and now we are standing here ill at ease not knowing what to say, how to say it. . . .
> **Denise:** Because we came from a place where words had a different meaning.

Unlike the experience of torture, which often relies on the complete physical isolation of the victim within a world of absolute pain, the camps forced this retreat of the consciousness into the world of the physical sensations of the body within a group context.[23] Recalling fascism itself, a mass movement relying on the submersion of the identity of the individual into the consciousness of the group, the play stages the way the camps worked to make the individual internees into completely anonymous and interchangeable bodies. Starved, heads shaved, and with numbers instead of names, the characters become cogs in the mechanism of the camp. This outward erasure of individuality amplifies the retreat into the world of the body, so that when one character glances outside of her body to reaffirm her subject position, she sees nothing but other dying, identityless bodies like herself or the SS and kapos (prisoner overseers) responsible for her torture. The resistance to such horror and loss of individuality in the play takes the form of continuous dialogue as the characters use language to reaffirm their own particularity as individuals, to build communal structures of support and resistance, and to address the audience as witnesses.

The "truth" of witnessing (the idea that testimony is telling the factual truth of what happened) is crucial to the problem of the inability of survivors to feel that they can adequately bear witness to their experience. As the character Denise states, "we came from a place where words had a different meaning." In a world where even basic words had a meaning understandable only within the context of the camps, once outside the camps the survivors feel that they must learn a new language, that the language of the camps is lost, and along with it is lost the ability to talk about and describe their experiences. Wyschogrod describes this as a function of the camps' absolute difference from the symbolic structures of the outside world:

In the death-world, new meanings become affixed to the body through the systematic substitution of pain for the ordinary complex of meanings that constitutes our corporeal transactions. This fixing of meaning through the language of pain lies outside any linguistic referential system. In fact it is first noticed as a gap in linguistic possibility: there seems to be no language which can make sense either of the death-world as a whole or of the particular experiences it generates.[24]

Sara Nomberg-Przytyk, in her testimony, devotes a chapter called "New Words—New Meanings" to this crisis, writing that "the new set of meanings provided the best evidence of the devastation that Auschwitz created in the psyche of every human being. No one was able to resist totally the criminal, amoral logic of everyday life in the concentration camp . . . [which was] a bizarre transformation of reality."[25] Such implication in the murder of oneself along with everybody else—what Dori Laub has referred to as the "coercively totalitarian and dehumanizing frame of reference within which the event was taking place"— leads Laub to conclude that there could be no witness from within the frame of the event itself.[26] To the extent that the Nazi system forced all prisoners to feel complicit in their own murder and that of others, it effectively removed from them the ability to feel that they were credible witnesses who could tell the truth of the event. Laub describes this as the loss of the internal "thou" that makes possible the prisoner's ability to be a witness to her- or himself.[27] Testimony enacts a resistance to this loss of the ability to witness while staging, paradoxically, the impossibility of witnessing by demanding a dynamic, implicated witnessing that acknowledges difference and instability—that takes place from within the "gap in linguistic possibility" that Wyschogrod outlines.

Delbo's play implicates the audience in this witnessing immediately through its title. "Who will carry the word?" is not just a mystery of which characters will survive to the end of the play, which is already partially dispelled by the prologue; it is also a direct question for the audience. Through watching the play, will they remain aloof spectators or will they (we) acknowledge the ethical demand of the characters to become witnesses to and therefore implicated in the struggles and atrocities the play presents? As the title of the play implies, it is the survival of language—and by extension the world—that is at stake for these women and perhaps for us. The address to the audience that comprises the epilogue of the play is important not just as a resolution to the play—to prove that a character has survived—but as a dialogue. It is two women who have survived, and with two they form a community, one whose language is inadequate and unbelievable even to themselves but through which a future is possible.

The irony of their situation is that the very humanist system that proved constitutive of fascism is the culture these characters must speak and write themselves into in order to reconstitute themselves as subjects. They must write themselves back into the juridical system, reconstructing what the Nazis devastated, preserving the "Word," with all its implications of the Law and the Father, in order to regain a ground from which to speak and to act. In the very act of preserving the word, however, they disrupt the totalizing systems it implies.

Thus the play stages language and memory as a crucial site of resistance to the Nazi imaginary and death camps, the "coercively totalitarian and dehumanizing frame of reference," and builds a performative space of witnessing between the actors and the audience. Although Laub's argument that testimony is as much an exploration of differences as an exploration of identity is similar to the acknowledgment in many survivor testimonials that they are speaking from an unstable witnessing position, by foregrounding the importance of community, Delbo's play does not address differences between women that might disrupt the supportive nature of this community. Only at one time in the play, very near the end, does a character make reference to the constructed nature of the community of women who make up the cast of the play: in scene 2 of Act III, Françoise asks: "What use is it ever to read truth in a face? In life, who needs to see through people, to know in one split second if they'll share their bread or help others to walk?" Their community is a self-selecting one, where one's willingness to give support and help to others is the primary condition of belonging.

Common memories and the sharing of memories are also an important part of the group and depend partly on a shared language and culture (in the play, that of French women, many of whom were members of the Resistance). Thus the women maintain national or ethnic and political affiliations within the universe of the camp. This is perhaps a double-edged sword, as is so much about the camps that the play explores, where inclusion based on common cultures means exclusion of others who do not share them and where the maintenance of national, ethnic, class, and other boundaries provides both a site of common cause and resistance and also the weaknesses of division, hierarchy, intolerance, and so on. While common values are foundational of the characters' community, they also preserve difference within the all-encompassing physical and emotional pressure of the camps to become deindividuated and dehumanized. While enforcing a radical individualism of survival at all costs, the camp's submersion of individuality is resisted by the characters through a shared community that recognizes the particularity of its members' separate identities while building a community of common values.

The play is staged on a bare set with an inclined plane in the background and boxes with an aisle between them that serve as bunks in the foreground. The only characters in the play are the women who are prisoners; the Nazis and kapos are present only through the use of lighting suggesting the shadow of their movement and through the reactions of the characters themselves. Unlike Nomberg-Przytyk and Buber-Neumann, whose occasional inclusion of Nazis or kapos in their testimonials reinforces their implication as perpetrators of atrocity by portraying moments where they act out of character to help prisoners, thus illustrating that at all moments they chose to make decisions to perpetrate atrocity, Delbo refuses to embody them onstage. Such bare staging serves to focus all the audience's attention on the characters themselves while circumventing both the problem of spectacle (and its attendant erotic attachments) that is always a possibility when representing Nazis and the problem of recreating a "realistic" death camp on stage. Not only does the attempt to use realism to portray a death camp risk the same spectaclization as does representing Nazis and their violence, it also risks doing the injustice of claiming to have "realistically" or "accurately" recreated or conveyed the authentic death camp experience. Such a claim runs counter to testimonials' insistence on the incommensurability of the experience as fundamental to engaging the witnessing position.

In the Author's Note that precedes the play, Delbo herself precludes any possibility of realism. Not only are there no sets, but the women's faces are to be powdered grey, including lips and eyes, and their dress is to be almost identical—tunic or smocklike with gray slippers and stockings and monotone headscarves. While this helps to reinforce visually the strong theme that the community, not individual women, is the emphasis both of the characters struggling to survive and of the Nazi death camp itself, it also serves to undercut any idea the audience might entertain that what they are watching in any way approximates an actual experience of a death camp. Despite the fact that this is a theatrical space, the play rejects verisimilitude as the first and most important fact of the camps themselves. As Delbo states, this camp is "nowhere . . . a place that no one can imagine." Drawing attention to the highly fictionalized nature of theatrical representation, she goes on to direct that "in a light of unreality, the groups [of women] mill about then move into formation."

Such incommensurability is basic to the play's structure, which uses a combination of monologues, direct audience address, prologue and epilogue, and dialogue between characters. Rather than providing the audience with a progressive narrative that reinforces through the structure of narrative itself the fourth-wall illusion by eliding what is unseen, offstage, inconsistent, or linearly out of time, the play presents an experience that is composed of the fragments of the characters' thoughts and experiences combined with their demands to the audience actively to engage with their struggle to witness. Drawing attention to the fragmentation of the text (in this case the performance) that is conveying the testimonial, the play physically embodies the crisis of witnessing that is performed in its prologue, as the character Françoise articulates her despair at the uselessness of the "knowledge" the play is about to provide.

Act I, scene 1, opens the play with a discussion of the merits of suicide—as a form of individual resistance and mercy—versus the importance of surviving so that the group of women will be stronger and increase the likelihood that somebody will survive. Françoise, who also performs the prologue and epilogue, wants to kill herself before she is murdered by a Nazi or by starvation or disease. Claire, however, argues that it is her duty to the group to stay alive as long as possible, increasing the strength of the group and serving as a role model for the young girls. The rest of Act I consists of scenes of the women at roll call and at night in the barracks. Claire is killed by a kapo, the women consider their former lives and the foods they miss, and Mounette, a girl Françoise has befriended, ends the act with a monologue about her nightmares. She repeats the common nightmare that many survivors remember: that of returning home to her family only to have her mother not see or hear her. She has become a ghost in her own future/past.

Act II consists of several scenes where the women verbally and physically support each other during the morning lineup and ends with Françoise addressing the audience after the others have left the stage to return to the barracks in the evening. She recounts the way in which the women were left to stand all day in the freezing weather and then made to run to the barracks with the Nazis and kapos pulling all of the weak women out of line. Fourteen of their group are lost. She ends by asking the audience "Can we act a play where the characters die before you've had time to know them?" Throughout the play, beginning with the direct address of the prologue, the audience is asked to participate actively as witnesses to the testimony of the characters, and with her question Françoise breaks any illusion of the fourth wall that might have developed to remind the audience that passive identification with the characters is not what is being demanded of them. They are positioned as witnesses—and even here as judges—of the play's crisis of representation.

Can a play exist under such circumstances? And what are the implications of spectatorial pleasure inherent in the terms "act" and "play"? Surely the audience is present for some sort of pleasurable experience, but the site of the pleasure does not reside in any of its traditional areas. Or does it? And if not, then where is it situated? Françoise suggests that while spectatorial pleasure is not to be gained from a play where "the characters die before you've had time to know them," the audience might find a form of pleasure in engaging with the characters over the very impossibility of their project. This is not the pleasure of identification but of a self-conscious decision on the part of the audience to engage dynamically with the characters over the central struggles of representation, language, survival, and witnessing that they embody.

Act III begins seventy days later with a long monologue from Denise detailing the gruesome and violent deaths of some of the characters. Denise, Françoise, and Gina are the only three characters who are left, but before the act ends Gina has killed herself rather than join the "White Kerchief Kommando" that is responsible for undressing the small children before they are burned alive in a pit at the edge of the camp.

Despite their loss of visual individuality for the audience, the play presents each woman as a distinct individual. The women are dressed identically in shapeless gray dresses and headscarves, but through their dialogue we learn their individual histories, fears, and needs. Throughout the play, each woman is presented as an integral part of her community, necessary for its survival. The play itself functions as an act of resistance in its stubborn refusal to focus on anything other than the mutually supportive community of women. Delbo's play resists what Laub has called "the unique way in which, during its historical occurrence, *the event produced no witnesses.*"[28] Laub goes on to state: "Not only, in effect, did the Nazis try to exterminate the physical witnesses of their crime; but the inherently incomprehensible and deceptive psychological structure of the event precluded its own witnessing, even by its very victims."

Laub's work describing the witness/survivor's testimonial dynamic with a witness/listener suggests that there is a necessary performative element to witnessing. Through the performative space, a dynamic relationship is constructed between the audience and the characters/witnesses. The witnessing that the play enacts is exactly the witnessing by the audience of the characters' struggle to witness. Laub suggests that the experience of the Holocaust precluded the ability of its victims to bear witness, even to themselves, to the event while it was occurring, and that the importance of testimonial for the survivor is in the performance of the testimony with a witness. This testimonial performance serves to rebuild for the survivor her or his own position as a witness.[29] By staging this witnessing dynamic between characters and an audience, the play performs the ethical demand of witnessing for the audience—that the audience accept implication within the testimonial dynamic by relinquishing the position of spectator in favor of that of witness—to witness the characters' struggle to witness and actively to engage them in it.

Who Will Carry the Word? stages this struggle to reclaim the position of a witness through a fragmentary content that mirrors the fragmentary structure of the play. The play is a medley of narrative dialogue between characters, direct audience address, everyday discussion of food and one's family, bitter discussions of the impossibility of understanding the experience of the death camp even while it is happening, and lists of the dead and the way they died. From this medley emerges the process of rebuilding a witness to the event. By exploring it using the format of a play, Delbo puts herself as a survivor at a double remove from the audience. Her testimony is fragmented and mediated by her characters and their portrayal by actors whose own relationship to the Holocaust and to atrocity is completely beyond her control. She herself has written it, but once written, it leaves her to be performed over and over by different actors, before different audiences, in countless different places and circumstances. Unlike the written testimonial, where this performative act of witnessing occurs "privately" between the reader and the text, the play builds a community of witnesses who participate in the event, but at a different level of remove from the written survivor testimony.

The audience, then, collectively becomes witness to the testimony of the play. As a testimony predicated upon the importance of community to survival, the play builds from the audience a community of witnesses. This performative space of interaction holds the potential for remembering the Holocaust differently, as more than an event out of time whose survivors cannot even be sure it really existed. As an experience that happens within a narrative frame, no matter how fragmented, the audience of the play participates in the characters' rebuilding of the witness's relationship to language and the past. Trauma and the performative aporias which suggest it are not evacuated but are managed through this witnessing dynamic. Rather than claiming an "authentic" and fixed historical narrative of their experience of the Holocaust, the characters, by claiming the experience as "unbelievable" even to themselves from their position as survivors, speak from a witnessing position that embraces the instability of traumatic experience as the basis of witnessing even while they resist it.

The anxiety of language and remembering that begins and ends the play is recounted by Laub as symptomatic of the process by which the Nazi system succeeded in a genocide that effectively carried over into the psychic lives of survivors long after the event and that testimony is one method of working to overcome. He states:

> The Nazi system turned out to be foolproof . . . in the sense that it convinced its victims . . . that what was affirmed about their "otherness" and inhumanity was correct and that their experiences were no longer communicable even to themselves, and therefore perhaps never took place. This loss of the capacity to be a witness to oneself and thus to witness from the inside is perhaps the true meaning of annihilation, for when one's history is abolished, one's identity ceases to exist as well.[30]

The infliction of overwhelming pain on the human body physiologically destroys the self's relationship to language. Once this relationship to language has been destroyed, the self's capacity to function as a subject of language is also disrupted, even after the pain has dissipated.[31] The Holocaust, as Laub outlines its functioning in relationship to witnessing in the above passage, combines the experience of acute, ongoing, bodily pain with a coercive encompassing ideology that makes absolute victims of its targets. Because they are implicated within the totalitarian frame of mass death and atrocity, they are denied the position of witness as somebody with a perspective outside the frame of the encompassing atrocity event itself. Trauma, resulting not just from this fundamental break with language but from the radical disenfranchisement of the atrocity experience, not only breaks the narrative frame of the present for the survivor as experiences of the past intrude into present time, consciousness, and memory as ongoing phenomena, but adds a delusional quality to the events remembered.

The traumatic ground of the Holocaust, where survivors can remain convinced on a fundamental level that their experiences, through being incommunicable, perhaps "never took place," needs a witness from beyond the event itself to acknowledge the survivor's testimony. As people with the ability to witness the characters from beyond the stage of the Holocaust, then, the audience members in Delbo's play are crucial to the witnessing project of the characters. These characters inhabit the paradox of resisting and yet believing this formulation of their own inhumanity and inability to witness. Through the stories they tell of their past lives, told to remind themselves that they are still alive in the world—part of a contiguous history—the women resist, within the frame of the play and through breaking it to address the audience, this formulation that they are "other," outside history, and removed from the world.

This careful attention by Delbo to the self-conscious staging of the always fictionalized nature of historic events, even for the participants, and her insistence on the inability or failure of realism goes beyond the often discussed problem of Holocaust texts representing the unrepresentable experience of the Holocaust. Edith Wyschogrod's analysis of the relationship of the "death-world" to the structure of modern global consciousness, which argues that the mass-death events of the twentieth century have radically reconfigured our relationship to language, time, self, and culture, provides a lens for reading the ways that Delbo's play presents a problem of representational structure that is fundamental to the structure of modern consciousness and society. Within this formulation, the cliché of the "unimaginable" nature of the death camps becomes a nostalgic wish. They are unfortunately very imaginable, and while the individual experience might not be accessible to our imaginations, as no other person's experience ever is, the grotesque physical violence and the scale are very accessible to us as the audience. Even for the characters within the play, their history is marked by the historical atrocities of World War I—by previous events of mass death on an unimaginable scale. As the characters insist, however, there is never any knowledge of the event until one is inside it. Although the true horror of the event of massive physical atrocity is not accessible to those outside the event and even to the survivors on some level, the physical images and strong psychic residue of the horror have proliferated in the wake of such events. To too easily claim the unimaginable nature of a slaughter such as a death camp is to push it away, to relegate it to the outside of culture, where it can no longer trouble us in our daily pursuits, just as the survivors themselves are pushed away, becoming "ghosts" (as Françoise claims in the epilogue) in the cultural imaginary. From this vantage, we can choose to try to ignore it (as Delbo's characters have done with the atrocities of World War I) or turn it into iconography in the service of various goals, but we cannot claim that it is unimaginable.

While Wyschogrod suggests that these mass-death events have led to a dangerous reformulation of the individual's imaginary relationship to death that is reflected in our current social and political formations, Delbo's characters insist upon a different kind of relationship to mass atrocity. Speaking of the survivors of Verdun, who returned and "never stopped talking" about it, despite the fact that their listeners were "bored" and "never understood," Delbo's characters are hyperaware of the spectral presence of the survivor as the marker of the trauma that can never be communicated. This contrast—of a model of traumatic memory and survival versus the model of masses of individuals collectively damaged through the overawareness of mass death as a possible (and, in their imaginary, probable) method of dying—is also a contrast of focus. The model of trauma, as Delbo's characters formulate it, moves from the individual out to the community as each individual recognizes the necessity of speaking and of ties to those around her, both to maintain their connection to history and to the dead and to make the future possible. Delbo's is a model of communities of individuals, while Wyschogrod's model is of an event of death so overwhelming in its experience that it blots out all possibility of individuality, so that the historical spectators to—survivors of—the event lose, through extension, their own individual relationship to death.

Delbo's play clearly posits the survival of communities of the future as dependant on the witnessing of mass death through her articulation of it as a necessity for the survival of the character Françoise. The ongoing argument of other characters against Françoise's intention to commit suicide is that of the necessity for someone to return to bear witness to the event and for the dead, and therefore for all of the women to attempt to survive and to ensure the survival of others for as long as possible. Laub has provocatively suggested that "the survivors did not only need to survive so that they could tell their story; they also needed to tell their story in order to survive."[32] Although this remains undeveloped in his essay, he also suggests that one of the important elements of survival might have been the recognition of this untenable paradox set up by the Nazi system and the attendant imperative to survive and bear witness to the history that was being eradicated. In Act I, Claire asserts that "there will be one who will return and who will talk and who will tell, and who will make known, because it is no longer we who are at stake, it's history—and people want to know their history. . . . none of us is alone and each must render an account to all the others."

This is an account of community that exists parallel to and simultaneously with that of the Nazi Volk—in direct competition with it—and the characters of the play recognize that the war continues within the death and concentration camps as well as on the battlefields. Within the camps, the war waged by the women is that of keeping this competing history alive; they trust that the power of truth is that of testimony and that if one person is to survive it will mean at least the partial defeat of the Nazis. Consequently, each time Delbo's play is staged, it performs the history of this struggle over history, and the testimony performed by the characters with the audience serves to enact the memory of the event.

As Delbo's play suggests, the Nazi system was not perfect and contained within it the possibility of resistance. The emphasis in her play is not upon the loss of identity and retreat into the body exemplified by the Muselman, the inmate who has become completely unresponsive to the outside world and waits to die, but upon the strong community that the women in the camp form in response to this pressure. Throughout the play, the women who are stronger support and hide those who cannot stand alone or are more vulnerable. Language itself, that final link with the world that is broken in torture and for the Muselman, becomes necessary for survival. The women talk to each other continually about the need to survive, about their histories and fears, about food and daily life, continually reaffirming themselves as individuals and subjects who have some link, however tenuous, to a world outside that of their own physical pain. As Mounette says, when Françoise notes that they should take advantage of their brief opportunity to sleep, "talking is as important as sleeping. It helps as much. If I did not talk, it would seem to me as if I was no longer alive. I say anything; we say anything." The play reads, in many ways, as a manual for survival under such extreme conditions. It opens with a discussion between Claire and Françoise as to why Françoise does not have the right to commit suicide—because, as Claire says, "There must be one who returns. . . . Would you want millions of people to have been destroyed here and all those cadavers to remain mute for all eternity, all those lives to have been sacrificed for nothing?"

This is a valorizing of the needs of the community over those of the individual, but it is of a very different order from that of the fascist community and has very different results from those the fascists are trying to achieve through the camp system. The responsibility of the living is an ethical responsibility to the mass dead, who have died without voice or individuality as sacrifices to the totalitarian violence of the Nazis. Rather than sacrificial victims of an all-encompassing ideology of dominance and atrocity, Claire wants to recuperate their position as people who have been murdered. The "one who returns" resists the death-world of the Nazis as Wyschogrod elaborates it—and resists the configuration of sacrifice—by testifying to the murder of millions through the particularity of individual experiences. The survival of history makes the future possible—a future that resists the death-world through the ethical responsibility of bearing witness to the dead and therefore to justice and the human. Such witness-bearing ensures that the dead will remain "people" rather than mute cadavers, and suicide in the face of such responsibility is an unethical act that acknowledges accountability only to the individual self.

The direct addresses to the audience that begin and end the play painfully confront the difficulties of being a witness and of using language as a medium of communication. The performance of the play has not altered or overcome the problem, yet it has been performed anyway, and this lack of resolution suggests that any hope for dialogue or understanding lies within the paradox itself. In the prologue, Françoise confronts both the psychic dangers of witnessing and the inadequacy of testimony to have any meaning outside the camp when she says "The light seared the eyes that dared to seek. / So why should I speak? / For the things I would say / Could not be of any use to you." In the epilogue, she ends the play with the question: "Why should you believe / those stories of ghosts / Ghosts who came back and who are not able to explain how?" The play betrays a deep ambivalence about the issue of survival and the despair of the survivor; for Françoise and Denise, the only hope for survival even after returning from the camps is in finding a community of other survivors who can help to support each other. The women know that to survive alone is not enough.[33] They have been radically removed from the culture and life they once had and will not be able just to step back into the lives they had before.

Françoise's feeling of being a ghost who has returned to the world of the living only as a shadow driven to compulsively retell her story to people who cannot really see or hear her echoes the dream of the camp inmate, recounted by Mounette at the end of Act I, who returns to her family only to be ignored and go unseen. This dream, signifying the temporal space of trauma, prefigures the excessive and spectral position of survivors after their return from the death-world. Only by building ties with other women who have experienced this deep schism of cultural violence and dislocation can she hope to live some semblance of a life of "normal" communication and routine. The narrative of shared experiences works (imperfectly) to bridge the chasm between the worlds she has lived through and to build a third life that encompasses both of the first two. With Denise, she must construct a third language, one that remembers both her history before Auschwitz and the radical difference that was Auschwitz, and that confronts the paradox of speaking a truth of witnessing that they can no longer themselves believe is true.

This "third language," like the position of the third term elaborated by critical studies, marks the excessive position of the survivor within the postatrocity cultural imaginary. As trauma haunts the narrative frame of the individual memory of atrocity, the survivor is a living presence that haunts the narrative frame of the atrocity event in cultural memory. Françoise's statement that they are "ghosts" who have survived the unsurvivable, speaking a third language constructed from experiences bridging wholly incommensurate worlds and experiences, challenges the audience to engage with them as more than ghosts—as fully embodied living witnesses. Such a challenge demands that the audience members take an ethical position in relation to their witnessing.

This process is an obsessive focus for the characters of *Who Will Carry the Word?* and is both exemplified and resisted by the following, when Françoise declares:

Here everything is true. . . . The executioners are executioners. They don't try to conceal it, to pass for human beings. They are executioners without hypocrisy. They never try to flatter, they never try to fake a smile. They don't see us although we see them and how different they are from us. The victims are victims, brutalized, defeated, humiliated, disgusting, lice-ridden. And those among the victims who succeed in crossing over to the other side, they immediately take on the badges that distinguish their new office: armbands, sticks or whips, and the faces to go with them.[34]

Françoise is instructing the spectators about how to view the play—as a world of absolute difference, both from that of the spectators and between the perpetrators and the victims. For these women the camp is a space of absolute difference, where truth is the truth of the uncrossable divide. This formulation points toward the problem of language often addressed by the characters, as it speaks of a world where absolute difference means absolute loss of the ability to comprehend anything other than one's most immediate bodily circumstances. By beginning with the phrase "here everything is true," however, the passage also suggests exactly the opposite. Simultaneously there is absolute difference and absolute relativism, and the victims' complicity with their own victimization likewise forestalls their ability to testify to their experience. However, despite her claim of the absolute difference of the victim—of one who has no possibility of witnessing to the wrong she has suffered—Françoise herself gives this dialogue from the position of witness. And part of that to which she witnesses is the formulation of the human as an ethical category. The executioners fully perform their identities as executioners, they make no effort "to pass for human beings." The "human," in this play, is an ethical category that entails responsibilities toward other members of the human community, and that is performatively enacted onstage throughout the duration of the play.

Claire and Françoise begin the discussion that will continue throughout the play to outline for the audience the play's main preoccupations: the death-world versus the life-world, history and memory, trauma and recovery. This schematic series of discussions, the grounding narrative of the play, at first addresses the basic issues of how survival and ethics can be meaningful concepts within the daily murderous routine of the death camp. The narrative structure encourages us to sympathize with Françoise, in contrast to whom Claire seems almost aggressively naïve although she is the most important character in this opening scene of the play. Not only does her position make strong moral claims, but it is Claire who most strongly argues against the radical individuation of the camp and, by extension, the mass-death consciousness outlined by Wyschogrod. Claire occupies the role of the woman who insists, against all reason, on the necessity of maintaining ethical relations within the camp despite their seeming impossibility. Françoise insists that suicide is the only ethical option within a system that requires complicity for survival. Counterintuitively, perhaps, it is Françoise, through her insistence upon the necessity of choice and her belief in the possibility of the "free act," who is already within the logic of radical individualism promoted and insisted upon by the mass-death consciousness of the camp.

Within the context of a death camp, ethics can become a structure complicit with the workings of the camp. Françoise's insistence on her "right" to make ethical decisions about her own existence is countered by Claire's argument that such a position facilitates the larger project of fascist mass death. Joan Copjec, reading Kant on universalism and ethics, states that "the universal defines the terminus of moral action; it is the goal toward which actions are directed and without which the decision to act would be irresolvably stymied. . . . as the final end of all moral acts, this notion grounds ethics in practical reality without reducing the question of what we ought to do to the question of what is currently acceptable, without resorting to relativism."[35] Claire's position echoes this argument that a universalism that preserves particularity is necessary to a notion of ethics. The "free act" that Françoise articulates is located within the camps, a site of the relativism that Copjec marks as inherent to ethical structures that do not position such a universalism as "the terminus of moral action."

In other words, Françoise's decision does not partake of the "we" of the question Copjec locates as one of the central questions of ethics—that of "what we ought to do." By insisting on the necessity of the "we," Claire bridges the chiasmatic boundaries of the camp temporally and physically, locating a community of women inside the camp as a community and linking them to the human communities of the past and future outside the camps, as a "we" that can and must respond to this question. As such, she resists the alternate symbolic order of the death-world as Wyschogrod outlines it and locates the site of such resistance in the gap—that physical, linguistic, symbolic, and historical space—between the worlds within the Holocaust and outside the Holocaust.

However, Claire's argument for the maintenance of the individual meaning of death even in the death camp runs counter to Wyschogrod's description of the modern break with the individuality of death, a break that is caused by the phenomenon of mass death. When Claire argues to Françoise that "You aren't free . . . you are part of a chain that links all men—that links them far into the future," she uses the death-world to maintain a connection to a pre-mass-death understanding of the vital connection between individuals' lives and deaths. Through such a move, she also links the death-world—the world of the camp these characters inhabit—to life, history, and the future. Claire's insistence on an ethical position that is located in the acknowledgment of the universal responsibility to the human runs counter to Wyschogrod's assertion that such a position can always only be a bracketed position of fantasy. Wyschogrod writes that in the camps

> as soon as survival is no longer an end in itself but a means, a sense of solidarity with the dead develops. [However] in the absence of the assured continuity of a symbolic system of meanings, this means stripping away sentiments that usually accompany ethical acts and leaving the acts to stand for themselves. . . . In order to ascribe value to other persons, the newly constituted conditions of the death-world are bracketed, put out of play however briefly, in order to reinstate in fantasy the older symbolic continuities as if they alone prevailed.[36]

Claire, however, rejects this formulation of the absolute difference separating the world of the camps from the world outside. Arguing that "there are no free acts," Claire claims an encumbered consciousness, which she retains in the camp. She struggles to maintain her position of witness even within "the event to which there could be no witnesses from within," and in doing so, Claire rejects the position of "victim" as Lyotard defines it and claims herself as plaintiff and witness.[37] This insistence by Claire on the importance of witnessing serves a function similar both to the function of the boy discussed by Dori Laub, who carries with him throughout the Holocaust a picture of his mother that he talks to each day, maintaining an "internal witness," and to the importance of storytelling between herself and Milena Jesenská that Buber-Neumann relates.

Claire, a character in a play speaking these words of dialogue, performs resistance to what Wyschogrod calls "the destruction of meaning [which] is the *telos* of the death-world."[38] The performance of the absolute difference of worlds—between stage and audience, actors and characters, historical camp and play—creates possibilities for the differences of repetition from which new meanings can arise. To locate resistance in the gap between these worlds is not a bracketing off of the new meanings of the death-world in favor of the fantasy of old symbolic systems but a location of witnessing, like ethics, in the space of difference. Wyschogrod notes that for Derrida, "difference is not unrelated to the logic of presence. Difference, that which is past and cannot be reversed by representation, makes meaning possible since that which is present is related to that which cannot become present by way of negation."[39] Claire calls for an ethics of "meaning" defined by engaged responsibility to the human within a world composed of its destruction.

Against the phantasmic freedom of the death camp that Françoise outlines, where one is "already dead" and occupies the radical individualism of the ghost, Claire claims an even more oppressively weighty responsibility to past and future generations. Derrida's "ethical responsibility to the specter"[40] echoes Claire's position that from within the death camp the only way to maintain the connection to human community is by taking upon oneself that very excessiveness of meaning that marks the position of the survivor. To Françoise's claim that suicide is "the only right I have left, the only choice. The last free act," Claire responds "You have nothing left. No such choices, nothing. You are not free to do it. You don't have the right to take your life."[41] Claire's argument from within the Holocaust, from within the position of victim demanded of her by the totalizing fascist imaginary—that where one is stripped of all choices, one has nothing left but responsibility to the history, the others, that have been banished by this phantasmic structure—places her in the position of a soldier for the nonfascist symbolic realm. Rather than being "fighters off the battlefield, useless," as Françoise claims, Claire positions herself and the other women as battling for the very foundations of culture and historical memory—and, by extension, for the survival of humanity itself. Through the device of the play, this responsibility is demanded of the audience, as we are asked to choose between spectatorship and the witnessing that survival demands.

This survival is a survival posited on the ethical responsibility to testify and to witness, which places it in a fluid and difficult place. Against the radical or hyperindividualism of the camps, as articulated by Françoise, Claire juxtaposes the anti-individualism, or lack of importance of the individual, articulated by the imperative of testimony. This is not a survival based on the constant hope for a slight advantage that formed the fundamental structure of the camps. Instead, Claire posits survival of the human community, as she recognizes it, as dependant upon no single woman or group of people but instead upon the continuation of its individuals and of the mass dead within the memory of whoever might survive. Resistance, for Claire, is to maintain an affiliation with and memory of this community even under the extreme, impossible pressure of the camps. Claire recognizes that the reality of the human community exists in the historical memory of its members, not in the material reality of individual lives, noting that "it is no longer we who are at stake, it's history."[42]

For Françoise, the most horrifying aspect of the death camp is its dissolution of boundaries: "other people in other places . . . *they* have lost their reality. Everything has lost its shape, its depth, its sense, its color." She and the other women have been forced under the extreme physical and psychic trauma into a radical retreat into their own bodies, where nothing seems real outside the experience of their own unbearable physical sensations as their bodies dissolve around them. Yvonne notes that "You can no longer look at yourself when you gradually dissolve, turning into dirty water, when diarrhea is dripping from you night and day. . . . I am turning into dirty water. My strength is ebbing, stinking, it flows, right here, right now. . . . My strength and my will are going. I am emptying."[43] Not only has the world outside the camps ceased to exist for these women from within the radical otherness of the camp, but the camp itself is a place of abjection—both all boundaries and no boundaries.

Françoise's argument that suicide is her only option, the only "free choice" left, is founded on her notion of a private body, and the final option left to her, the only avenue of control over her own body that she has left, is to decide whether it lives or dies and in what manner—in this case, suicide. As Claire argues, however, when her physical options have been curtailed to such an extreme extent that suicide is the only avenue left through which she can maintain the illusion of free control over her own private body, her strongest choice is to let go of this fantasy of free individualism. For Claire, individualism and free will are luxuries that one can afford in the normative world outside the camp, but they are far too expensive in the death camp. She understands that they have been stripped of all freedoms, placed in the position of absolute victims, and within this place of disappearance into abjection, there can be no such thing as free will or unencumbered choice. Claire's insistence on an ethics that understands individuality only in relation to the continuation of history and the symbolic order through which it is constituted counters this through her insistence that it does not matter which individual women survive, as long as at least one does. To survive to testify is to move one from the position of victim to that of plaintiff. To use Lyotard's formulation, "A plaintiff is someone who has incurred damages and who disposes of the means to prove it. . . . In general, the plaintiff becomes a victim when no presentation is possible of the wrong he or she says he or she has suffered."[44] If no one survives the death camp, if the fascists win the war and their symbolic becomes the dominant order, Claire recognizes, her history and that of all the other women will end. They will in totality become nothing but victims. She says "Of these 15,000 women from all countries of all the languages of Europe, how many will survive? 15,000 women more or less, 200 women more or less, what difference does it make? You, me; it doesn't matter who—no one matters. They will only matter if there is one who returns."[45] Claire argues that the only choice, the only responsibility left, is to the group, and this is not a free, unencumbered choice. The importance of testimony is paramount to the survival of history and community. And one cannot testify from within the event.

Dori Laub has described this as a primary reason that the Holocaust, as an event, could take place with no witnesses. He writes:

> The very circumstance of being inside the event . . . made unthinkable the very notion that a witness could exist, that is, someone who could step outside of the coercively totalitarian and dehumanizing frame of reference in which the event was taking place and provide an independent frame of reference. . . . One might say that there was, thus, historically no witness to the Holocaust, either from outside or from inside the event. . . . To understand [this] one has to conceive of the world of the Holocaust as a world in which the very imagination of the Other was no longer possible.[46]

Who Will Carry the Word? reconfigures the experience of Auschwitz as an experience where the struggle of the characters is one of the continual formulation of witnessing even while acknowledging the impossibility of this act. The imagining of the future after the end of the war and the camp provides the bridge of possibility through which a witnessing to the events can be possible. Despite the fact that the characters reside in a "world in which the very imagination of the Other [is] no longer possible," Claire's demand is for an ethical engagement that insists on the phantasmic imagining of this Other even when she or he does not exist.

The temporal confusions and elisions of the play mark the site of the performance as zone of trauma. Act I ends with Mounette's account of her dream of returning home, only to discover that her family cannot see her, prefiguring the survivor's position as excessive to cultural frames. Associated with the mass dead of whom they bear witness, they are culturally marked by the wound of the atrocity event they have survived. Act II ends with Françoise's direct address to the audience that notes the passage of time and the winnowing of the community through a series of brutal murders and disease. This address emphasizes the temporal confusion of the play—we do not know how much time has passed—and associates it with the deaths of the various characters. The passage of time is marked by death; associated with trauma, it is not bound within our normal frames for understanding its passage. Yet Act III begins with a direct statement of the passage of time encompassed by the play—seventy days—which begins Denise's long monologue opening the act.

Explaining that "we kept count of the days so as not to feel a break in time between what we were before and what we have become," Denise locates herself outside the traumatic space that ended the first two acts and declares the keeping of time to be integral to resisting their death-world positioning as victims. Ending the monologue with a graphic account of finding a rat having eaten her living sister's ear in the infirmary, Delbo begins the final act of the play not with traumatic markers but with a graphic emphasis on conscious, embodied witnessing of corporeal atrocity. Denise is clear, concise, and factual, although she notes all of the slippages in her account. While Françoise has been given the role of enunciating trauma, Denise is articulating linear witnessing. The epilogue, a dialogue between Françoise and Denise, combines the traumatic with ordered experience in a shared act of testifying that locates witnessing as occurring both within community and from the merging of traumatic and ordered experience, bridging the linguistic gap of the camp.

During this epilogue, the audience is not invited to understand the experience of the characters as survivors. We are told that we cannot and that the survivors themselves cannot. Françoise and Denise understand that their desire to be heard and understood is impossible, unbelievable even to themselves, yet they bear witness anyway. Marked by trauma, they recognize that they embody a cultural symptom of the trauma of the death-world, excessive even to themselves as they mark themselves as spectral—the "ghosts who came back and are not able to explain how."

Yet while Wyschogrod discusses the death-world as a space of trauma within society and modern consciousness—unincorporated but structural, entailing repetition, and recognized through its symptoms although it cannot be approached directly—Delbo's play stages the characters within the death camp as resonating between these worlds. To stage the death camp as she has done creates a communal, social frame for the experience of witnessing. As a staged play, this is a different form of testimony from that of the book-length published narrative. By speaking for the dead through the living bodies of the actors, the performative context adds a "theoretical" gap between the "bodies" of testimonial texts and those of the play.

Milena: Passionate Friendship, Resistance, and Ethical Humanity

The testimonial *Milena*, like *Who Will Carry the Word?* focuses on the importance of difference and othering to survival. Buber-Neumann's book is a testimony to her relationship with Milena, a relationship that is emphatically homosocial and possibly lesbian. Although conventional accounts of the lesbian subject often consider lesbianism in terms of sameness, so that relations between women are either narcissistic, hopelessly imitative of heterosexuality, or a passing fancy on the way to the more proper domain of difference—that is, heterosexuality—such accounts are inadequate.[47] Such formulations fail to account for the constitutive role of othering in the constitution of lesbian subjectivity, an othering that is not simply present but is often the subject of a "lesbian" text precisely because such a lesbian text bears an uneasy relation to the realm of "proper" difference. As such, I am using *Milena* here to talk about the constitutive nature of difference in witnessing and testimony. Rather than trying to posit a belief in the stability of identity and the ability to reclaim such stability after an experience of radical trauma, the strength of *Milena*, as of *Who Will Carry the Word?* is that it is not concerned with reclaiming a stable self and identity but instead with exploring difference as crucial to survival. And as I will continue to argue throughout this book, it is exactly this exploration of difference that is at the heart of the act of witnessing itself.

111

Buber-Neumann's *Milena,* subtitled *The Story of a Remarkable Friendship,* is unusual to the extent that Buber-Neumann's testimony is also largely the testimony of someone else's life and experience. It is unique in its position as a Holocaust testimony by a woman that directly addresses issues of desire and lesbianism among the women inmates. A German communist who fled to Moscow in 1937, Buber-Neumann spent three years of forced labor in Stalin's gulags before being handed over to the Nazis in 1940 and sent to Ravensbrück, where she became close friends with Milena Jesenská. As in Delbo's play, the emphasis in this memoir is on the importance of friendship and community to survival. The strong impulse that the women in Delbo's play feel to remember and witness for the dead finds a very full expression here in a book that testifies to the shared love and experiences of the two women during their time in Ravensbrück, recounts Milena's life up through her arrest, and narrates Buber-Neumann's memories of the camp from her position as a survivor. While Delbo's play is a performative study of some of the central problems of testimonial and survival—the impossibility of language to convey experiences of mass death adequately, the fissures of memory, and the horrific pressures of such a death experience on relationships, identity, and community—Buber-Neumann's book textually performs pleasure as the most crucial site of resistance during her time in Ravensbrück.

By focusing on the love and friendship between herself and Milena, Buber-Neumann can recount her own experiences of the camp with a focus on interiority and concern for another that is less prominent in other testimonies. The development of the strong and uncompromising "passionate friendship" that Buber-Neumann documents goes against all of the pressures of camp life and of our understandings of its "conventions," by which the camps were designed to isolate individuals and turn them inward, destroying communal support networks and family ties and increasing the vulnerability of the individual person. This focus on interiority is figured as a radical form of resistance in Buber-Neumann's narrative, and one that, she writes, she and Milena were well aware of at the time. Noting, "It can be said without exaggeration that a frightened, cringing look seemed to invite blows," Buber-Neumann quotes from Milena's writings that to be strong, "you mustn't dissociate yourself from others, you mustn't forget that you're a member of a community. Once you feel alone, you start looking for a pretext to run away."[48] Rather than the radical drawing inward of the Muselman, the inmate who has completely disassociated him- or herself from the camp environment, often neither eating nor obeying any orders, the interiority described by Buber-Neumann has a strongly nurturing quality based on this self-conscious commitment to community.

In the complicated passage above, Buber-Neumann illustrates and reconstructs an exemplary exchange between herself and Milena that carries their dialogue beyond the camp and the death of Milena into the present through the use of Milena's published writings. Not only does the passage illustrate a central tenet of Buber-Neumann's testimony—that she and Milena resisted the death-world of the camps as much as possible by building and maintaining communal bonds—but it continues to resist the absolute death of the camps by writing this dialogue on resistance into the testimonial. Thus the historical memory of the camps as a site of absolute abjection is refuted in favor of a complex portrayal of the women's lives within the camps—in dialogue not just with each other but with other inmates and certain members of the SS.

Claiming a unique relationship with Milena during her time in the camp and relying on research into Milena's life that she conducted following the end of the war, Buber-Neumann provides the reader with a testimonial that, through her reliance on "outside sources" and biographical format, sidesteps some of the problems of memory usually associated with testimonial. In this passage, rather than reconstruct dialogue based on her memories of their conversations, Buber-Neumann utilizes published materials of Milena's that provide Milena with her own voice in the testimonial. Carrying their conversation beyond the camps, the passage encompasses three different temporalities—the time before the camp when Milena wrote her material, the time within the camp that is under consideration in the passage, and the time following her release from the camp during which Buber-Neumann writes. While Delbo's surviving characters worry that the witnesses/spectators will not believe stories that seem unreal now even to them, Buber-Neumann's authoritative manner often belies questions of the idiosyncrasies of memory. In this testimonial, time is less an enemy of memory than a shifting series of planes that slide back and forth across each other in various stages of overlap.

Eleven pages of the memoir, however, directly concern fifteen weeks of Buber-Neumann's experiences in the camp that occur in solitary confinement, when she is almost completely cut off from all human contact. As she writes of her own experiences when she is isolated from Milena and the other prisoners, memory becomes a slippery arena where one day slides into another, and hallucinations and terror brought on by isolation dominate her memories. Noting that she has already written in her previous testimony of her experiences of imprisonment during three years in a Siberian gulag, she states that here she "will speak of it only briefly."[49] As Dori Laub and others have remarked, there is a danger of retraumatization that occurs each time a survivor tells the story of her/his experiences of atrocity, and the fifteen weeks under consideration here—through the very brevity and ellipses of their telling—are marked out as particularly traumatic for Buber-Neumann because she is cut off from all community.

Buber-Neumann attempts to suture over the gap in the telling here by claiming her authority—both literally, as an author who has already written of similar experiences, and materially, as a survivor of previous long stretches of traumatic isolation—in deciding which parts of the narrative are important enough to be told. She leaves it to the reader to imagine the horror and trauma of the terror of starvation and total isolation or to read about it elsewhere, rather than recounting it. She recalls that initially her previous experiences gave her some advantage over other prisoners experiencing isolation torture for the first time: "I didn't scream, I didn't weep, I didn't hammer the iron door with my fists, I repressed all self-pity, because I needed my strength, I had to survive for Milena's sake."[50]

Initially she is able both to control her responses to the torture, since she already knows what to expect, and to continue to feel sustained by her bond with Milena, but she quickly acknowledges that there is no possible way to resist the torture. "But when the body is weakened, the strongest character ceases to be an impregnable fortress,"[51] she states. Lacking the language to describe the experience of torture by starvation and isolation, she notes that "I lost all sense of time. One hallucination followed another. . . . All sensation went out of me. . . . A great sense of peace came over me. . . . The angry voice of the SS overseer shocked me into consciousness."[52] This sequence, taking place in one paragraph, moves from temporal dislocation and hallucination to near-death catatonia to the shocking realization that the SS have her under careful surveillance, watching to see just how far they can allow her to slide near death before bringing her back again. The language of the passage consists of short, abrupt sentences filled with the articles "I" and "my," unlike the majority of the testimonial, which is written in third person and utilizes large amounts of dialogue and quotation. Suddenly, in this section, she is writing only about herself, and the tenor of the testimonial changes accordingly.

She testifies to the memories and experiences of her torture, but in a spare, affectless style. Her memory of this time, following the first seven days of starvation discussed in the paragraph above, is of the few objects and experiences that punctuated her isolation. She recalls the exact amount of food she was given at midday every four days and the amount she conserved for each of the foodless days that followed. Her physical and emotional state can be discerned from her brief notation that "in the darkness of the cell every minute had to be lived through. I distinguished night from day by a faint glimmer under the door. . . . in the end I lay flat, pressing my lips to that faint vestige of beloved light."[53] Here each minute becomes an eternity, beyond language, and the physical act of crawling to press her lips to the crack under the door where a glimmer of light enters is her entire world.

Also punctuating the nonspace/totality of her dark cell are the screams of the other inmates being tortured with whippings in "a special room." In a paragraph, she both gives concrete, material detail as to the layout and routine of the "bunker" where she is held and testifies to the tortures carried out there. Despite the problems of memory and language that mark this section of her testimonial, her provision of detailed information as to the layout of the prison, "concrete," "about a hundred cells," "arranged in two tiers around a court," and "acoustically . . . like a swimming pool" provide evidentiary weight to her account. She also establishes her own authority as an eyewitness by noting the acoustic nature of the building and her ability to distinguish the direction and distance of the sounds she was hearing.

Having established her authority as a witness, she testifies to the torture being inflicted on the inmates. "Beatings were dealt out on Fridays in a special room. . . . Such offenses as theft, refusal to work, and lesbianism were punished by twenty-five, fifty, or seventy-five strokes. . . . The screams of the victims resounded through the building. It did no good to stop my ears; I heard it all the same, heard it with my skin, with my whole body; the pain went to my heart."[54] The screams take on a material form, "resounding through the building," and her body becomes a single organism for hearing, penetrated throughout by the screams, which cause Buber-Neumann a pain that blurs the physical and the emotional as the screams penetrate to her heart. She testifies to the fact that the tortures occurred with ordered regularity, to their severity, and to her own—and, by extension, other women's—responses to them. She does not claim to have been physically tortured herself during this time, nor does she testify to the outcome of the beatings, many of which must have been death for the women being tortured. That lesbianism was one of the "crimes" singled out for such specific "punishment" marks both its regularity in the camp as a form of relations between women and its acknowledgment by the SS as a form of relationship, since the Nazis did not generally criminalize lesbianism as they did homosexual relations between men.[55]

Following this two-and-a-half-page passage that details her isolation, Buber-Neumann spends the remaining nine and a half pages of this section detailing her growing escape into a fantasy world of dreams punctuated by two incidents when Milena manages to break her isolation by getting the Jehovah's Witness who is detailed to the building to pass her small packages. The lifesaving interventions by Milena are juxtaposed with the danger of escaping into a world of dreams from which one is unable to return. Although Buber-Neumann originally began the storytelling exercises that gradually led to her slide into fantasy as a way to discipline herself and regulate the day so as not to slide into apathy, such an extended stay in solitary confinement cannot be resisted alone. Buber-Neumann eventually occupies the position of both characters in the Maxim Gorki story she is retelling and reliving, saying that she "slipped into the skins of the protagonists. . . . From that point on I was two people, two fugitives from reality."[56]

Such a splitting is presented by Buber-Neumann as a self-protective measure by her mind, so that she is no longer alone and can engage in dialogue and communal sharing. However, her fantasy world becomes so real to her that she is no longer willing to "return" to the isolated world of her cell, finally refusing even to eat the food that is provided to her: "I lost all sense of time and reality, I no longer knew if it was morning or evening . . . why bother with my bread ration when the table was groaning under the choicest dishes?"[57] Months of starvation, isolation, and the torture of listening to the screams of other prisoners account for such a self-protective retreat from reality, but even so, the escape she recounts is a fantasy of community and mutual aid, rather than one of individualism, violence, or revenge.

Buber-Neumann credits Milena with her release from the isolation cell through her dangerous intervention with the SS officer in charge. However, by the time of her release, Buber-Neumann is so lost in her dreamworld that Milena must spend considerable time and attention returning her to the world of the camp; Buber-Neumann is very resistant to reentering, declaring that she "hated the daylight and the ghastly reality" of the camp.[58] Milena gets her admitted to an annex of the infirmary where she works, and visits her whenever she is not working. Buber-Neumann says: "Over and over again, I would tell her about the life of my heroes by the seashore, and she would listen with infinite patience. In this way she enabled me to return slowly to the reality of concentration camp life."[59]

Such careful, patient attention to storytelling is both what Buber-Neumann credits with her survival and what is so impossible for most of the inmates. By exteriorizing her internal world for Milena, Buber-Neumann is able to rebuild her linkages with the communal structures that facilitate her survival in the camp. But only through a set of lucky circumstances could these conditions have occurred. Milena was brave and well-liked enough to stand up to the SS officer and convince him to release Buber-Neumann, she had a privileged job in the infirmary that allowed her some freedom of movement and some influence with other inmates, and so on. By detailing both the temerity and the chance that ensured her survival, Buber-Neumann gestures toward the near-total impossibility of survival in the camps even under the most auspicious set of circumstances.

Community as a site of resistance, such as Delbo stages it, becomes in Buber-Neumann's testimony even more, as the pleasures of an overwhelming "passionate friendship" are located as the primary site of her survival. This friendship between Milena and Buber-Neumann allows them not just to support each other but to take risks and break rules, which gives them a sense of being alive and having an identity; "because it was so strong, because it filled our whole beings, our friendship became something more, an open protest against the humiliations imposed on us" writes Buber-Neumann.[60] This sharing and support work to resist "the Holocaust as a world in which the very imagination of the *Other* was no longer possible," as Dori Laub has formulated it, and instead bolsters Buber-Neumann's ability to be her own witness to the events in which she participates. The primacy of her relationship with Milena is based on a complex set of remembered attractions: her physical presence and her devotion to Buber-Neumann are explicitly cited, but her role as Buber-Neumann's "witness/listener" and the intellectual project—the coauthored testimony they plan following their release from the camp—are located as equally important.

Delbo figures the camps as the site of the ultimate expression of patriarchy, the symbolic order of language and the "word" that survivors have been both radically and violently removed from and must speak/write themselves back into in order to return. Thus they must willingly reenter the symbolic order while recognizing that this same structure has been the cause of their experience of atrocity. Buber-Neumann's testimony foregrounds both Milena's ongoing struggles against patriarchy and oppressive strictures of language and her own resistance to the violences, both physical and discursive, of totalitarian ideologies. Buber-Neumann locates Milena as the guide who helps her to put her experiences of atrocity into language and makes possible for her the belief that she can write about them. Through a consistent focus on Milena's femininity as existing in continual tension with her difference from social, gender, sexual, national, and intellectual norms, Buber-Neumann testifies to Milena as the "site" through which Buber-Neumann finds her own testimonial voice.

This performative act of testimony occurs between Milena and Buber-Neumann while they are still within the concentration camps and is situated as an important locus for pleasure between the two women and for resistance to the absolute difference and alienation of their world in the camp. Buber-Neumann recalls that her friendship with Milena was formed around Milena's insistence on hearing the story of her life, especially her experiences in Soviet Russia. She writes that "[Milena's] imagination threw her back into the past, and she was able to flesh out my memory of things I had long forgotten. . . . Her manner of questioning was a creative act; *it enabled me for the first time to give form to my recollections*" (emphasis added).[61]

Milena's questioning is important in that it helps Buber-Neumann to remember and narrativize her experiences in the gulag. She externalizes her experience, putting it into language as she builds the story under Milena's "creative act" of questioning. In this passage she remembers both her experiences with Milena and her experiences of the gulag, doubling the testimonial moment. As she herself testifies to her experience with Milena in the camps, she also testifies to her experiences in the gulag. Buber-Neumann attributes Milena's skill at building the testimonial dynamic to her skills as a journalist, remarking that "as a journalist she was interested first and foremost in what others said and did . . . [and was] utterly devoted to her calling."[62] Thus she also locates Milena's ability to keep "her grip on life" to her ongoing work as a journalist collecting testimonials, which keeps Milena from speaking about (and therefore, Buber-Neumann implies, focusing on) her own suffering. Milena's ability to survive the initial shock of her entrance into the camp is attributed to her continued prioritizing of her responsibility toward others. Buber-Neumann reports that "in every interview she created an atmosphere of intimacy, because she invariable identified with the person she was questioning. She had a remarkable gift of empathy."[63]

Buber-Neumann attributes her ability to remember things she had "long forgotten" to Milena's detailed questions about all aspects of the gulags, including the other prisoners. Milena is thus positioned as the perfect witness to testimony, neither intrusive nor overly empathic, whose questions bring forth daily chronological installments of Buber-Neumann's experiences in the gulags. Such witnessing is located by Laub, among others, as crucial to the survival of trauma, and Buber-Neumann locates it as a crucial site of resistance to the ongoing trauma of life within the camps, which has been formulated by Laub as a position from which unencumbered witnessing is not possible. Milena's and Buber-Neumann's friendship both is predicated upon and opens the space for them to continue the ongoing project of (re)building themselves as witnesses and is located as the most important element of Buber-Neumann's survival of Ravensbrück. Buber-Neumann's relationship with Milena and her extreme pleasure in it and need for it are formulated as resisting the impossibility of "the imagination of the *Other*" within the Holocaust, instead positing their friendship as the site of a recognition of difference, of "the Other," that is crucial to their active witnessing and therefore ongoing survival in the camp.[64]

Unlike Delbo's play, the bodies in Buber-Neumann's testimony are largely whole. Delbo's characters, physically disintegrating onstage through their dialogue, challenge the spectators' imagination to recognize the continuing humanity and individuality of each woman as their bodies become increasingly abject. Buber-Neumann, however, does not foreground the physical deterioration of the characters of her testimony. Instead she focuses on the emotional and physical pleasures of their lives under conditions of horrific distress. Resistance, for Buber-Neumann as for Delbo's characters, becomes a series of daily, individual acts aimed at prolonging lives. As many of the women in both texts are political prisoners, they bring a sophisticated scope of analysis to bear on their status as death camp inmates and reformulate terms such as resistance, ideology, and loyalty under the pressure of the camps.

Buber-Neumann's emphasis on stolen time and pleasure is not cast as heroic or out of the ordinary in the lives of the other women in the camp. Indeed, despite her focus on the relationship she shared with Milena and her emphasis on Milena's unusual character, her testimonial suggests that many women were sustained—for whatever length of

119

time they had left—by such daily acts of support, friendship, exchange, and necessity. Thus, although her book (even more than most, perhaps) emphasizes the particular individual experiences she and Milena shared, like many testimonials her text makes the claim that while the story she tells is particular to her own experiences, any of the other women in the camp with her could have told a similar story. Her book, like other testimonials, speaks for all the other women who also experienced the camps. She says:

> The combination of monotony and constant terror favored strong friendships among the inmates. Our prospects were as uncertain as if we had been shipwrecked on the high seas. The SS had absolute power over us, and every day could be our last. In this situation, we developed mental as well as physical faculties which tend to remain untapped in normal life. Under these circumstances the feeling that one was necessary to another human being was a source of supreme happiness, made life worth living, and gave one the strength to survive.[65]

By emphasizing "strong friendships" that are the result of "mental and physical faculties that tend to remain untapped in normal life," Buber-Neumann acknowledges that the erotic bonds between women that she has earlier noted flourish in the camps are a site of resistance that in "normal life"—that is, heteropatriarchy—remain "untapped." Under the extreme, coercive, gender violence of the camps, however, such bonds become a crucial site of humanity, of "feeling that one was necessary to another human being." Rather than emphasizing the abjection of circumstances that force women into modes of friendship that in "normal life" would be at best hidden and ostracized, if not violently acted against, Buber-Neumann valorizes such "strong friendships" as a site of difference—of recognition of the Other—which is necessary to a survival figured as the maintenance of humanity through the recognition of the basic humanity of the Other. Such recognition of the Other "was a source of supreme happiness, made life worth living, and gave one the strength to survive." All three of these claims are shocking in the context of a death camp and figure prominently in Buber-Neumann's testimonial project to resist the historical memory of the camps as a site of absolute abjection, erasure, and inhumanity for women.

Rather than testifying to the radical selfishness of inmates fighting each other for any scrap that could improve their immediate material circumstances, as some authors do, Buber-Neumann's testimony works as a form of historical resistance to the death camps. For the camps to be figured as a site of absolute abjection where all inmates lost their humanity under the extreme pressures of survival in an environment of extreme violence, coercion, and death, Buber-Neumann's testimonial suggests, is to allow the Nazi project to win. By emphasizing the ways in which they and the other women consciously worked to maintain their "humanity" under such conditions, Buber-Neumann, Delbo, and Nomberg-Przytyk provide us with definitions of "humanity" to counter the "inhumanity" of the common representation of the death camp inmate. Thus these testimonials refute the historical memory of the camps as a site of an absolute difference that becomes sameness— both the difference of the inmates from each other, radically individuated yet indistinguishable, and of the inmates from the Nazis—where both descend into an absolute inhumanity of total powerlessness subject to total violent control.

To cede such absolute power to the Nazi project of the camps while acknowledging their own descent into complete inhumanity, these testimonial authors suggest, is to allow the Nazi project to have historically succeeded despite the Nazis' loss of the war. In the quotation above, Buber-Neumann acknowledges both the absolute power of the Nazis over the inmates and the development of reserves of resistance that remain "untapped in normal life." Despite such absolute power over the women's physical survival, the Nazis inadvertently create a situation where the women find new ways to resist that they might never have known otherwise. Buber-Neumann, like the other authors discussed here, never figures survival as a form of heroic resistance. Instead it is an elusive, stolen impossibility that occurs moment by moment, not as part of a conscious pattern of resistance but as a necessity for maintaining each woman's sense of herself as a basic human being. Such humanity is figured as the conscious decision to engage an act of material or emotional support that serves to recognize the basic humanity and right to life of another person.

The rigidity of systems of oppositional political and religious ideology is portrayed much more explicitly by Buber-Neumann than by Delbo as complicit in the violence of the death camps. Buber-Neumann's testimony traces a trajectory of communist "opposition" within Ravensbrück that actually endangers the survival of inmates. Her testimony moves from stories of some women's refusal to aid non-communist-affiliated women, to the persecution of communist-affiliated or

121

previously affiliated women who are perceived as deviating from the political ideology, to outright complicity with the Nazis. By differentiating such organized opposition from the resistance she locates as occurring between women through mutual bonds of friendship, Buber-Neumann highlights the ways in which previous structures of political affiliation must necessarily be reconfigured within such a radical death environment. Affiliation across lines of difference—national, political, religious, sexual—and recognition of one's own basic "humanity" through acts that acknowledge the right to life and basic humanity of the other become the foundation for the politics of survival and witnessing developed in her testimonial. For example, in a chapter titled "Zealots," she attributes the same qualities to the Jehovah's Witnesses as she has to the communists.

After an incident in which Buber-Neumann persuades a dying Jehovah's Witness to renounce her religion and be released after she has been placed on an extermination list, earning the vitriol of other Jehovah's Witnesses, she states that she and Milena "discussed the utter intolerance of these people, their lack of sympathy for anyone who did not belong to their sect, and their cowardice when given an opportunity to perform an act of true Christianity. We came to the conclusion that they were very much like Communists. The only difference was that they worshipped Jehovah instead of Stalin."[66] She attributes such actions to the women's adherence to a rigid ideology that is incapable of adapting to changes of circumstances and is too inflexible to recognize the vital importance of affiliation across lines of difference under circumstances of mass death. Upholding allegiances and grievances from the world outside the camps without recognizing that within the camps, under the pressure of atrocity and mass death, perhaps the most overriding concern is that of basic survival both of oneself and of others regardless of ethnic, religious, or political affiliations (all meaningless in the death camp) is portrayed as a form of complicity.

All former beliefs and behaviors become suspect in the camps, as Buber-Neumann and Milena recognize the role that certain social and political structures have played in abetting totalitarian violence. As such, they formulate an alternate ideology of resistance and politics, born in the camps, that recognizes the survival of other humans as a primary political and ethical obligation that both respects and transcends the boundaries of identities. Such a development is invariably attributed to ongoing conversations between herself and Milena as they work out together the problems of political, ethical, and personal engagements and responsibilities in the camp.

Buber-Neumann portrays the results of these conversations to be an evolving formulation of ethics and politics based on the recognition of the responsibility of each person for the basic well-being of others and the rejection of both rigid political ideologies and "bourgeois sentimentality."[67] Such a rejection both of liberal models of sympathy based on individual nostalgia and of reigning political systems, coupled with systematic critique of the effects of structures of power on the lives and identities of the people within them points within the testimonial to the beginnings of what could be described as a politics of human rights.

Like Nomberg-Przytyk, Buber-Neumann relates stories of Nazis and SS who also stepped out of their roles to help individual inmates, complicating even further the boundaries between actors in the death-world as well as the easy identifications of the reader: "Not all the women overseers and SS men in the concentration camps were evil by nature. I believe that one of the worst crimes of the dictatorship was to have corrupted average human beings and made them into its tools."[68] This serves to implicate Nazis even more severely in the genocide, since some are shown resisting through small acts when the possibility arises. Thus resistance to the genocide was possible for SS and Nazis, and their choice not to resist it but to further it was an ongoing process of daily decision-making. Also, such portraits of Nazis and SS who engaged in acts of humanity, as the testimonials define it, again works against the historical memory of the camps as an absolute site of abjection where everybody involved was beyond the realm of "humanity."

Originally published in Germany thirty-two years after the end of the war, the book highlights the problems of memory associated with testimonial projects. Buber-Neumann's choice to emphasize discussions that lead to rejections of absolutist ideologies in favor of proto-human-rights concerns is on some level influenced by post-1948 developments in human rights. However, the testimonial claim that there is a remembered truth of experience that one can access after the closure of the physical event of the atrocity itself should not be discarded because of temporal distance from the "death event" itself. Instead, Buber-Neumann's testimonial can be read as a vital link in the development of human rights discourses. The experiences of survivors, not just those of intellectual and political elites horrified by the mass atrocities

123

and genocide of World War II, must remain at the forefront of our understanding of how these discourses develop.

Passion, Testimony, and Memorial

The book reads both as testimony and as memorial. To the extent that it is testimony, it provides an account of Buber-Neumann's experiences within Ravensbrück with some mention of her imprisonment by the Soviets. Equally, however, the book is a memorial to Milena Jesenská, and Buber-Neumann intrudes herself occasionally into the text to remind the reader that it is being written long after the events actually occurred. She insists upon both the "truth" of the story she tells and the possible inaccuracies of memory brought about by time and changing perspectives. This odd mix of testimony and memorial places the "I" of the witness in the uncomfortable position of reconciling the story of Milena's precamp life, which Buber-Neumann recalls from their conversations and from research done after the end of the war, with the story of Buber-Neumann's own experiences of the camps mediated through her narrativizing of her friendship with Milena.

Buber-Neumann's awareness of the pitfalls of memory and the time that has lapsed between her experiences and her testimony is due perhaps in part to this difficult relationship between testimonial and the thirdhand recounting of another life. The physical structure of the book takes the form of fragments rather than a continuous linear narrative. Employing such devices as epigraphs, biographical sections, quotations from letters, testimony, and commentary by the author from her current perspective, Buber-Neumann highlights the fragmentary nature of knowledge, memory, and identity, performed for the reader through the physicality of the text itself.

In the translation and publication of the book from German to English, the subtitle of the book changes from *Kafkas Freundin* to *The Story of a Remarkable Friendship*. This changes the emphasis of the book for the reader's first encounter with it—from Milena as an appendage of Kafka's to the primacy of her friendship with Buber-Neumann. Perhaps the translators meant the "remarkable friendship" to be that of Milena with Kafka, but it is also clearly that of Milena with Buber-Neumann. It also highlights the inherent complexities and inconsistencies of all translation—including that of the testimonial experience itself.

The testimony obliquely (and sometimes not so obliquely) suggests that Milena and Buber-Neumann were themselves lovers. In the language for homosexuality that has developed throughout the course of the twentieth century, however, same-sex love is usually equated with sameness and the denial of difference. Precisely what is important in the text for the relationship between Milena and the author, however, is the emphasis on difference that their relationship provides. Milena's intense questioning of Buber-Neumann allows her to testify, within the concentrationary universe of Ravensbrück, to her experiences in the Soviet gulags—and to develop, along with Milena, the structure she will later employ in writing this testimonial to their time in the Nazi camp. Milena's differences from her, rather than her similarities, and her exploration of Milena as a site of difference form one of the basic structures around which Buber-Neumann's testimonial is written.

Milena's prior relationship with Kafka, portrayed by Buber-Neumann as intensely erotic but unconsummated, and her use of epigraphs by Kafka testifying to various aspects of Milena's character and persona and their shared love and understanding position Buber-Neumann as Milena's second important extended erotic relationship (as opposed to Milena's relationship with her husband, which is portrayed as hopelessly mired within the coercive structures of patriarchy and heterosexuality—he is a philanderer who fails to respect her and is notable mainly for making her unhappy, uprooting her, and giving her Honza, their daughter). Buber-Neumann's use of fragments of Kafka's writings on Milena as epigraphs both supports her own claims for Milena's character and testifies to Milena as an object of lost love and unattainable desire. By incorporating Kafka's writings about Milena into her own testimony, Buber-Neumann not only speaks her own love for Milena in deeper more complex ways through the voice of a former lover, she also gives a voice in new ways to Kafka's own writing about Milena. Just as testimonial speaks for those who experienced the atrocity but did not survive, Buber-Neumann's testimony incorporates Kafka's voice into its testimonial project—highlighting even more the fragmentary nature of the testimonial act.

In this testimony, Ravensbrück becomes a crucible where, in an all-female environment under immense pressure, women prisoners form intense homoerotic and homosexual bonds that enhance survival through the affirmation of affection, the recognition of difference, and the physical support that was generally necessary to survival. In many testimonials, love is portrayed as an almost impossible emotion within the violent coercive structure of the camps, and the love for lost ones or between family members is the most common form taken by such anxieties about love's dissolution into responsibility under the pressure of the camps. Sex, when it is mentioned, is almost always a violent, proprietary act that takes the form of rape or enforced prostitution. And in the case of many men's memoirs, women figure as a site of anguish and emasculation. But Buber-Neumann's focus on sexuality implies more than the importance of the reaffirmation of affective bonds in a world of absolute degradation and atrocity. While most testimonials focus on the destruction of the body, such as the disintegrating bodies of the women in *Who Will Carry the Word?*, Buber-Neumann portrays bodies as sites of resistant pleasure.

Locating bodies in such a way serves to recuperate them from the universalized sameness of bodies that is enforced through the camp's violent ideology. It also positions them as sites of difference and particularity that are more than the site of intense pain and the unendurable horror of the ultimate betrayal—the body turned against the self. Buber-Neumann's testimonial powerfully and counterintuitively focuses on the resistant possibilities of pleasure as site of survival within a concentration camp—the pleasure in building new relationships, in small (and sometimes large) acts of resistance, in physical expression, and in sharing memories and identities. She does not downplay the atrocity of the camp through this emphasis but instead refuses its overwhelming and all-consuming violence.

Milena presents both women, Milena and Buber-Neumann, as already marginalized from patriarchy in their erotic relationships with men. Milena's identity is presented as an extended self-conscious negotiation with and resistance to normative structures of patriarchy and law, and her three primary relationships with men have been with her autocratic father, her philanderer husband, and in her asexual affair with Kafka. Buber-Neumann, through the intensity of her focus on the priority of her relationship with Milena, by extension affiliates herself with this history, although she does not approach the subject of her own divorce and the murder of her second husband in the testimonial. Buber-Neumann also insists on the nonsexual nature of her own relationship with Milena, although her text continually (and nostalgically?) recalls the various possibilities of lesbianism as a sexual relationship. Although reticent about relating her own story (not mentioning her first marriage), Buber-Neumann has lost two husbands—the second murdered by the Soviets after they fled Germany for Moscow in 1937.

Such ellipses of her own story within the testimonial frame the silence of the spaces that Milena, who was to write the biographical sections on Buber-Neumann in their planned shared testimony, was meant to fill had she survived.

Buber-Neumann thus also effectively presents herself as "unmarked" by past relationships in the memoir—not referencing her previous marriages and erotic or romantic ties. Through such "unmarking" she associates the story she tells of Milena's unconventional sexuality with herself as well. As Buber-Neumann is alienated from her previous communities, including the communists who should be her allies in the camp, Milena suddenly becomes all of her world and community. Her testimonial presents their bond as more than the survival bond of two women who together form a "community of witness" (and here I am thinking of Dori Laub's formulation of the external witness to trauma as an important element of survival). By using so much of her testimonial to narrate Milena's life prior to her incarceration, Buber-Neumann links her story with Milena to the story of Milena's past life, binding them together into a single organic narrative. Such an act does more than provide us with an unusual testimonial that goes beyond the bounds of the camp experience to tell the story of Milena's (not the author's) life; it provides Buber-Neumann with an extensive link to Milena herself, both as an authority on Milena's life and experiences, and as Milena's most intimate companion since Kafka—and her final companion.

The structure of the testimonial itself is also fragmentary, skipping between chapters of Milena's autobiography as told to Buber-Neumann in the camp and supplemented by her post–World War II research, stories of their time together in Ravensbrück, epigraphs about Milena written by Kafka, Buber-Neumann's own testimony of her experiences, and pieces of Milena's own published writings. Thus Milena herself is given a testifying voice in the text—through quotations that Buber-Neumann writes in her voice, through selections of her writings, and through the testimonies of people who knew her. Utilizing a structure of fragments of narrative that can never be whole, Buber-Neumann weaves a testimonial of numerous voices speaking from gaps and fragments. The identities of these speakers, even central ones like herself and Milena, remain fragmentary, and yet through the testimonial they speak strongly and coherently about their experiences and their lives.

Milena's public sexual self-presentation is portrayed by Buber-Neumann as a consciously political act that bridges personal and public ethical engagements. Milena's adolescent rebellions against middle-class culture and her father mature, according to the testimonial, into the basis for her strong ethic of liberationist politics. Within the context of the extreme pressures of the concentrationary universe of Ravensbrück, Milena is presented as a strongly resistant figure. Thus Buber-Neumann, the narrator, while valorizing and condoning Milena's sexually transgressive self-presentation, links it to a politics of resistance very different from that of the communists with whom she herself has been affiliated. Stating that "she was far from unique [as a teenager] in her rebellion and wild urge to live," Buber-Neumann notes that "this urge to break away from the old social patterns can be explained at least in part by the then prevailing atmosphere in Prague. The whole Czech nation was living in hopeful anticipation of national independence. . . . a minority at least of young Czechs were beginning to form ties with the German and German-Jewish writers living in Prague. National boundaries were giving way."[69] Milena's "deliberately boyish look," the "wild stories told about her," and the fact that it is she who "sets the tone" among her circle are linked to a world of transnational intellectuals, the dissolution of national boundaries, and the shifting borders of national identity. Her performance of self becomes a public representation of these political formations.

Buber-Neumann here risks presenting Milena as operating fully within gender norms and stereotypes; as little more than the iconic female representation around which many strongly patriarchal movements have cohered. Her immediate textual recuperation of Milena from this model is awkward. With such hyperbole as "among . . . quite a few shining lights . . . Milena outshone them all," and "she was gifted with a sixth sense that enabled her to detect pretense . . . and [see through to the] core of the human being," Buber-Neumann places Milena in a position of uniqueness that seems to defy her membership in ordinary human communities yet is also akin to the language of a lover describing her beloved.[70] She also, however, locates her both within the feminist movement and within, for a time, "the radical political left." Such positioning of Milena as both a unique figurehead and an open, flawed, political, and deeply caring woman parallels her own relationship to Milena that Buber-Neumann describes in Ravensbrück.

Throughout the testimony of their time together in the camps, Buber-Neumann presents Milena as the leader in their friendship, herself as follower. In her narration of Milena's life prior to her arrest, Milena is portrayed as always at the center of an admiring circle of friends and onlookers, not despite her deviance from social norms but because of it. She is presented as an object of desire by both men and women, her sexuality subject to continual speculation and regulation—including her confinement to a sanatorium by her father for her romantic friendship with another adolescent girl and her defiance of her father's authority. Milena's position as social rebel is presented as an ethical position, one in which her politics and relations to others are exemplified by the most mundane aspects of the way she lives her daily life—even within Ravensbrück. In addition, by making Milena the "visible" marker of difference—the ethical place-marker in the testimonial—Buber-Neumann herself becomes visible as exceptional without the danger of claiming such contested terrain for herself. Buber-Neumann's relationship to the law, her position as claiming from within the absolute difference of the world of the camps a relationship to the other that carries over into the normative world she once again inhabits, is marked by her recalling of Milena's insistence on difference.

The focus on pleasure within the concentration camp and later death camp of Ravensbrück is highly unusual in the extent to which Buber-Neumann emphasizes it as a site of survival, resistance, and individuality. By placing the story of Milena's affair with Kafka at the center of the narrative, Buber-Neumann draws a parallel between Kafka's love affair with Milena (his "great love") and her own. She spends considerable time exploring the reasons why Milena and Kafka never physically consummated their sexual relationship, although they were clearly lovers and in love in every way. This seems to parallel and give a romantic turn to her own relationship with Milena, both relationships of whom are implied to have existed on another plane beyond that of the ordinary physical world. In Kafka's case, this "other plane" was his own particular being, described in a letter by Milena as "resolutely self-contained and self-sufficient, devoid of all artifice that might enable him to misrepresent life, either its beauty or its misery."[71] For Milena and Buber-Neumann it is Ravensbrück.

Their love is both a profound source of strength for both women and a means of resistance. Buber-Neumann falls in love with Milena because she is an "unbroken spirit" in the camps and because of the deep bond they share when she tells Milena of her imprisonment in the gulags. Her description of the progression of their relationship is erotic partly because of the transgression they commit in pursuing it. In a world where radical separation was demanded, and lesbianism, when recognized, resulted in death or severe beatings and solitary confinement, the transgressive and resistive nature of this relationship would have profound psychological effect. In fact, in the first pages of the testimonial Buber-Neumann shockingly states that "I was thankful for having been sent to Ravensbrück, because there I had met Milena."[72] Lesbianism itself becomes muddled here, as it is a category under the pressure of several competing definitions. The Nazis have violently organized for themselves all definitional power and exercise the right of naming in the camps. Lesbian as a category is articulated by Buber-Neumann as defined by Nazi punishments and by sex acts committed for immediate physical pleasure and advancement—such as the commodification of sex through prostitution. However, pleasure as a site of resistance is a complex formulation, and while Buber-Neumann generally articulates pleasure as a politically aware act of survival through a focus on the well-being of an other, she does not condemn acts of pleasure that seem more immediately focused on sex.

The emphasis in Delbo's play on dialogue and community as crucial sites of resistance finds a parallel in Buber-Neumann's focus on dialogue and homosexual/homosocial community as sites of resistance in the camps. Just as "the word" for the characters of *Who Will Carry the Word?* becomes crucial for rebuilding their relationship to history and juridical culture, in *Milena* the recognition of "the love that dare not speak its name" is the most revolutionary of acts. The camps enforced both a rigid separation between the sexes and a complete prohibition of same-sex contact. As Buber-Neumann notes, however, "Despite the horrors of the camp, the close quarters at which thousands of women were living made for an erotic atmosphere."[73] Locating the camp as a site of erotic transgression "despite the horrors," Buber-Neumann documents same-sex love as a positive, redemptive act that denies the formulation of prisoners as nonhuman and as sexual commodities in the service of the totalitarian system. She does not posit a naïve form of "redemptive lesbianism" as the key to survival; she does suggest that in the possibilities for intimate sharing, risk-taking, and support, homosocial relationships could be crucial to the rebuilding of an imaginary where the Other was still possible, to use Laub's formulation.

She writes: "It was toward the end of November, during our evening exercise, that we dared for the first time to walk arm in arm. This was strictly forbidden in Ravensbrück. It was dark, and we walked in silence, with strangely long steps as though dancing, peering into the milky moonlight. . . . For me nothing existed but Milena's hand on my arm and the wish that this walk might never end."[74] The eroticism of the passage quoted above is located in the romantic description of their environment, the darkness and "milky moonlight," the physical pleasure of touching, the pleasures of transgression in a situation where it is extremely dangerous, and the language of romantic love, where nothing exists outside one's awareness of the beloved. Such a combination of romance "despite the horrors," where language is unnecessary and they walk "strangely" "as though dancing," uses a clichéd language of romance to heighten the unreality of existing simultaneously in two seemingly incommensurate worlds—a death camp and a romantic moonlit stroll. In the concentration camp, where all physical intimacy is "strictly forbidden," such action takes on the heightened meaning of remembering the normative world outside the Holocaust and of reaffirming the women's position as its members despite their current location. Physical intimacy that was of the most casual kind outside the camp becomes an act fraught with danger and resistance.

But there is a tension in the testimonial between the portrayal of their relationship as a self-aware site of pleasure and resistance, and a profound need that goes beyond the women's ability to control or explain it. Following the passage quoted above, Buber-Neumann goes on to say that when the siren to return to the barracks sounds, "we hesitated, holding each other tight, unwilling to part." They make an appointment to meet later, and Buber-Neumann notes that "it didn't even occur to me that this meeting might end with a flogging or solitary confinement or even death. It didn't cross my mind that someone might see me. . . . In my haste and excitement I tripped over a stump and fell into Milena's arms." As they take more risks and spend more time together, Buber-Neumann writes that "our longing to spend time together became more and more imperious." They develop a relationship that defies all boundaries within the camp, and yet she never portrays it as a source of anxiety or fear beyond the fear that the other will be discovered and harmed.

This introductory section in the book, introducing their relationship, culminates in the creation of a space where Milena can tell her story to Buber-Neumann. After several pages describing their growing intimacy with each other and the profound risks they have taken to be together over what seems in the text to be a year since they first met, they manage to spend a night together. In a moment of physical intimacy, Milena takes Buber-Neumann's hand and places it on her hair, initiating a space where Milena gives her testimony to Buber-Neumann. While over the course of the past year Milena has, through a series of interviews, witnessed Buber-Neumann's testimony, now Buber-Neu-mann hears Milena's. The intense intimacy that Buber-Neumann artic-ulates as necessary before Milena can tell her story and the locating of Buber-Neumann in the position of Milena's lost mother (the placing of her hand on Milena's hair on the spot where her mother used to touch her) allow Milena to relinquish her control over the relationship and tell her story through the spectral mediation of her mother. Here the dynamic performance of testimonial is articulated through the ghosts of the past and the present time, as Milena tells her story to Buber-Neumann in a stolen, interstitial space, "as though safe on an island," that is both carved out from the concentration camp and yet subject to its intrusion at any time.

Buber-Neumann writes: "I realized that what fascinated me most was the aura of mystery surrounding her whole being. . . . Sometimes, when I saw her from a distance on the camp street, it seemed to me that she had just popped out of nowhere. Even when she was happy, her eyes were always veiled by some bottomless grief. . . . This evasive, water-nymph-like quality captivated me completely, for I knew I could never get through to her. All my dreams of Milena are haunted by this feeling of hopelessness."[75] Milena functions in an uncanny capacity in this passage and in Buber-Neumann's text, haunting it with her pres-ence recalled through the testimony. Popping out of nowhere, she uncannily signifies the non-Holocaust world as the participant in Buber-Neumann's testimonial dynamic within the camps. A cipher or a mythical being, "water-nymph-like," whose eyes are seen by Buber-Neumann as the scene of incommensurable grief, she continues to haunt Buber-Neumann's dreams as the site of difference, marked by the present tense of the last sentence. This "feeling of hopelessness" is Buber-Neumann's acknowledgment, in the unconscious of her dreams and in her testimonial, of the difference of the other, her knowledge that she "could never get through to her." The text is haunted by the physical ways that Buber-Neumann and Kafka did not get through to her, but also by the abyss of language, of knowing, and of memory that must be acknowledged by Buber-Neumann's witnessing.

For Buber-Neumann and Milena, the stolen time together that other women use for sex is used for testimony. But she does not con-demn sex; rather she valorizes it as an act of love, even documenting rare affairs between SS and inmates. The objectivity of tone that she uses in discussing affairs between women, sex with Gert the prostitute, and between SS and inmates is extraordinary to the extent that it does not condemn the relationships out of hand as perversions, exploitation, or coercion. Rather, she suggests that all erotic relationships are commodified in some fashion, and while the form of her relationship with Milena is articulated through the testimonial dynamic, she suggests that other formations within the camps also meet the same ethical criteria if they involve the recognition of the other.

This is not to say that she herself explicitly addresses her affair with Milena as lesbian. It is life-affirming, necessary, and resistive to the totalitarian structure, but she remains bounded by the cultural prohibitions against openly declaring it as other than a heterosexually framed, if extremely close, relationship between two women. Buber-Neumann addresses women's relationships in the camps in the following remarkable paragraphs:

> Far from ceasing with the loss of freedom, the need for love and affection becomes more imperious than ever. Some of the women in Ravensbrück took refuge in passionate friendships, others eased their heartache by talking endlessly about love, and still others resorted to political or even religious fanaticism.
>
> The passionate friendships of the politicals usually remained platonic, while those of the criminals and asocials often took on a frankly lesbian character. Such relationships, when discovered, were punished with flogging.
>
> In my next to last year at Ravensbrück, when conditions were becoming more and more chaotic, I heard of a lesbian prostitute. Her name was Gerda, but she called herself Gert. She serviced a number of women, but not for money. Every Saturday and Sunday her customers brought her their rations of margarine and sausage, which were distributed only on weekends.[76]

In this passage, universalism becomes an act of resistance. Rather than situating the universalism of sameness with the erasure of particularity upon which some critiques of human rights discourse depend, Buber-Neumann locates difference as a site of resistance through an appeal to basic, human, emotional needs. Love and affection are absolutely antithetical to the functioning of a death camp, and while the camp's power and devastating psychological attack rest largely in the erasure of all differences between prisoners while insisting upon their absolute difference from the world outside the camp, Buber-Neumann locates universal ideas of love and affection as a site of resistance where differences between the women can be recognized and affirmed. Such affirmation is fully in line with her emphasis throughout the testimony on Milena as a teacher of resistance through the continual reaffirmation of difference.

The universal reference to "love" and "affection" in the first sentence of the extract above introduces the homosocial and homosexual bonding between the prisoners as strongly resistant acts. Compared to the options of "talking endlessly about love," implying a passive self-indulgent behavior that does not benefit others, or "resorting to political or even religious fanaticism," both of which have been strongly condemned by her in the testimony, engaging in passionate friendships is presented as active and affirming as well as something widely supported by women within the camp. Her ambivalence toward these relationships and toward her participation in them is clear from the passage, despite her open discourse of romance with Milena.

In the second paragraph, whose first sentence ends by stating that relationships between criminals and asocials "often took on a frankly lesbian character," the conjunction of lesbian with criminal/asocial leads the reader to expect condemnation from Buber-Neumann. Her distinction between platonic passionate friendships and those with a "lesbian character" seems to participate in a long discourse of homosexuality that attributes to "passionate friendships" of the upper classes attributes of a "higher" a/sexual platonic love, while the lower classes engage in the crass physicality of actual sex. In the following sentence, however, she notes that the camp did not recognize such differences of class and behavior and punished all such relationships with flogging. While Buber-Neumann may want, in the objective tone of the observer, to distinguish between the physicality of homosexual relationships in the camp depending on the political and intellectual commitment of the participants, she also recognizes that within the disciplinary structures of the camp, all relationships that lead to "love and affection" are a threat to the proper functioning of the death camp and will be punished without distinction.

This does not mean, however, that Buber-Neumann uncritically celebrates all moments of community-building between prisoners. Rather, she leaves open the possible meanings of various identifications. Hers is a witnessing that refuses collusion with the beatings that end the second paragraph, even if love in the camp has become a form of material exchange embodied by Gert. The women who resort to "political or religious fanaticism," the communists and Jehovah's Witnesses, are reviled by Buber-Neumann for their lack of solidarity with and sometimes destructiveness toward women who are not members of their party line or religion. While nowhere in the text does she condemn "frankly lesbian" relationships, she implies that their more carnal nature puts them below the level of "passionate friendships" such as the one she shared with Milena. The criminals and asocials, in her experience, do not have a political consciousness and therefore their lesbianism may be transgressive and dangerous but does not carry with it the same life-affirming nature as do the passionate friendships of the politicals. However, lesbianism is figured throughout the testimonial as a site of resistance to totalitarian violence.

Gert, the lesbian prostitute, is an exceptional figure who seems to exemplify Buber-Neumann's claim that the close quarters of the camp made for an erotically charged atmosphere. The "chaotic conditions" of the last year of Ravensbrück were a time of massive overcrowding and death, when the camp went from a concentration to a death camp and the camp authorities began ordering mass executions of prisoners, receiving Auschwitz evacuees, and finally building a gas chamber that began operating in February of 1944. Under increasingly threatening and chaotic circumstances, the appearance of Gert supports the contention that intimacy was an important site of resistance and support for the prisoners yet suggests that in a time of frantic competition for scarce resources, the valuable intimacy that Buber-Neumann celebrates was as much commodity as resistance.

The definitions of transgression and resistance in this testimonial are left deliberately open by Buber-Neumann as she rejects totalitarianism and absolutism in any form as coercive and violent. For the prisoners in the camp's world of absolute difference, transgression of authority is very different from the transgressions indulged in by people in dominant positions, where it is often an act of privilege and even a game of power. In *Milena,* it is an act of self-affirmation and resistance at great personal risk. Any of the meetings that Milena and Buber-Neumann kept over the three and a half years of their "passionate friendship" could very well have resulted in their deaths if discovered, as could Milena's act in rescuing Buber-Neumann from solitary confinement.

Buber-Neumann relates a complex relationship to popular culture, memory, and love in the testimonial that serves as a bridge between her present existence as a survivor and her time in the camps. Because she left Western Europe in 1935, it was not until her return as a prisoner in a concentration camp that she heard the songs that had become popular in her absence. Although the trauma of the camps could serve as a break with memory—marking the time within the camps as absolutely different from the time before and after it—in Buber-Neumann's formulation, the songs serve as a bridge reminding her of her time in the camp. And remarkably, she writes of them as markers of pleasure among the horrors of the camp:

> Even now, forty years later, the tune carries me back to the first years of my friendship with Milena, to those unreal days when, prisoners among prisoners, we lived in a rich world of our own. Every gesture, every word, every smile, had its meaning. Constantly being separated and yet so close together, living always in anticipation of a brief meeting, even the bell of the little railway train running along the camp wall while we—Milena a few hundred yards away from me—were lined up for roll call seemed like a loving message from one to the other. In that existence without a future, we lived entirely for the present.[77]

Marking the unreality of the situation, despite the fact that she lived through it, for Buber-Neumann the song triggers not traumatic memories of atrocity and horror but romantic memories of taking pleasure in her relationship with Milena.

This testimony is focused around the resistant possibilities of love and pleasure in situations of extreme atrocity, and Buber-Neumann quotes Milena as saying that "love is indestructible. It is stronger than any barbarism." But the testimony is also formulated around a subtext in the form of a question, as articulated through Milena's understanding of Kafka, that might be stated something like this: "What ethical person can continue to live in the knowledge of the mass atrocities of the twentieth century?" Buber-Neumann quotes Milena as writing that Kafka was "clear-sighted, too wise to live." And the bodies of Kafka and Milena seem to be given as the answer to this question. But the book also structures the survivor as occupying an ethical position in relation to atrocity. Buber-Neumann claims an ethical position for herself by articulating her love for Milena and by engaging in the act of testimony that resists the absolute abjection and death of the concentration camps.

Buber-Neumann rarely mentions her own role in camp as part of a network of prisoners who sought to protect other women, often submerging her acts as backup to Milena's actions. She notes, for example, that "As I was physically stronger than Milena, it was only natural that I should try to take care of her. That sounds so simple, but with the strict camps regulations it involved considerable risk." She goes on to state that she steals bread from the kitchen both for Milena and for the other women in her barracks with the complicity of a woman who worked there. However, she immediately undercuts the courage of these actions by ending the paragraph with a story of Milena carrying a bowl of coffee with milk and sugar through the camp during working hours to bring to her as a gift. An act that would have, as she notes, resulted in extreme punishment if she had been caught. This impulse to undercut her own actions by emphasizing Milena's is not unusual, perhaps, in such testimonials, which emphasize the actions of others rather those of the authors.

The passage quoted above conveys a defensive tone, placing her desire to care for Milena in the realm of the "natural." Such caretaking, at risk to oneself, is completely "unnatural" in the world of the camps and can be read as both upholding and disrupting gender norms. Women themselves, within patriarchy, are positioned as caretakers, and thus it is "natural" for a woman to take care of somebody who needs it. However, in the terms of a same-sex relationship that occurs within heteropatriarchal structures, to take care of the "weaker" feminine partner is a masculinized and therefore "unnatural" role. The assumption that physical strength entails the responsibility of caring for those perceived to be weaker is itself a traditionally masculine position.

The movement of tense in the passage above—from the past tense of the first sentence above, to present tense in the following sentence ("that sounds so simple"), and back to past tense for the second clause of the sentence—marks Buber-Neumann's awareness that she is writing for an audience that can never understand the world of the concentration camp about which she is writing—including the relationships that occurred there. "That sounds so simple" conveys an anguish both about the impossibility of communicating the gravity of the situation to contemporary readers as well as her own anguish as a survivor remembering her possibilities for action, which could never be enough. And as a survivor outside the world of the Holocaust, she now inhabits the world of Delbo's surviving characters, for whom the experiences of the Holocaust no longer seem real, even to themselves. Thus her testimonial acknowledges and sutures over these chasms of identity through the performance of witnessing.

Ethical Choices, Performative Witnessing, and the Human

Delbo and Buber-Neumann figure resistance as emerging from the maintenance of interiority, of storytelling, and of support networks.

Germaine Tillion, in *Ravensbrück, An Eyewitness Account of a Women's Concentration Camp,* also claims the support of other women prisoners as vital to her survival: "The fact that I survived Ravensbrück I owe first—and most definitely—to chance, then to anger and the motivation to reveal the crimes I had witnessed, and finally to a union of friendship, since I had lost the instinctive and physical desire to live. This tenuous web of friendship was . . . almost submerged by the stark brutality of selfishness and the struggle for survival, but somehow everyone in the camp was invisibly woven into it."[78] Near the end of the war, Tillion recounts that Buber-Neumann, at great risk to herself, hid Tillion at the foot of her bed to save her from the certain death of a selection, yet throughout *Milena,* Buber-Neumann refuses to tell most stories, such as the one told by Tillion above, that relate individual acts of resistance and solidarity on her own part without Milena's participation.

Dori Laub's suggestion, that "[t]he survivors did not only need to survive so that they could tell their story; they also needed to tell their story in order to survive," is borne out by the contentions of Buber-Neumann and Tillion. From within the camps, Buber-Neumann and Milena plan a coauthored book about their experiences that becomes a central theme of their interactions, and Tillion begins documenting the camps, taking notes and even a role of film, while she is still a prisoner. Testimonial in these texts is a dynamic performative act that occurs 1) within the camps between women; 2) between the author and the testimonial text; and 3) between the testimonial text and the reader/spectator (such as with Delbo's play) to build witnessing communities from the fragmented experiences, voices, and memories of trauma and atrocity.

Sara Nomberg-Przytyk's *Auschwitz: True Tales from a Grotesque Land* is not structured by a single narrative but instead consists of a series of vignettes—"true tales"—some of which are the mythic stories of Auschwitz that have been told in different ways by a variety of survivors. This form that her text takes functions as an analysis of both how memory works and how the various communities within Auschwitz attempted, despite the enormous resources directed at destroying them, to form a space for an imaginary within which they saw themselves reflected as human beings with a past and a future. As James Young notes, "each telling adds new dimensions both to the events and to our understanding of them and their effect on the prisoners themselves. Each version establishes a different set of moral implications, a different frame of critical reference; each raises new questions and is witness to a different act: of resistance, of rage, of courage, of revenge, or of desperation."[79] Nomberg-Przytyk questions the role that memory plays in constructing the events perceived as history and suggests that it is not the minutiae of the event as it occurred that are important so much as the perception of that event by its individual witnesses and the role that the memory of the event plays within future communities.

The stories of acts of resistance that Nomberg-Przytyk recounts are stories that circulated immediately and for considerable periods of time among the inmates, providing them with a heroic alternative to the life of momentary existence demanded by Auschwitz and the strength to resist the Nazis in some way themselves. As Young comments, "As we see in legendary stories that deviate widely from other versions, whether or not events transpired precisely as the author relates them ultimately matters less than the paradigms by which they have been recovered, even reinvented."[80] The acts of resistance and heroism in tales circulated among the camp inmates serve the important purpose of opening up the possibility for resistance in locations where it was otherwise unimaginable.

The examples Nomberg-Przytyk gives of resistance are of people whose actions are easily given mythic proportions.[81] When recounting the story of the woman who shot two SS in the undressing room of the gas chamber, she describes her as a dancer who is beautiful, young, and brave; the two lovers hanged by the Nazis after escaping are described as romantic heroes: "Their love affair, their courageous flight, and now their torment had all the elements of the tragedy of Romeo and Juliet, set in Auschwitz. Like the Greek heroes in the face of unyielding fate, we were completely helpless to do anything about the death that surely awaited them."[82] Unlike the stark "truth" Delbo's women discuss, where executioners and victims are fixed in one role with no room for ambiguity, while the characters of Nomberg-Przytyk's tales are vividly delineated within their roles, the reasons for their actions are never clear-cut to the narrator. Instead the text itself works to form the framework within which Nomberg-Przytyk and her readers can evaluate people's actions.

In Nomberg-Przytyk's text, the Nazi ideology seems to operate upon a base where the normal laws of transgression have been transcended—they attempt to create their own symbolic order within which to ground the logic of their community. In normative culture, society intrudes upon the individual's control over her or his body in various ways but only within certain limits that still allow for a perception of individual autonomy. A certain level of murder is also accepted, both legally, such as in war, and illegally, such as the murder rate of everyday life outside the context of war. The Nazis, however, attempted radically to replace these moral codes with others of their own creation. Especially in her portrayal of SS who step beyond their roles to aid prisoners (once to save Nomberg-Przytyk's life), she complicates our easy acceptance of victims and perpetrators in fixed roles. Instead, by narrating moments when perpetrators choose to step outside their roles to help prisoners, Nomberg-Przytyk highlights the absolute responsibility of perpetrators for their actions at all times. She writes against the too easy acceptance of our own distance from perpetrators as stereotypes of unfathomable evil by relating events where they break this frame. Textually through such stories, together with her intrusion of questions into the text, she asks us to consider our own position not just as readers of the text but toward the dead whom the text embodies and perhaps also toward our own positions in the material world in which we live.

Over and over, Nomberg-Przytyk uses her vignettes to address the fundamental crisis of understanding and judging the actions of herself and others in the camps. As the narrator says (of Orli, a kapo), "I would like to describe her behavior toward various prisoners, and in so doing, arrive at some kind of judgment of her." Because the narrator as a survivor is no longer sure of her own moral value systems, she feels she has no criteria with which to judge Orli, unless perhaps by a consensus of her actions. When she tells the story of how Orli and other women working in the infirmary restrained Magda, a young woman, from leaving to warn a newly arrived transport that they were headed to the gas chambers—an attempt to break the silence and make a space for resistance—she asks: "After all, was it fair to take all hope from those people for the short time that divided them from death? One was speaking of an honorable death. But was death so dishonorable in this situation in which a fight was impossible? That is how we thought at the time. What is the case, really? It is hard to find the right answer."[83] Her testimonial consists of the act of witnessing combined with storytelling as an attempt to produce not a consistent or coherent narrative but an exploration of the world in which "the imagination of the Other was no longer possible."

This is the dilemma faced by Françoise and Denise at the end of *Who Will Carry the Word?* The performative potential for witnessing that is enacted through the staging of the play takes place for Nomberg-Przytyk through the storytelling dialogue of the vignettes. She is in continual dialogue with herself in the stories; like Buber-Neumann she is conscious of her position as a survivor, recounting incidents from memory, from a position where the events she recounts often seem, as Françoise and Denise say, unreal even to herself. From the tension between what is remembered as real and the imperative to "tell the truth" and between normative language and the unrepresentable nature of camp existence emerges an interplay between the survivor's memory, the narrator's continual questioning of events and their contexts, the storyteller and the reader within which the act of testimony occurs.

Nomberg-Przytyk develops a definition of humanity in her testimonial—based on decisions to act in ways that recognize the basic humanity of another person—which resists a historical memory of the camps that would further the Nazi project past the war by claiming them as site of absolute inhumanity and abjection (thus placing too much emphasis on the perpetrators). Delbo, Buber-Neumann, and Nomberg-Przytyk do not dehumanize the Nazis by "casting them out" of the ethical category of the human. Instead they argue that the Nazis deliberately dehumanized themselves through the continual decisions they made to act against humanity. Thus there is no single action that permanently banishes one from the category of the "human"; it is always contingent—unlike totalitarian categories of belonging.

Driving a wedge into the monotonous drone of daily survival and routine death that comprised camp life, stories of resistance—like the love between Milena and Buber-Neumann, the documentary work of Tillion, and the stories told by the women in Delbo's play—are portrayed as vital moments in rebuilding an imaginary where the Other was still possible. Lesbianism and "passionate friendships" are figured as a site of resistance and survival—maintaining "difference," pleasure, and interiority within the camps (as opposed to the forms of sexual violence endemic to the atrocity, exemplified within the camps, perhaps, by the infamous brothel in Auschwitz—a site of rape and violence against women by inmate men). These testimonials invite us to engage with them in such witnessing—not through the overidentification of guilt and voyeuristic pleasures of horror but through a conscious performative stance of witnessing to the witness of the dead and of survival.

4

State Terror and the Ethical Witness

Testimonio and the Testimony of Atrocity

The term "testimony," as I am employing it in this book, is a very particular genre of testimonial writing—the writing of atrocity—that sometimes falls within but is not synonymous with the genre of Latin-American *testimonio* as critics such as George Yúdice, John Beverley, and Doris Sommer have defined it.[1] As I noted in the first chapter, I would like to make a distinction between *testimonio*, as a distinct generic form of expression that has been well elaborated by critics in the context of Latin-American studies, and the term "testimony" as a term that applies within literary, critical, and cultural studies to the witnessing of the specific experience of atrocity (massive, deliberate infliction of violence against people's selves and bodies by state actors in the context of this book) by its survivors.

Latin-Americanist critics have defined *testimonio* as a genre that includes, for example, "an effort to recognize and valorize the aesthetics of life practices themselves"[2] along with the narration of the personal and collective story of atrocity and violence to which the speaker/author witnesses. As Yúdice nicely summarizes it:

> testimonial writing may be defined as an authentic narrative, told by a witness who is moved to narrate by the urgency of a situation (e.g., war, oppression, revolution, etc.). Emphasizing popular, oral discourse, the witness portrays his or her own experience as an agent (rather than a representative) of a collective memory and identity. Truth is summoned in the cause of denouncing a present

situation of exploitation and oppression or in exorcising and setting aright official history.[3]

In contrast, testimonial as I am defining it shares many of the characteristics outlined by critics as paradigmatic of *testimonio* but also tends toward a very different portrayal of authenticity and of the experience of mass atrocity itself. Both genres engage in similar representational practices that make them distinct from other forms of literary representation, but they have a different set of foci for their primary concerns.

In addition, while Latin-Americanist critics such as John Beverley and Doris Sommer have discussed the importance of *testimonio*'s extraliterary elements to our understanding of the literary in Latin America and to disciplinary definitions, *testimonio* is a cultural production that merges the aesthetic with the production of "authenticity" in order to create a literary production that, largely through its extraliterary elements, seeks to move readers to intervene in the ongoing situation of disenfranchisement that the text portrays. As a hybrid literary production that makes use of disciplines such as anthropology and claims a strong political position from the voice of a member of the disenfranchised community whose story is being told, *testimonio* has helped to reconfigure our understanding of Latin American literary and Latin Americanist critical production.

As Alberto Moreiras notes, "testimonio always already incorporates an abandonment of the literary. Testimonio provides its reader . . . [a] region where the literary breaks off into something else, which is not so much the real as it is its unguarded possibility . . . which is arguably the very core of the testimonial experience [and] is also its preeminent political claim."[4] *Testimonio* "works" through the promise of this "unguarded possibility" of the real for the reader—that we must recognize ourselves as witnesses and then choose our relation to the "secret" that Sommer elaborates. Using *Me Llamo Rigoberta Menchú* as a paradigmatic text, Sommer rigorously details the ways the text's continual re-marking of secrets that will not be told marks a site of absolute difference for the reader that requires a conscious choice either to respect this difference (secret) through an act of responsible (ethical) reading or to deny it, calling into crisis the reader's own self-identity as a proper reader. Moreiras reads this critical move of Menchú's, the secret, as "the key to the real as unguarded possibility" that marks a border that "must be understood as a limit to the expansion of knowledge as a war machine: a limit to be overcome by further expansion, or else a limit to be defended and protected from conquest."[5]

As the responsible readers Sommer outlines, we are asked to partici- pate in this defense. Through the continual assertion of difference— cultural, class, identitarian, and so on—*testimonio* seeks to construct readers who respect difference and unknowability and who engage in an act of political solidarity with the speaker(s) of the text. But this hybridizing of literary text (which forces a reading practice of respect for an absolute of cultural difference, claiming an always already fic- tional authenticity of cultural difference to mobilize a politics of solidar- ity) is based as much on liberal discourses of anthropology and the exoticizing of the other—and the mobilizing of guilt and fascina- tion—as it is around an ethics of relations with the other. And as such, in its production as well as our reading and codification of it, *testimonio* depends on aesthetic apparatuses to mobilize such identifications even as it rejects them.

Testimonio is usually claimed as a mediated text, a spoken testimony told by the witnessing individual to the transcriber who takes down the story and translates it into a written narrative.[6] I use the term "witness- ing individual" rather than the also common "testimonial subject" to note the distinction that while the person testifying makes the claim of speaking for all members of her/his community, who would tell sub- stantively the same story, she or he is still speaking as a privileged wit- ness (to the extent that she or he has the opportunity to witness) and is telling a personal as well as collective story of experience.

And while *testimonio* is always a textual genre with literary claims and attributes, which is transcribed from oral interviews upon which its claim to authority rests (while complicating the notion of authority in its dual speaker/authorship), testimony of atrocity, as I am outlining it for this book, sometimes includes no literary dimension at all and at other times makes a much stronger claim to the literary than does *testi- monio*. Testimony of atrocity can range from individual oral witnessing that is not transcribed, to therapeutic sessions, to recorded and/or tran- scribed interviews, to authored texts, some of which are quite literary, as is the case with Alicia Partnoy's *The Little School* and the works of Charlotte Delbo, Marguerite Buber-Neumann, and Sara Nomberg- Przytyk that are considered in the previous chapter (none of which are considered *testimonio*).

While *testimonio* witnesses to a broad range of injustices facing a self- identified community of class, ethnicity, and so on from and within the larger state structures, atrocity testimonial witnesses to the specific experience of overwhelming violence, such as torture, death camps, mass death, and so on, survived by the speaker/writer without a wider emphasis on the life experiences of the witness beyond the boundaries of the atrocity experience itself. Although details of the survivor's life before or after the atrocity may be included within the testimonial, they are included as part of the story of the experience of atrocity rather than to provide a wider scope for the testimony. The emphasis in such testimony on the extreme disenfranchisement—from body, self, and language—wrought by atrocity tends to focus the testimonial very specifically on particular topics, such as the materiality of the body, the importance of community to survival, the struggle with memory and resistance, and the perception of chiasmatic disjunctures in structures of language, knowledge, and experience that had previously been taken as continuous. As such, the testimonial of atrocity can have a much narrower (although very deep) critique of structures of power and disenfranchisement than the *testimonio*.

Rigoberta Menchú's testimonial, for example, which has been appropriated by many critics as a paradigmatic *testimonio*, tells the story of her life as a political organizer and her peasant community's struggle against state (outsider) oppression and violence while emphasizing "the aesthetics of life practices themselves."[7] The representations of atrocity in her testimonial are graphic and personal and are used to illustrate the massive repression, violence, and disenfranchisement faced by her community. They are mobilized toward a particular, textual, political goal, that of raising the consciousness of her readers and encouraging them to take responsibility for intervening into the political situation that enables such violence.

While this is very similar, in some ways, to the testimonial recounting of atrocity, testimonials of atrocity do not employ representations of violence in such a utilitarian fashion and are much more suspicious of its complexities and textual representations. The community from which the survivor of testimonial is speaking and for whom she or he speaks is the community of people with whom she or he experienced the atrocity rather than an ongoing life community of ethnic, class, national, or geographic origin. While sometimes, such as in Alicia Partnoy's case, these are also people who share the same political concerns and were arrested for the same reasons, this is certainly not always the case and is not the primary reason for the solidarity of community portrayed in the testimonial. Community and solidarity are formulated by Partnoy and others as fundamental to the resistance of the self against the massive attacks of violence and involve everybody who is a victim of these attacks.

The political struggle for the speaker or writer of the testimonial of atrocity is against the fundamental structures of culture and politics out of which the violence of the atrocity has emerged and which has been violently enacted against his or her own body in the most horrific and alienating ways. Through the profound alienation of the voice and self from the body that torture enacts, the survivor's witnessing is a much more deeply embodied struggle than that of political struggle against repression in the public sphere as it is traditionally framed through, for example, armed struggle, peaceful resistance, and the organizing of blocs of communities of common interest against external oppression.

I am not seeking to valorize one form of testimonial writing over another and I would include the Latin-American testimonial of atrocity under state terror as a possible subgenre of *testimonio* as Yúdice and others outline it. Just as Rigoberta Menchú in her *testimonio* has little interest in critiquing underlying norms of gender and patriarchy that lead to oppression and violence against as well as within her community, writers of atrocity testimonials may have little interest in examining whatever structures of privilege they may benefit from that are implicated in various forms of violence and atrocity. Both forms are profoundly personal and political interventions into representational forms and material structures of power and utilize performance as the dynamic through which witnessing takes place. But the narrow focus on the individual body as the site of struggle, violence, and resistance that is inherent to the testimonial of atrocity entails a different set of concerns and difficulties from the broader scope of *testimonio,* where the testimonial witness continues to occupy a position within the community despite the atrocities visited upon that community by the state. Although their entire community might be violently under siege, he or she can still speak from a position of identity within and as a member of this community with shared history, memories, and cultural norms.

In a crucial difference, the witness of testimony has been excised from his or her community, and his or her identity itself is violently attacked as part of the ongoing experience of atrocity. In the case of state terror such as Alicia Partnoy experienced, the witnesses have literally disappeared. Their bodies have become the tools for the reordering of the symbolic that the violent regime is attempting, and as such, as survivors, their witnessing must address a complex set of movements between the individual and the various communities with which they are affiliated and sometimes have come to be affiliated through extreme coercive violence.

Diana Taylor, speaking of the way the bodies of the disappeared are necessary to the reordering of the symbolic, writes that "the gendered violence taking place in the discourse of the symbolic *Patria* was being played out on the 'real' bodies of the victims in order to shape a new symbolic entity: the national being."[8] The identitarian politics that Moreiras locates as replacing the politics of class in Latin America as the strongest site of resistance to globalization, exemplified through the *testimonio,* is something about which witness survivors of atrocity tend to express a strong suspicion. Having been excised from the cultural, juridical, and symbolic fields through state violence, such survivors voice continual suspicion of the body as a ground for "authenticity," which is the claim of identity politics, and speak from a fractured position of instability where the body is no longer a site of knowledge, despite their excessive awareness of its materiality.

Rigoberta Menchú, for example, positions herself as a testimonial subject who, by virtue of her difference as an indigenous peasant, has forms of knowledge—secrets—that she will not share, thus marking herself as an "authentic" subject of the community for and from which she speaks. Her transcriber, Elizabeth Burgos-Debray, facilitates and expands this move, positioning Menchú in her introduction to the testimonial as a fetishized organic peasant woman with access to more "authentic" forms of knowledge by virtue of her closeness to a "natural" cycle of land, history, and culture. Conversely, in her introduction to *The Little School,* Partnoy warns us, "Beware: in little schools the boundaries between story and history are so subtle that even I can hardly find them."[9] Partnoy questions the authenticity of "history" as well as warning readers to beware of all claims to authority, including her own. The bricolage of stories and voices she writes into her text provides a multitude of fragments of perspective and experience rather than a single voice or historical record to be refuted or denied.

When Yúdice notes that "the speaker [of *testimonio*] does not speak for or represent a community but rather performs an act of identity formation that is both personal and collective,"[10] he describes a process very similar yet not identical to the act of performative witness that I am outlining in this book and that is described by Dori Laub and others as inherent to the process of testimonial itself. But writing against atrocity from the position of the personal survival of atrocity blends the intensely personal and psychic with a very public telling and remembering that are undertaken in a way that is profoundly unsettling for the material experience of their body for the survivor. Trauma, guilt, shame, feelings of complicity, and profound crises of language merge the political project of speaking the unspeakable and witnessing for the dead with the necessity of acknowledging and addressing the deep ways that atrocity and mass violence disenfranchise and damage victims and survivors.

The obscene conflation of the private with the public upon which torture and other forms of atrocity depend, including the destruction of the safety of the everyday objects of life that many survivors as well as Scarry in *The Body in Pain* outline, is a nightmare inversion of the process of writing and testifying itself. While writing and testifying can be life-affirming acts and are often valorized as such, to engage in them as a survivor is to face the profound dangers of reactivation of trauma, alienation from language and communities, and the shame or guilt associated with having been victimized through atrocity, which calls into question the ability to write and speak at all after the experience of mass violence.

The authors of testimonies of atrocity do not seek reconsolidation of voice, identity, or community as the result of their witnessing. They state openly in the text their skepticism about the possibility of such reconsolidation. Instead they embrace fragmentation, confusion, gaps, complicity, and powerlessness simultaneously with their performance of resistance, memory, voice, and identity as survivors. The trauma of atrocity is enacted through such witnessing, which textually performs the gaps marking speech and memory and the haunting of consciousness by unincorporated trauma.[11]

Testimonial Intervention: Language and Witnessing

Diana Taylor, writing on Partnoy's use of both documentary and literary forms in her testimony, notes that "Throughout the 'tales,' there is a tension between the testimonial intent to record the disappearance and death of a group of individuals and the literary effort to make those individuals come alive once again—this time for the reader" and goes on to state that "Unlike Menchú, however, she had no mediator, no one to chronicle her tales and make them available to a reading public."[12]

Taylor claims that Partnoy makes a dual move in utilizing two different forms of writing—documentary testimonial reports (testifying before human rights commissions, the "factual" appendices and introduction of *The Little School*, etc.) and literary autobiography, where she "encapsulates and backgrounds the violence. Recomposing the disap-peared, rather than documenting their destruction, is what matters." But although Partnoy is Argentinean, it would be wrong to try to read her testimony only through the rubric of Latin-American *testimonio* and the critical and disciplinary discussions that have surrounded its possible emergence as a genre. Partnoy's work is testimony to atrocity, and the fragmentation of her work in *The Little School* is a textual em-bodiment of the process of testimonial that goes far beyond the need for the "recomposition" of her voice as a survivor.

Within the context of Latin-Americanist discussions of *testimonio*, to note the duality of textual forms makes great sense. But I would like to remove Partnoy's work from the expectations of this disciplinary, politi-cal, and identitarian rubric. As testimony produced as the result of the experience of state terror in Argentina, it occupies a position alongside *testimonio*, but in its focus on the embodied experience of overwhelm-ing atrocity, on the remembering of the dead, and on the struggle to use language to speak the unspeakable, finding its articulation of resis-tance and identity within the fissure of this paradox, it is very different from either *testimonio* or autobiography. If we no longer have the ex-pectation that it fit either the autobiographical or the *testimonio* model, of which Taylor follows Doris Sommer's articulation, we can consider it as a testimony alongside other testimonies witnessing to the specific experience of mass death and atrocity.

Although Diana Taylor, writing of *The Little School,* calls it "an odd mix of autobiographical and testimonial literature," not applying the term "testimony" to the book as a generic distinction, she also notes that "Partnoy's stories differ from *testimonios* in that, though they struggle *against* those who directed or participated in the atrocity, they are also a *struggle to* deal with the long-lasting effects of violence. Thus perhaps they have more in common with the testimonies given by Ho-locaust victims."[13] Taylor notes this similarity to Holocaust survivor tes-timony because of the ways both forms of testimony grapple with the effects of massive violence on the voice of the witness. But this struggle to deal with the effects of violence goes beyond the personal struggle to reclaim a voice that Taylor marks in her reading and is ultimately located in the immense difficulties for the survivor associated with the articulation of overwhelming pain and disenfranchisement after the to-talizing experience of embodiment associated with the infliction of atrocity through torture.

The body of the text/testimony must speak through a body that has been abjected, made voiceless and other, and situated as the ultimate,

final ground of experience where articulation fails. Such a violent imposition of power on the body of the victims and survivors is replicated in
the spectatorial move made by many in the face of the testimonial demand for witness; by us, the audience for the testimony, in our location
of the bodies of survivors as the ultimate ground of unknowable, extreme experience—as the abject we both reject and fetishize. As one
survivor, interviewed by Marguerite Feitlowitz, states, "In every case
. . . you are the living symbol of everything society rejects. Dead or alive
you can't win. . . . No one could *determine* to live. They stripped us of
that power. We who did survive are the emissaries of the horror. The
horror. That too society rejects. So the isolation of the messenger never
really ends."[14] To write testimony into this spectatorial field and from
such a position might itself be a traumatizing act and one where the
ethical demand issues from the fissures of the testimony itself rather
than from the site of *testimonio*'s demand of solidarity with the "secret."[15]

Taylor attributes the "duality" of form in *The Little School* and in
Partnoy's other testifying in part to a concern over audience, to Partnoy's fear that she should write about what people "can relate to."
Taylor goes on within the context of *testimonio* criticism to locate this
as a concern over publication demands for more autobiographical chapters and to quote Partnoy's concerns that the book retain its testimonial
qualities as a horizontally shifting "we" of communal experience rather
than the vertical "I" of elite literary texts, to use Yúdice's terms. Partnoy's anxieties about the elevation of an autobiographical "I" over the
communal "we" of *testimonio* are not hard to understand in the context of Latin-American literary and critical studies and production. But
we do her a disservice to bind her production within these terms. What
she has produced is a testimony of atrocity, and her direct experience
of atrocity and attempt to write about it are responsible for her testimony's differences from *testimonio*.

As Taylor notes, "readers in *testimonios* are asked not to identify but
to act as witness to event," which hopefully leads to a form of active
intervention by some readers into the injustices articulated in the text
and which is also Partnoy's goal. But the similarities between the two
forms of testimony, if one wants to preserve the category of *testimonio*
as it has been articulated, should not be a cause for attempting to wedge
testimony of atrocity into a generic category. The very nature of trauma
itself makes testimony slippery, and to position it as the limit point of
representation is to demand that it occupy textually the position within

literary and cultural studies that the scar of atrocity left on the body occupies in our globalized cultural imaginary.

Taylor quotes Partnoy as not only concerned about writing what people "can relate to" but as going on to state that "I don't know how to write about torture."[16] Yet Partnoy's concerns about writing about torture—and about not knowing how to—convey a much larger set of concerns about representation, voice, and materiality than Taylor takes up. The very fragmentation of Partnoy's text, the multitude of gaps between styles of text and form of testimonial, that babble of voices and absences, textually embody this crisis of not knowing how to write about torture. And this very "not knowing" is itself an acknowledgment of the atrocity, of the radical disenfranchisement from language that torture performs.[17] Partnoy's fragmented text embodies the radical break with language, knowing, and certainty that torture enacts. Resistance and the reclamation of voice and identity, both for herself and for those she was imprisoned with, are an important function of Partnoy's text. But this is not the only function. Equally important to the constitution of the witness through the text, both for herself and her demand of her readers, is the fragmentation of forms and the gaps and silences of the text itself.

Marguerite Feitlowitz, detailing the changes to daily language that have entered the Argentinean lexicon since the Dirty War, writes:

It seems to me that such changes, such ravages of the language are manifestations that what happened in the camps did not just happen to those imprisoned there. . . . The repression lives on in such aberrations of the language, in the scars it left on the language. When a people's very words have been wounded, the society cannot fully recover until the language has been healed. Words mark the paths of our experience, separate what we can name from ineffable terror and chaos. . . . When, like skin, the language is bruised, punctured, or mutilated, that boundary breaks down.[18]

Partnoy's text enacts this profound damage and alteration that has occurred in the language. Just as words took on different meanings in the camps and torture chambers of the Holocaust and no longer hold meaning outside the context of the camps, so Feitlowitz documents the same process occurring in Argentina during and after the Dirty War. As such, Partnoy experiences a crisis of language similar to that faced by Delbo, Buber-Neumann, Nomberg-Przytyk, and the other survivors who testify in language to the Holocaust.

But the systematic destruction through torture that was endemic to the state terror of Argentina is different in its attack from the systematic destruction wrought through the concentration camps and death camps of World War II. Although the Nazis widely employed torture and the Argentinean dictatorship held the disappeared in concentration and death camps, the differences between these formations of atrocity and mass death affect the experience and writing of survival. While the Holocaust survivors, along with many survivors of atrocity, express their inability as survivors to reintegrate back into society in a normative way, feeling they occupy a "marked" position as "ghosts" who carry with them the stench of mass death into a world that works to seal the atrocity into a historical past, they also reentered a world that has slowly come to acknowledge the enormity of the genocide. For the victims and survivors of the Dirty War, which was carried out with the knowledge and disavowal of the majority of Argentineans, they must "reenter" a culture that has largely denied their existence as victims, whose citizens largely refuse to acknowledge their own complicity in the terror, and who themselves were terrorized into paralysis through the mechanisms of the dictatorship.

State terror in Germany itself ensured that the vast majority of the population stayed docile and complicit, but the totalitarian violence of the Third Reich enacted a genocide that touched many different national, ethnic, religious, sexual, and class identities in many countries. The state terror of the Argentinean dictatorship was much more contained (it stayed largely although not completely within Argentina) and pervasive, consciously employing and elaborating on Nazi techniques of terror as well as those of other more recent mass atrocities. Thus the systematic use of torture against prisoners, enacting the radical break with language, the total betrayal of the self by the body, and the destruction of culture that Scarry outlines, created a specific set of difficulties with which survivors must grapple if they are to testify to their experiences and witness for the victims.

All testimony marks the crisis for the survivor of her or his body as the overdetermined materiality of truth—the "authentic" document that witnesses the truth of her or his story is the body itself. The numbers tattooed into the arms of Auschwitz survivors, the scars left by whippings and brandings on the bodies of American slaves, and the scars from torture on the bodies of survivors of state terror and others have all become fetishized in various ways as markers of a "truth" of experience. But for the people who inhabit these bodies, truth is a

much more complex negotiation than the seemingly transparent validation of "seeing it with one's own eyes" would suggest. The scar on the
body both makes visible the "authentic" claim to experience of the
survivor and obscures further seeing of the difficulties of such experience. The expectation that survivors' bodies are marked in some way
by the experience of atrocity is a burden not just of the overly visible
but of the expectation of the visible. Many survivors' bodies are not
visibly marked by the experience of atrocity, but the lack of physical
traces does not imply a lesser experience of atrocity. And as the medical
and legal professions become more adept at reading the signs of torture
in the quest to prosecute perpetrators, the perpetrators become more
adept at inflicting pain without leaving visible traces.

The burden of the visible goes beyond the simple expectation of the
readable scar. By witnessing to their disappearance from the juridical,
cultural, and social fields, survivors must witness to their own profound
lack of voice and knowledge in the face of what appears to be transpar-
ently visible experience. Partnoy's claim that she does not know how to
write about torture is a witnessing to the crisis of representation that
underlies the testimonial act. The testimony becomes the scar and trace
of the experience, marking the survivors while simultaneously serving
as a vehicle for their reentry into the arenas from which they have been
excised by extreme violence. Much torture rehabilitation therapy literally uses the testimony as the trace of the experience, transcribing it and
then giving a copy to the survivor to do with as she or he pleases, one
use of which may be to allow people to read it as a surrogate for having
to tell the story of the atrocity when asked.[19]

Our expectation of "knowledge" in the readability of the scar recalls
the crisis faced by Delbo's characters at the end of *Who Will Carry the
Word?* Audience members do not want (or "need") to hear the stories
of survivors because they already "know" the story. The iconic representation of atrocity, beginning with the Holocaust imagery of emaciated bodies behind barbed wire and dumped into piles that Barbie
Zelizer has carefully parsed out, serves a spectatorial as much as or more
than a witnessing function.[20] This "already knowing" when faced by
the visibility of the scar relieves us of the burden of bearing witness to
the witness of the survivor. It marks the survivor as supplement, as both
excessive to and foundation of the symbolic, and disappears her or him
once again through the spectatorial act of distanced identification.

To write about the torture or the camps risks replicating this "transparency" of knowledge for the reader/spectator as well as entering vio-

lent representation into a specular field burdened by voyeurism and erotic identification. The language of the camps, to which the survivor no longer has access, will never be available to us, the witnesses of and spectators to, the survivor's testimony, and the testimony itself must witness to this fact. In this context the blindfold Partnoy is forced to wear during her time in the camp occupies an important metaphorical function, standing in for the "blindness of seeing" that in all ways marks her experience as a survivor.

State Terror and the Writing of Pain

In the conclusion of chapter three, I suggest that there is a value to be gained in reading the works of Holocaust survivors alongside those of survivors of more recent instances of state-sponsored human rights abuse. While I do not want to imply by reading these texts alongside each other that there is a leveling or sameness of experience that occurs in women's writings about trauma despite the historical conditions of their experience, I do believe there are similarities between certain texts that create the grounds for a fruitful analysis of their parallel formulations of voice and fragmentation. Accordingly, this chapter considers writings that speak to the experience of political imprisonment and public silence during the years of state terror and military dictatorship in Argentina from 1971 to 1983.

Both Alicia Partnoy's *The Little School* and Griselda Gambaro's *Information for Foreigners* oppose the monolithic discourse of the state with a fragmented collage of texts and voices.[21] In this way, like Delbo, Nomberg-Przytyk, and Buber-Neumann, they betray a suspicion of the juridical language of state culture from which they have been disappeared and fight for a voice that will encompass the fragmentation of their experience rather than simply trying to replicate the voice of coherent, seamless identity required for full visibility within humanist, juridical systems.

Alicia Partnoy wrote *The Little School* in 1984 in the United States after her release from the concentration camp and prison and subsequent exile in December 1979. She was arrested in her home on January 12, 1977, by uniformed army personnel, detained without trial, and sent to the concentration camp, the Little School, for five months. During this time she was "disappeared," meaning that nobody was informed of her whereabouts or condition, there was no record of her arrest or imprisonment, and no official or unofficial body claimed responsibility or knowledge of her whereabouts. During her time at the Little School she, like the other prisoners, was blindfolded at all times, forbidden to speak, and forced to spend her time lying prone on a bunk bed. She was also subject to continual physical and mental abuse, threats, and periodic torture. After five and a half months, for reasons she does not know, her family was informed of her whereabouts, and she "reappeared" and was transferred to a prison for the next two and a half years until she was forced into exile.

Discussing her activities following her exile, she states that "I soon learned more about the widespread use of disappearance as a tool for repression in Latin America. As a survivor, I felt my duty was to help those suffering injustice."[22] Writing this in the introduction to her testimonial, she makes explicit her position regarding her status as a survivor. She is not writing as the autobiographical individual narrating a private life but as a member of a collective of voices that have shared and are sharing an experience of oppression for which she can provide a testimonial voice. In this way, she hopes to create some ground for further intervention into such sufferings.

Griselda Gambaro, a prominent Argentinean playwright, wrote the play *Information for Foreigners* from 1971 to 1973. Although the play was never performed in Argentina, when she was forced into exile in 1977 she smuggled it out of the country with her but continued to withhold its circulation and publication for fear that it could endanger members of her family who were still in the country.[23] Her play explores the role of terror in facilitating the acquiescence of citizens (and spectators) to state violence as Argentina moved during the 1970s increasingly and with the tacit support of the U.S. government in the direction of massive totalitarian violence. In December 1970, for example, Nestor Martins, an attorney, and his client, Nildo Zenteno, were kidnapped from the street by a band of armed men escorted by a car that had pulled out of a Federal Police parking lot. This event is revisited by Gambaro in scene four, where it is footnoted in the play as marking one of the first "disappearances." Between 1973 and 1976 there were four presidents of Argentina, during which time the violence of urban guerrilla organizations and police and military repression continued to escalate. In March 1976, the military seized the government, marking the beginning of the state-run Dirty War (1976–1983), during which time up to thirty thousand people were disappeared, tortured, and murdered.[24]

There are also some interesting differences between these texts and the Holocaust texts I explored in the previous chapter, many of which revolve around issues of form and collective experience. The Holocaust texts are more similar to each other in form, focusing intently on their dual function as memorial and testimonial. While Partnoy's and Gambaro's texts also embody these concerns, memorializing especially is not necessarily the primary element in either work, nor is it presented as the driving force behind their creation. This is due to several factors: the more radically individual and isolating nature of the experience of disappearance and political imprisonment; the seemingly ongoing and less totalizing nature of the historical event; the awareness by the authors of a community of readers and spectators aware of and concerned about human rights abuses that could not have existed during or immediately following the Holocaust; and the radical break with language that occurs during torture.

As Scarry argues, torture is a deeply isolating and radically individuating experience.[25] She explores the way in which the language and history of the torture to which a body is subjected come to be inscribed upon the body itself and the way in which the process of torture involves a necessary deconstruction of civilization by the torturer. During this process the most basic markers of civilization, which Scarry identifies with the domestic realm, are turned against the individual; for example, a kitchen table, a bathtub, and so on are used as instruments of torture. In this way, "culture" and its objects come, for the person being tortured, to be weapons of pain in the hands of the torturers. Conversely, the "private" realm of one's thoughts and bodily functions is made public through torture, as the torturers gain control of all aspects of the body's functions including one's voice. This process contributes to the extreme humiliation that accompanies the physical pain of torture. As Scarry states, "This dissolution of the boundary between inside and outside gives rise to . . . an almost obscene conflation of private and public. It brings with it all the solitude of absolute privacy with none of its safety, all the self-exposure of the utterly public with none of its possibilities for camaraderie or shared experience."[26]

In a move that mirrored this dynamic, the discourse of the state during the dictatorship also removed the boundaries between the private and the public through its rhetoric of "bad" children who had to be controlled by the intercession of the state into the "privacy" of the family unit.[27] Thus, while the state, through terror, conflates the public with the private on the collective cultural level, torture works this terror and conflation on the level of individual bodies. While the terror of the state uses the weapons of the domestic—children, spouses, neighbors—to attack and control the body of the citizenry through humilia-tion and fear, the torturer uses weapons that also serve as signifiers of domestic life to dominate and destroy the person being tortured. The authors I discuss in this chapter and the previous one all repro-duce traditional paradigms such as the sanctity of motherhood, the strength of women's communities, and the importance of family as im-portant modes of resistance and survival, yet they remain suspicious of such reifying discourses, which carry with them structures of power and hierarchy. In her work on resistance and the family structure during the dictatorship, Judy Filc questions the ultimate efficacy of discourses of privacy and the family that resistance organizations such as the Mothers of the Plaza de Mayo relied on, noting that their ideal family and that of state rhetoric were largely the same.[28] In a similar fashion, this book questions the efficacy of discourses of individuality and privacy, as they are formulated in the Universal Declaration, truly to protect bodies from human rights abuses.

Partnoy's text provides an example of resistance to such discourses through the text itself, with its pastiche of narrative voices and genres that destabilizes the single "private" voice of the author into just one fragment in a stream of fragments that combine to form the text of *The Little School*. Throughout her book, for example, Partnoy writes against the experience of torture and dehumanization by narrating the private world she maintained for herself in the camp. Rather than focusing on her experiences of torture and trying to represent them in some way, her narrative focuses on her experiences of sharing and camaraderie with the other prisoners, her thoughts of her daughter and husband, and the long stretches of solitude she endured by remembering her past and inventing games for herself.

The radically isolating experience of torture that Scarry describes is very different from the experience of the concentration camps during the Holocaust, where the prisoners were forced to live in conditions of intense overcrowding and competition among themselves. In the Holocaust, the break with language that occurs for the survivors results from the radical representational chasm between the world of the camps, the "concentrationary universe," and the world outside the camps, that of normative culture and narrative history. The break with language is the result of the incommensurability of parallel worlds rather than the "private" internal destruction that Scarry argues is the result of extreme pain. Thus Holocaust authors must address different obstacles to their writing from those of the authors who write about the experience of torture and disappearance. While Charlotte Delbo's characters must find a way to use language to tell the story of a world where "words had a different meaning," Jacobo Timerman states that "it's impossible to convey what I know now. In the long months of confinement, I often thought of how to transmit the pain that a tortured person undergoes. And always I concluded that it was impossible. It is a pain without points of reference, revelatory symbols, or clues to serve as indicators."[29] For Timerman, although he can and does testify to his experience of imprisonment and abuse, there are no words to convey any meaning in his experience of the pain of torture. It is beyond and before language and any system of symbols that convey meaning.

While in the Nazi concentration camps of World War II words were created or took on new meanings to describe the universe of the camps and therefore lost their meaning outside this universe, the pain that Timerman cannot convey is the pain that Scarry argues happens prior to and after the destruction of language. Through this process of extreme pain, she argues, the consciousness of the person being tortured shrinks to include only an awareness of the pain of the body itself, and the person's links to the world outside his or her body become completely severed. Ultimately, the individual's relationship to language is completely destroyed, as pain—which is inexpressible—becomes the totality of the perceived world, and the body is reinscribed into a system where it occupies the position of the tortured body recognizable through the signs of torture that have been inscribed upon it and defined only by the representational system of the torturers.

Scarry argues that pain defeats language in one of two ways. Either it is so powerful and overwhelming that it destroys language altogether and thus is inexpressible, or, when it is given voice in language, it becomes so overwhelming that its voice silences all other discourse. Pain's power and its destructiveness thus lie in its alterity to discourse, either destroying or silencing it. Her analysis of the radical break from language effected by extreme pain stands unchallenged in texts such as *The Little School* and *Prisoner without a Name, Cell without a Number* through their resounding silence toward its representation. Unlike the Holocaust literature in chapter three, in which documenting the daily reality of the camps and the degradation of prisoners' bodies and minds is an obsessive preoccupation of the authors, these texts refuse the attempt to represent the experience of torture. The break with language that occurs for the author/experiencer happens during the intense physical attack that is torture and cannot be recovered, even immediately following the torture while she is still imprisoned. For Delbo, Nomberg-Przytyk, and Buber-Neumann, this break/disruption of language is something they truly become aware of only upon leaving the concentrationary environment, when they suddenly find themselves once again in the world of normative communication outside the camps.[30]

The differences between Holocaust texts and the texts of this chapter can also be accounted for, I believe, in the different formulations of the way that the event is not "over" for the survivors of torture and state terror as it is for survivors of the Holocaust. Although the psychic trauma of the Holocaust is not in any way—and may never be—over for its survivors, the event itself, with the ending of World War II and the death camps, is decidedly over. The more diffuse and omnipresent state terror that Partnoy, Timerman, and Gambaro experienced in Argentina, however, is not over in the same way. As survivors of torture, political oppression, and the totalitarian state formation of the military dictatorship, they have no guarantee that the terrorism of state-sponsored paramilitary organizations and antidemocratic government oppression will not recur. The formative relationship of these state structures to transnational capital, patriarchy, and the internal imbalance of power has not changed significantly between the time of the last military dictatorship and the present.

Torture survivors, therefore, have every reason to expect that state terror could recur again at any time. As Wyschogrod argues, the omnipresent threat of mass death with which we all live has altered everybody's relationship to death and survival. For the survivor of state terror as well as the survivor of the Holocaust, this might create an amplification of the trauma with which the survivor struggles.

Aside from historical differences between the instability of Latin-American states such as Argentina and the reconstitution of the European nations as monolithically "stable" following the end of World War II and the beginning of the Cold War, the state terror and violent repression that happened in Argentina in the 1970s is an ongoing problem in Latin-American countries in general. As Partnoy writes in her introduction, "I knew just one Little School, but throughout our continent there are many 'schools' whose professors use the lessons of torture and humiliation to teach us to lose the memories of ourselves."[31] Even if the "event" is over for the speakers of these texts, it is not "over" in any way for many millions of other people in South and Central America. Thus the temporal differences embodied in these texts—the Holocaust texts are memorial in tone while the Argentinean texts are combative and interventionist—mark the historically different situations in which these survivors find themselves.

Also, unlike the Holocaust survivors, these authors are writing from a post–Universal Declaration global positionality. They are aware of the existence of human rights discourse as a juridical discourse administered through the United Nations that attempts to formulate international guidelines for the behavior of states toward their subjects/citizens. As such, their projects bear with them from the outset the imperative not just to bear witness to past injustice but to intervene into ongoing situations of abuse and to stop it from happening again. While Holocaust survivors were writing into a void—the Holocaust itself and their early testimonies were one of the imperatives out of which the Universal Declaration was written—more contemporary survivors of torture and human rights abuse know the crucial political role their testimonies can play for international human rights organizations. These survivors are also painfully aware of the role torture and disappearances play in reinforcing state oppression through terror and fear. Their writings, therefore, must address this terror as an ongoing attack against the peoples of the nations experiencing it. Their writing serves partly as a resistance to this terror.

The Little School: Memory, Bricolage, Resistance

Like Sara Nomberg-Przytyk's *Auschwitz: True Tales from a Grotesque Land,* Alicia Partnoy's *The Little School: Tales of Disappearance and Survival in Argentina* also claims to consist of "tales." As with Nomberg-Przytyk's book, Partnoy's "tales" take the form of brief, two-to-four-page chapters documenting her experience of incarceration and abuse in one of the concentration camps operating during the military dictatorship (1976–1983) in Argentina. The use of the term "tales" to refer to her writings highlights the contested nature of the stories they tell as well as the phantasmic nature of the events in her own memory. Against "official history" Partnoy opposes "tales," with their connotation of the colloquial, fictional, and imaginary (folktales, fairy tales, tall tales). While still claiming the veracity of her experience, she highlights the problems of memory and the fragmented nature of her text that are endemic to the witnessing of trauma and violence. While the "official" history of the dictatorship claims one story—that there were no concentration camps or disappearances, that the people arrested or detained were violent subversives who posed an immediate threat to the civilian population of the country, and so on—Partnoy claims many pieces of stories, a bricolage in direct opposition to that of the state.

The first epigraph of her book, a quotation from the *Final Document of the Military Junta on the War against Subversion and Terrorism* (April 1983), denies the existence of disappearances and detention camps and blames the stories of them on subversive elements seeking to undermine the rule of the state. The stories, poems, and drawings that follow this epigraph constitute the rest of the book and refute its claim through their very existence. Yet to draw attention, as Partnoy does, to the competing histories and the struggle for memory that define postdictatorship Argentinean culture is to refuse the idea of any one "true" history or memory of events. The power of the state and its oppressive hierarchy is invested in the control of history and truth, the insistence that there is only one story—the right one—to be told. By positing the notion of competing histories and truths, Partnoy does not undermine the credibility of her claim to experiences that the government denies ever took place. Instead, she opposes the singular, state-owned story with an accretion of fragments of many stories, both her own and those of other people, told through a variety of artistic mediums (drawings, dialogue, poetry, vignettes, author's preface), creating a flexible, sedimentary collection of truths that surround, cover over, and eclipse the monolithic "official story" of the state.

In this fashion, her book as a communal project cannot be divorced from her book as a political project. She includes in her text not only illustrations by her mother and the quotations of other people's poetry that serve as many of the epigraphs to chapters but also the dialogue of people who were murdered and no longer have voices of their own with which to tell their stories. Parallel to the witnessing impulse evident in the Holocaust testimonials I discuss in chapter two, *The Little School* is impelled by the imperative of the survivor to bear witness to those murdered—both to give them voices through Partnoy's own voice and to bring their deaths back into memory. Like the countless millions murdered by the Nazis, made nameless, and removed from memory, the disappeared of Argentina have been forcibly removed from the text of history. In naming them as disappeared and recounting pieces of their lives from beyond the moment of disappearance (from her contact with them in the concentration camp), Partnoy writes them back into the story and into the framing text of collective memory.

They are not, however, miraculously reconstituted as whole/complete subjects; instead they remain fragmentary, serving a dual purpose. Politically, they function as the return of the repressed, haunting the "seamless" present of current national history as ghosts whose only semicorporeal existence makes them difficult to oppose with the rigid weapons of state repression. Communally, these resubstantiated voices and subjects of memory serve as a foundation from which Partnoy, as a survivor, can begin to bear witness to her trauma and reconstitute herself as a subject who has a voice and a place within memory and history. Reconstituting herself as a subject with a continuous narrative—linking who she was before, during, and after disappearance—is not, however, her goal. Having been "disappeared" from the official history of the nation—as well as disappeared juridically as a subject—Partnoy builds an alternative community that functions not just to "reappear" people as juridical national subjects but to build alternative structures of memory, subjecthood, and family that counterpose those of the existing state discourse.

While the state attacks and destroys families, dissolving generational links by killing teenagers and young parents and stealing their children, justifying its actions with the rhetoric of protecting the traditional family, Partnoy and other survivors build new families bonded from similar experiences of loss, suffering, and survival.[32] In her introduction, Partnoy notes that when she was reunited with the mother of two friends who were murdered, the mother told her that even though she did not have any daughters left, she still had Partnoy. These new families, then, form the foundations of new communities, operating both within the interstitial spaces of the traditional family and state hierarchy and beyond its disciplinary frame. Countering the existing state discourse of families whose children are out of control and must be controlled by the state—the subtext of which is an attack on women and mothers as both out of control and not occupying their proper place within the hierarchy, which is as subjects to their husbands—Partnoy's book foregrounds the intergenerational ties between women as sources of strength and resistance. The shared experiences of gender become the site of bonds that help to resist the humiliations and tortures of the camp as the women become "sisters" and "mothers" to each other, sharing words of support, passing on articles of clothing, worrying about pregnancy, menstruation, and other members of their families.

Partnoy does not valorize these new bonds and familial constructions as a "new" hierarchy with which to counter that of state discourse. Instead her construction of a fluid community in text and memory offers multiple possibilities for identification. The multiplicity of genres that create the book appeals to a wide range of readers, both asking them to identify with whichever literary (or visual) form they are most comfortable and demanding that the reader let go of a narrow preference for genre and read expansively—allowing the various texts of the book to speak together as a bricolage. Rather than being composed of a single narrative form that demands coherence and a singular way of reading, *The Little School*'s form invites the reader to consider what is not written down—the silences that exist outside the frame of the texts—as an integral part of the stories being told.

Likewise, the voices of those memorialized in the book inhabit the interstitial spaces of the narrative as much as they inhabit the narrative itself. They exist variously as the person with whom the narrator snatches a few moments of precious conversation, as the subject of the narrator's thoughts and memories, as the subject of a story that is being told as though the teller were present as it happened, as the "I" voice of a series of events, as the subject of a note in Appendix A, or as pieces of poetry or drawing interspersed throughout the text. She opens the first chapter with the sentence, "That day, at noon, she was wearing her husband's slippers," bringing herself and her story into the narrative in the third person.[33] Her husband, we learn, has already been kidnapped, and by wearing his slippers, she is almost "in his shoes" but not quite. The domestic objects of his slippers stand in for him in his absence, and she loses them, one by one, as she flees from the paramilitary through their house and yard, leaving behind their daughter. Already Partnoy is dispersed throughout the text as third person "she" and as the mechanism through which her husband enters the narrative.

Elsewhere in the text, people such as Vasca and Hugo enter as the hands that hold Partnoy's hands while the guards force them to run in a chain through the camp.[34] Even more interstitially, "Eduardo" enters through a sentence that appears alone in poetic form on an otherwise blank page between chapters, in the same way that other fragments of poetry and dialogue are placed throughout the text: "Eduardo says that on a cell wall / at the police station where he / was tortured when arrested, / someone had written: / 'Take heart, my friend, / one day more is one day less.'" The use of poetic form highlights the foundational position of gaps and the unsaid to the telling of tales of trauma and violence, foregrounding the reader's awareness of the narrative drive to suture over the gaps and interstitial moments upon which poetry depends and asking us to pay as much attention to what is un-said—to the gaps that structure Partnoy's narrative—as we do to the narrative itself.

Partnoy writes these voices into the text to take them out of the realm of private, individual memory and place them within the spaces of collective memory. As she writes in the introduction, "the voices of my friends at the Little School grew stronger in my memory. By publishing these stories I feel those voices will not pass unheard." The emphasis here is on publishing, the making public of the stories, as the method through which the "voices will not pass unheard." This points both toward a recognition that those alternative communities that have formed and that Partnoy inhabits do not exist as separate from the hierarchies of state (public) discourse and toward the book as a vehicle for building and inhabiting larger communities with people in very different times and places from those Partnoy inhabits. These voices, however, are not fixed within the text; they are "passing" through it, their movement marked by a verb that denotes boundaries and their crossings—one passes over, into, through, and across things—with fluidity. The ghosts and voices of her text travel in these ways across space, time, and memory, given new life after their disappearance and refuting the discourse that has excised them from the juridical field.

Following the body of the text of *The Little School* are two appendices. The first contains the names, histories, and fates—to the greatest extent possible—of the other prisoners of the camp where Partnoy was detained. The second is a list of the guards and officers of the camp, their aliases, and whatever information about them Partnoy has collected. These appendices resist the "official" story of the Junta with the specificity of the information they contain, which bears witness to those who died and the manner of their death as well as listing other survivors/witnesses to the camp. By listing the guards, Partnoy tears at the veil of anonymity that protects them and threatens them with the continual possibility of exposure. Turning the Junta's methods of terror back on itself, where "each pebble of information" is gathered until it creates an "avalanche" of information leading to the uncovering of the hidden/anonymous person for whom they are searching, Partnoy adds as many pebbles as she can to the pool of knowledge about the guards' identities.[35]

The collage of stories and forms that create the main body of *The Little School* is bookended by the introduction, containing a brief history of the dictatorship and Partnoy's biographical information, and the appendices, filled with their "pebbles of information." This format serves to ground the "tales" of the text with the more traditionally authoritative first-person testimonial voice of the survivor. Throughout the text, however, Partnoy questions just what this "authority" of experience is; although she never suggests that her experiences were not the "truth" of what happened, she questions the meaning of competing truths and how one decides from among them what to believe. In the transition from the "I" of authorizing experience in the introduction into the multiple voices that compose the "tales" of the text, she writes, "Beware: in little schools the boundaries between story and history are so subtle that even I can hardly find them." Although she claims the boundaries as hard to find even for herself as a survivor, she does not claim that she cannot find them. Her sentence, however, suggests that the accretion of stories becomes history, while at the same time, in the words of Françoise from *Who Will Carry the Word?*, the truth has become unbelievable even to herself.

Unlike the experience of the Holocaust for the writers I discuss in chapter three, Partnoy's book does not present her time in the little school as representing such a radical break with her life before and then after the camp that they become completely discontinuous experiences. The devouring, all-encompassing world of the Nazi concentration camps is not recreated in the same way by the little schools. This is due in part, perhaps, to the different methods of control and humiliation utilized by the two systems. While the Nazi camps enforced exhausting physical labor and the isolation of the individual within a homogenous group context (roll calls, barracks, soup lines) the Argentinean camp enforced total isolation through stasis, blindness, and silence.

Thus Partnoy is left with the challenge of occupying her mind as the only activity that she is freely allowed. While for both Partnoy and the women of Delbo's play, "talking is as important as sleeping," for the women in Nazi camps, the rigors of daily existence left little or no time for self-reflection—and in fact it could be unbearably painful; for Partnoy there is little else to do. Thus, in the absence of sight and speech, her other senses become acute, as she must judge where the guards are and what they want from her to avoid some of the physical abuse of the camp. As with Nomberg-Przytyk and other Holocaust survivors, her strong sense of commitment to witnessing, should she survive, causes her to gather as much information as she can about the daily functioning of the camp and the guards and officials who maintain it.

Forming the foundation of Partnoy's text throughout her tales is a focus not on the grueling physical abuses of the camp but on the myriad ways she found to resist them, often through the "black humor" she refers to as a "shield" to protect herself.[36] Thus, in the chapter "A Conversation under the Rain," she focuses her narrative not on the fear and abuse she suffers after being caught talking by the guards but on the strength and comfort she achieves by engaging in the conversation. The rain leaking through the roof onto the beds is not a further source of pain and discomfort to the narrator but instead makes "the sweetest music she had heard in a long time," and as she washes her hands with some water she has collected in her palm, she feels she is "washing away some of the bitterness that—mixed with filth—was clinging to her skin."[37]

A recounted conversation with Maria Elena, reported in detail, forms the bulk of this chapter, while the punishment Partnoy receives when she is caught talking, with its overtones of sexual abuse and rape, seems to have been included only for its ludicrousness. She includes no mention of the punishment of Maria Elena or of the fear and pain she feels at being asked to strip or at being "kicked roughly several times." Instead she recounts being made to stand for a while under a roof leak, with the drops falling on her head, as the guards experiment with "Chinese water torture." Since water has already been figured in the story as energizing and a source of strength, to be forced to stand under a drip, when she has not encountered any water for over twenty days, rejuvenates rather than debilitates her. Narrating in the third person, she says that, "Black humor made her shield thicker and more protective. Drops of water sliding down her hair dampened the blindfold on her eyes. Threats and insults sliding down her shield shattered into pieces on the kitchen floor. She thought of little Maria Elena."[38] A paragraph recalling her relationship with Maria Elena follows. The only hint of the environment she is in at this time, of standing naked in the camp kitchen surrounded by guards that verbally abuse her, is her reference to the threats and insults that slide down her shield of black humor and shatter on the floor.

However, the third-person recounting of the story, distancing Partnoy from the narration, and the elision of rape and sexual abuse as a form of assault, despite its obvious threat, combine with her emphasis on protective humor and the memory of Maria Elena to highlight narrative gaps that the reader is invited to actively engage with. Partnoy describes herself as naked, with her hands tied behind her back, and subject to threats and insults, focusing on the water dripping onto her head from the roof leak and remembering Maria Elena as a teenager, then writes that "half an hour later they untied her hands. 'Put your clothes on.' She dressed very fast, as if she had suddenly become aware of her nakedness."[39] What happens during the half hour that remains unnarrated, except for her focus on Maria Elena, is left unknown, as the intense suggestion of sexual violence is subsumed into her narration of resistance to "the blows and restraints . . . filth and torture" through her focus on her links to community through memories and humor.

Sexual violence appears another time in the text in the form of a guard who, in response to her request for water, "put a knife to my neck to force me to kiss him" and is then interrupted from further action by the intrusion of his supervisor, and also appears in Partnoy's references to the use of electric prods on people's genitals, but it is not directly addressed. Instead Partnoy's text performs a form of resistance through an emphasis on group solidarity that is also described by one of the women interviewed by Feitlowitz: " 'We were 800 women, and certain things we had no choice but to accept—like vaginal searches in front of thirty men all aiming their guns. But on other questions we could resist; we were always analyzing, making decisions about where to draw the line. For us, the boundary was group solidarity."[40] The resistance practiced within the camps is maintained in Partnoy's testimonial witnessing, which enacts the practice of resistant memory when confronted with traumatic, humiliating, and self-destroying violence. While the sexual violence of torture attacks the victim at the most fundamental level of her gender and sexual identity, Partnoy's witnessing refuses such victimization through the narration of personal, private memories that are maintained despite the sexualized violence of the attacks.

The focus of the story returns continually to her relationship with Maria Elena, signified by their conversation, which reminds her, as does the rain, of her life outside of the camp and of how to survive inside it. The story ends: "In the corridor that led to the iron grate, Peine kicked her roughly several times. She thought he was mad because she had neither cried nor pleaded for mercy, because she had not even trembled. She thought he was upset because in spite of the blows and restraints, in spite of the filth and torture, both women had had that long and warm conversation under the rain."[41]

As is true of most of the tales of *The Little School,* "A Conversation under the Rain" figures relationships between the prisoners and Partnoy's memories of her family and relationships outside the camp as its most important and central focus. Rather than detail the abuses she suffers in the camp—throughout her text she states that she was kicked or beaten but does not describe it—she uses the abuses to form the background against which the stories are set. Within this chapter, the physical abuse brackets the narrative of Maria Elena from before the camp. Maria Elena becomes a whole character, a person with a history and distinct personality, not a victim or object of abuse, and through such memorializing, Partnoy herself maintains and builds her ties to an ethical humanity. While in *Who Will Carry the Word?* and other Holocaust survivor texts, the physical debilitations of the camp are an obsessive focus of the narrative, in *The Little School* they often serve as the trigger for recounting a particular conversation or event, thus highlighting Partnoy's emphasis on bonds of community and memory as privileged sites of resistance.

"Latrine," the second chapter, is a series of stories that center on the problem of bodily functions and the dangers inherent in the prisoners' routine journeys to and from the latrine. Beginning with "I've discovered the cure for constipation"—which we learn in the chapter was a serious problem the prisoners developed due to their enforced inactivity—the first story goes on to recount a joke Partnoy told to Maria Elena about imagining shitting on the face of one of the camp officials. "Just pretend that Chiche's face is inside the latrine and shitting becomes a pleasure." Rather than focusing on the physical debilities caused by their diet, the torture, and the enforced physical inactivity, Partnoy uses them as a moment to illustrate conversation and bonding among the prisoners. The other stories of routine abuse—about being beaten while forming lines for the latrine, being watched by male guards while she is using it, being forced to use sandpaper for toilet paper, fainting while being forced to run in circles (playing "choochoo" for one of the guards), and breaking a tooth from being pushed over an iron grate by a guard—serve as a backdrop for the moments of resistance they provide.

The fear and indignity of being supervised while using the latrine are secondary to the opportunity to feel a nice breeze and hear birds sing and the sound of a train. Likewise, the "little train" game of the guards is an opportunity to hold hands with other prisoners, passing along an imagined message of hope and encouragement through the circle of hands. The final story of the chapter is a tale of passive resistance; Partnoy has felt that she "couldn't bear the situation anymore," sleeping for eighteen hours in a row and refusing to go to the latrine. In the middle of the night, while dreaming of a clean and private toilet, she wakes up wetting her bed.

As is true in the rest of the book, these moments of resistance are not presented as uncomplicated. Partnoy balances the importance of maintaining her sense of integrity—allowing herself to be beaten rather than being bullied into hitting a fellow prisoner—against the impossibility of truly resisting the situation in its entirety. By escaping through sleep and refusing to go to the latrine, she has both given in to the despair of a situation that is consciously constructed to unbalance her mind and opened herself up to the abuse and discomfort she will face for wetting her bed. Rather than further unraveling the "lessons" of these stories for the reader, however, Partnoy usually allows them to stand as short vignettes without much commentary. Instead of allowing the "little school" to remain, in her memory and in the book, as a place whose "professors use the lessons of torture and humiliation to teach us to lose the memories of ourselves," as she states in her introduction, Partnoy writes a text that focuses on the lessons of friendship, resistance, and memory that she learned during her time in the camp.

"Latrine" is also the first entrance of the "I" of narration into the body of the text (the first chapter is written in the third person), which encourages the reader to identify with the narrator's experiences to the extent that by the end of the chapter it is as though the reader is in the camp with an author who is still trapped there. The chapter ends, "I'd rather not think of the latrine right now. I've been needing to go there for the past two hours. . . . There are still three more hours to wait."[42] The temporal confusion that ends this chapter is consistent with the temporal confusion that occurs throughout the text. Is the author speaking from inside the camp? Does this mark the way in which she is still psychically trapped within the camp even as she writes her stories from exile? Or is this a literary device meant to make the reader feel as though she or he is in the world of the camps?

In "Poetry," Partnoy recounts a moment when she and the other prisoners were allowed to speak among themselves by the guards and she spent the time reciting some of her poetry to them. Undercutting this triumphant moment, however, when poetry and her recital of it could be read as an unqualified resistance is the inclusion in the chapter of a torture session undergone by her husband. This session seems to be taking place at the same time as her recital and focuses on the insistence by the torturers that her husband admit that the poem they have from an old book of hers and that she has just recited was written to "honor some fucking guerrilla." His unwillingness to admit this is the excuse for his torture. The chapter ends with Partnoy's guilt over using their precious talking time to recite poetry, when she could have been explaining to the new prisoners what they need to do to avoid beatings, since a beating for a loose blindfold has just occurred. The irony of reciting poetry to raise the spirits of the prisoners while at the same time her husband is being tortured over the content of the poem adds to the temporal confusion of the chapter. Behind this irony lurks the irony that the poem, which was written in sorrow over the covering of a stream, serves through her contextual reciting of it the very political purpose that the torturers want to attribute to it. The temporal confusion is created over the labeling of the two sections as occurring at "noontime," although a day is never mentioned, so that the suggestion of their occurrence on the same day is caused by their proximity in the chapter, once again forcing the reader to "read" the gaps of the text and narrative.

The one chapter that most directly details the torture and violence that she and the other prisoners experienced in the camp stands out from the text by this very difference. "Ruth's Father" obsessively recreates the broken thoughts that run through her husband's head while he is being tortured. He continually tries to maintain his sense of himself by remembering his daughter through the words of a folktale he used to recite to her and which seems emblematic of his own experience. Part of the chapter reads:

> This little poem soothed you when you cried; you went to sleep listening to it . . . I've repeated it for a whole day but I still can't sleep. *Rib-bit rib-bit he sings on the roof* . . . I won't see you again . . . The electric prods on my genitals . . . Trapped, like the little frog . . . *but we hear him all the time.* I told the torturers if they took me to the meeting place I would point to him; then when I saw him I didn't do what I'd promised. Afterward, the electric prod again, and the blows . . . harder: "Where is he?" But my child . . . *Rib-bit rib-bit* . . . Where are you, my little girl? . . .
>
> But when they come for me . . . to kill me next time . . . No, please don't come . . . I'm not an animal . . . don't make me believe I'm an animal . . . but that's not my scream . . . That's an animal's scream.[43]

The obsessive, continually broken return to his daughter and the folktale and the sense of increasing velocity given by the text combine to create in the reader a feeling of being trapped within a mind that is desperately scrambling between trying to retain a sense of coherent identity and feeling broken, in pain, and immobilized. Once again, this chapter does not detail the physical violence of the torture but instead recreates the horror of the psychic violence that has been created, committing a form of violence on the reader as well. The jumping from focus to focus, combining the singsong lines of the tale with the repeated references to the electric prod and the fear of losing one's self so completely through pain that one is no longer human—that one becomes an animal—create the impression of madness, of a mind already slipping, at times, out of control. The memory of the time when he was in control, when he was "human" and had human ties, makes the nature of the breakdown all the more horrifying.

The complexity of issues raised by this dialogic and temporal confusion does not lend itself to easy unraveling. I would argue that the generic and narrative collage style in which the book is written works against instead of for strong reader identification with a single authorial voice whose experiences we also come to feel. Instead, Partnoy's text works to create an engaged and critical reader who is willing to do hard work to engage the multiplicity of different voices contained by the text and to juggle the fragments of stories they tell into a larger story that is nothing less than a lost fragment of the recent history of Argentina. The time and space architecture of "Poetry," the ellipses of "Ruth's Father," the temporal confusion of "Latrine," the ways in which the poetic fragments between chapters work as a kind of narrative ellipsis, and many other elements of the textual structure help to enable the possibility of a reader/witness. While one can read the book as a distanced spectator, eliding the gaps and reading only the basic narrative structure, the form of the text encourages a performative, engaged, witnessing relationship with the reader. Rather than allowing the state to disappear them, Partnoy lets a multitude of voices speak through *The Little School*, witnessing to the reader.

This is very different from the form that Sara Nomberg-Przytyk employs in *Auschwitz*; although the structures of the two books are very similar, Nomberg-Przytyk's text is focused on delving into the moral conundrums raised by the stories she tells and on issues of her own complicity and moral implication in the system of Auschwitz. Nomberg-Przytyk also writes of the importance of community and resistance to survival, but in the same way that Primo Levi refers to the camp as "a vast experiment" in behavior modification and social conditioning,[44] Nomberg-Przytyk is more concerned with the complex and paradoxical moral issues raised for her as an individual survivor than with the fragmentary speaking of many voices that make up the community of "disappeared."

This is probably due in part to the difference in historical circumstances out of which emerged the Nazi and Argentinean camps. While the Nazi genocide was aimed primarily at erasing entire "races" of people from their territories, the Argentinean "war against subversion" was aimed at people marked by their real or supposed political affiliations and activities rather than their race. While entire families in Argentina were arrested and "disappeared," prisoners such as Partnoy did not have to face the wholesale destruction of their entire community and way of life as part of their experience. From prison Partnoy can imagine a world outside her camp walls that goes on much as she has always known it to, including her parents and relatives, rather than living with the knowledge that all she has ever known has been murdered and destroyed. This difference in perspective allows Partnoy to build bridges— either imagined or real—between herself and the other prisoners based on their common resistance to a common enemy. The sense of absolute inability to influence one's chances of survival is similar to that described by many Holocaust survivors, but Partnoy's text resists the terror, paralysis, and trauma this can cause through her characters' insistence that they are imprisoned with reason—on account of their political and social commitments—rather than through the random actions of state terror. Another Argentinean survivor, interviewed by Feitlowitz, states:

> Every layer of our reality was death, . . . there was virtually no way to improve your chances of surviving. Your conduct had no effect on what happened to you. And their conduct was irrational. Why am I alive? My parents paid a ransom, and we have relatives in the army. But others had the same situation and were still massacred. Nothing you were or did mattered. They'd use it all—or not— and then annihilate you, if that's what they felt like.[45]

Rather than feeling she was rounded up and arrested without reason or warning, Partnoy can place herself as a vital member of a movement to improve the lives of the other members of the country from which she has been disappeared. This gives a reason to her imprisonment and suffering that is a significant source of strength for her. Her text continually references the importance of feeling herself to be participating in a movement, surrounded by acquaintances that share her commitments and experiences, and knowing that although she may die, she will be dying for a cause and moral integrity that remain for her, as she presents it, unquestioned.

For Nomberg-Przytyk, she and the other prisoners of Auschwitz can lay claim to no cause through which to justify their suffering and death, which seem to her to be without meaning other than the racism, sadism, and caprice of the Third Reich. I am not drawing this comparison to lessen the impact of Partnoy's experience or suffering, but I am interested in the different ways that Partnoy's and Nomberg-Przytyk's understanding and memory of their experiences impact upon the forms of their texts. Although Partnoy chooses not to detail the abuses she and the other prisoners suffered, they were constant, violent, and murderous.[46] I suggest that another reason for this difference between the texts, which I discuss in more detail in the conclusion to this chapter, is that while Nomberg-Przytyk is writing from the position of a survivor of a catastrophic event that she will probably not experience again, Partnoy is writing in exile about an ongoing situation—if not in her own country at the present moment, then in many others. This temporal immediacy between her text and the abuses it details lends it importance as a political document that details the experiences of other women who are imprisoned at this time, and she writes from an awareness of herself as a member of an international community that is working to intervene into and prevent these situations.

Information for Foreigners: From Spectator to Witness

Similarly, *Information for Foreigners* by Griselda Gambaro, written in Argentina from 1971 to 1973, right at the beginning of the most repressive years of the military dictatorship, proceeds from an awareness of the play as a performative political document. The title of the play itself suggests this status. Information for foreigners is both a reference to the naïveté of non-Argentineans from "stable" political systems who do not want to believe that things such as torture and state-sponsored military terror still happen and a reference to the "other country" created by this terror that most Argentineans themselves do not want to believe in and therefore tacitly support. It also anticipates a quote from 1976 by General Jorge Rafael Videla, one of the leaders of the military Junta: "The repression is directed against a minority we do not consider Argentine . . . those whose *ideas* are contrary to our Western, Christian civilization."[47]

The play, like *The Little School,* is collage-like and experimental in its form. Meant to be staged in an old house or building with many rooms in which scenes can take place, *Information for Foreigners* deliberately blurs the boundaries between what is staged and what is real, who is acting and who is audience, and what the audience's proper role should be. The drama itself is composed of many short scenes that are meant to be performed as though they are already in progress when the audience encounters them. In one room, the audience—led from room to room by a guide—views a young woman in a soaking wet dress sexually harassed and humiliated by her jailers. Along the walls of the hallways, boxes the size of coffins, leaning upright against the walls, contain the bodies of imprisoned men. The audience views the various psychological and physical abuses of each scene, but because of the coercive structure of theatricality—that we do not interrupt the action, it is not real—and the coercive structure of the play itself—the guide is the only person who knows the way out of the maze of the house—the audience members must feel a strong pull to do nothing to stop or alter the action.

Unlike Delbo's *Who Will Carry the Word?,* Gambaro's *Information for Foreigners* asks the audience to feel as if they are there, deliberately using the coercive nature of theatricality to attempt to make the audience experience on some level the fear and discomfort of being in a threatening situation from which there is no escape. This makes the audience feel both complicitous and oppressed. Through the promptings of the guide, the audience is asked to approve or disapprove of various scenes, to think about what is happening and what their role is, and to consider the ramifications for themselves if they were to do something to intervene into the situations being staged.

Because the play is staged in a building with many rooms rather than a conventional theater, the audience members must rely on the guide to lead them from scene to scene and ultimately to the exit. This dependency upon the guide is crucial to the staging of the play; as it becomes apparent to the spectators that the guide is an ambiguous figure whose position in the authoritarian hierarchy of the play is not clear, their reliance on the guide becomes fraught with moral dangers and fear. Each room encountered by the spectators contains an ongoing scene referencing some form of abuse, interrogation, or incarceration. The guide serves as the controlling force behind what they see or do not see and how they experience it by opening some doors and refusing to let the audience enter, stopping or controlling the action during particular scenes, insisting the audience exit a room in the middle of a scene for no apparent reason, and asking the audience to sympathize with and support his running commentary and the supposed difficulty of his position. Several times the guide explains the content of a scene being acted by stating, "explanation for foreigners," and quoting from a contemporary news report about the kidnapping and disappearance of the persons who are the subject of the scene.

The rooms themselves and the corridors between them are dimly lit and narrow, creating for the audience-group feelings of disorientation and claustrophobia that are distinctly threatening. Adding to this threatening feeling of possibly being trapped is the implied violence of the atmosphere; the coffin-shaped boxes interspersed along the walls have been shown to contain bodies, and the audience enters rooms to witness scenes containing actors who seem just to have been or soon to be the victims of some hinted-at and barely restrained horrible violence. The smallness of the spaces involved, with the group of audience members being led from small room to small room where they must crowd against the walls so as not to impede the action, gives an immediacy to the bodies sharing the space. Rather than the common distance between bodies that is maintained in traditional theaters between actors and audience, here the spectators must look at the girl who is being humiliated and abused with little distance between them. Whether they are horrified, interested, aroused, or feel personally threatened, they must confront these feelings with an immediacy that comes largely from their physical proximity to each other, the guide, the torturers, and the victim.

These feelings of discomfort heighten audience members' identification with the guide, who maintains, especially during the earlier scenes in the play, a pretense of distaste for and superiority from the actions taking place around them. Through this identification their dependence upon him is increased, so that as the play progresses and it becomes more apparent that the guide's position in the hierarchy is one of authority and possibly leadership, the audience is placed in an uncomfortable position. He has maintained the appearance of a "civilized" and rational man who shows distaste for violence and is solicitous of their needs and concerns. However, as their ongoing contact with him chips away at this persona and they begin to suspect him of a closer relationship to the authoritarian structure of the play's action, the audience is caught between wanting to pull away from their identification with him and their reluctance to do so. This reluctance stems from a combination of 1) the spectators' unwillingness to believe that some-one with whom they initially felt something in common and therefore trusted could be involved with something so repulsive as torture and organized state terror; 2) their feeling both of being trapped in their role as spectators, unable to break the action of the play, and of being unable physically to find their way out of the building; and 3) their growing fear that since the guide is not what he seems and his role is not clear, to oppose him—to break with the action—could bring the apparatus of terror down upon them, and they could find themselves singled out from the rest of the audience and possibly not allowed to leave.

Because of the confusion the play creates over the roles not just of the guide but of the actors and audience, the audience members cannot be sure if everyone who appears to be a member of the audience truly is one. At one time an actor who has seemed to be a member of the audience is set upon by a group of men who burst into the room and assault and carry off both the actor and a neighbor who has tried to protect him. At another time an actor opens and walks through a door in advance of the guide and is clubbed over the head and dragged off. At neither time does the guide do anything more than dismiss the incident and pretend it never took place. Since many of the actors are in the role of guards who control other actors through their violence, the audience's sense of group identity comes under assault. They cannot be sure that their "ranks" are secure and therefore do not know who is "really" to be trusted.

In another incident in scene 13, a member of the audience smothers to death a girl lying on a table and then returns to the group. Although the guide is distraught at the "inconvenience" of dealing with a body and the inevitable questions from the girl's family, the murderer is never again referenced and returns to being another anonymous member of the group. Audience members are also led to believe their lives could be jeopardized should they separate from the group. This is made clear not just by the clubbing of the actor who takes the initiative of walking through a door in advance of the guide, but also by a threat in scene 19, when a guard who is in charge of a group of prisoners calls to the audience "What about you all? Over here, young men" as the guide hurries them from the room. This contributes to the spectators' feelings both of being coerced into a role from which they cannot deviate—by intruding into the action or leaving—and of wanting to depend on and trust the guide.

Also under assault through this method of staging the play is the pleasure of voyeurism that maintains a traditional spectatorial position. The pleasure of watching and the feeling of control that is at the root of this pleasure are destabilized by both the violence and the proximity of the scenes being staged. To return to the argument I engaged in earlier about the discomfort of physical proximity, I would argue here that the voyeuristic pleasure that might be engaged in a scene that stages certain kinds of sexual violence or the threat of it is undermined by the viewer's physical proximity to the "victim." To watch from a distance, across the gulf separating audience from actors on stage or screen, carries a different weight of responsibility from watching from five feet away without the imagined separation provided by the "fourth wall." The physical immediacy of the scenarios makes the erotic element of voyeuristic pleasure more tangible, and any fascination an audience member might feel with the scenes would almost have to come with the knowledge that it stemmed from either a sadistic identification with the perpetrators or a masochistic identification with the victim.

This shift—from the relatively unconscious pleasures of theatrical voyeurism to either the unpleasure of being forced to watch a scenario that is threatening and uncomfortable or the more directly acknowledged pleasures associated with a sexual "perversion" that bears an uncomfortable resemblance to the scenes of nonconsensual abuse being staged—forces the spectators into a self-reflexive awareness of their position as spectators/voyeurs. The play, then, stages and complicates the overt theatricality inherent in torture that Scarry, Feitlowitz, and others have documented. As Feitlowitz notes, "this theatricality—of which language was an integral part—served several purposes: as a torment for the prisoners, a sadistic pleasure for some enforcers, and as a distancing, enabling device for others in the chain of command."[48] Audience members must wonder what they are doing wandering through a building as a group, peering behind doors and into coffins to see what interesting things they might find, especially when the "things" they find are inevitably people's bodies and psyches being violently attacked. What purpose is served by this curiosity? What is the "point" or "plot" of the play? What does it mean to be tourists of abuse?

The violence of the scenes, which uniformly contain the threat or trace of imminent violence even if none is happening at the moment, also works to disconnect the pleasure from voyeurism. Through their identification with the guide and with the victims or victimizers, the spectators also become participants in the action. Therefore, when the action is threatening or violent, they are also subject to the atmosphere of tension and threat that marks the various scenes. Combined with the possible fluidity of their position as spectators—since it becomes clear that some members of the "audience" are also actors—and the unstated threat to stay within the expectations of their role as audience, the situation of spectatorship becomes increasingly fraught and uncomfortable.

For the audience, then, the question of how easily they could become victims or victimizers instead of voyeurs becomes a crucial element in their experience of the play. Gambaro is writing for an audience that is being asked to and could attempt to do something to resist ongoing situations of state terror, despite the immediate personal dangers of resistance. As Marguerite Feitlowitz notes, "Terror does ghastly things to the human mind and heart. And Argentines were terrorized, had been since before the coup. The country as a whole was largely silent during the Dirty War. Since torture and death were castigations for *thoughts,* people tried to stop thinking. 'We knew but we didn't know,' would later become a refrain."[49]

By putting the audience into situations that force them, through discomfort and fear, to reflect on the role that passivity and noninvolvement play in supporting state terror and authoritarianism, the play works to compel the audience members to action. By insisting that everyone has a responsibility for the actions of the state and that deciding to take no action is in itself an important decision for which one can be held accountable, Gambaro seeks to undermine the authorizing silence that authoritarian regimes rely on and work to maintain through terror. Through its scenarios and its assault on the spectatorial position, *Information for Foreigners* insists that to take no action is ultimately as dangerous as taking action, since the randomness of state-authorized terror and the excesses of its violence are as likely to strike "nonsubversives" as they are "subversives." The arbitrariness of these terms and their cynical use in self-serving and obfuscating state rhetoric are excavated and exposed by the play, so that the crutch of belief in the "authentic" good intentions of a military state acting only to protect its citizens is removed from audience members as an excuse for their unwillingness to see and intervene into situations of atrocity.

The scenario that Gambaro dramatizes—of a hidden space where men in power deliberately inflict pain and humiliation on their prisoners, often only for their own amusement, while being watched by a passive audience that moves from scene to scene without question—is quite similar to the lived experience Alicia Partnoy writes of in *The Little School*. It is these neighbors—who are afraid to intervene when the soldiers come to arrest a family, who would rather believe the stories of a "war on subversion" that is being contained than admit that they live in a nation ruled by terror and arbitrary violence—who are the intended spectators of Gambaro's play. No person is safe from the charge that they willfully refuse to see and make conscious decisions not to resist certain instances of state violence and abuse of authority. While we all, perhaps, must "pick our battles" and decide when to resist authority and when not to, *Information for Foreigners* forces its spectators to recognize that they are responsible for each of these decisions, and that these decisions collectively create the environment we all must share.

Gambaro's play stages the deliberately theatricalized representations of violent spectacle and humiliation in what in many ways is presented as a "realistic" scenario. Thus it works to recreate for the spectators the feeling of an actual camp such as the Little School. In doing this, the play stages the process by which "hidden" violence and torture leads to public silence. As Diana Taylor notes, "Insofar as torture works through amplification, the systematic nature of the assaults also affected the voice of large sectors of the Argentine population who opted not to speak out against the atrocity."[50] Part of what makes Gambaro's recreation "work," however, is the construction of an oppressive and threatening atmosphere from which the audience cannot escape. Although Taylor criticizes this as a possible violence upon the audience, I argue that the form of such "violence" is itself an assault against the psychic mechanisms of spectatorship that facilitate the acquiescence of individuals to the silencing terror of the state.

In *Who Will Carry the Word?*, Delbo makes the decision not to try to recreate the camps realistically because it is an enterprise doomed to failure and fraught with the dangers of erotic identification with spectacle. Her play both preserves the traditional divide between audience and actors and works to disrupt identification. Gambaro's play combines an atmosphere of terror and oppression with deliberately absurdist, theatricalized scenes. This tactic makes the seemingly realistic transactions with the guide, the actors impersonating audience members, and some guards seem more real than the often grotesquely acted and staged scenes. At the same time, it refuses the danger of recreating violent scenes in a way that spectaclizes and makes fascinating the violence portrayed. Instead, the unsettling combination of common children's games, songs, and poetry with violence and terror increases the sense of unease and fear produced by the scenarios.

In a style strikingly similar to that of *The Little School*, the play is created from a collage of different elements. The dialogue and action combine quotations from news reports about disappearances, poetry by a woman who was arrested and tortured, pieces of *Othello*, poetry by Garcia Lorca and Garcilaso de la Vega, portions of common Argentinean children's games, and Tin Pan Alley songs. As with *The Little School*, this collage of different voices and styles creates an alternative to the violently rigid rhetoric of the dictatorship. Drawing attention to the ways in which the dictatorship turned commonly used words into words that had entirely different and sinister meanings—for example, "order" as terror, "security" as repression—by lampooning them, the play uses irony as an attempt not to reclaim the language but to reveal the ways in which it has been twisted to the uses of terror. Once again, this technique is directed toward pushing the spectators to a realization of their own complicity in the twisting and destruction of language in such a way that it conceals state violence and terror.

The play opens with the guide giving the following instructions to the audience:

Ladies and gentlemen. Admission is—, for adults. If you've paid, you can't repent. The cost is already incurred. Better to enjoy yourself. No one under eighteen will be admitted. Or under thirty-five or over thirty-six. Everyone else can attend with no problem. No obscenity or strong words. The play speaks to our way of life: Argentine, Western, and Christian. We are in 1971. I ask that you stay together and remain silent. Careful on the stairs.

The language combines solicitousness with subtle threat and marks the guide as allied with the dictatorship to the extent that he defines Argentinean culture as one that is necessarily Western and Christian. This will be an ongoing subtext of the play, referred to again in scenes 6 to 7 and 13, combined with the guide's (and so also his successor's) continual referencing of the catacombs that they enthusiastically seek to show to the audience. The catacombs that supposedly lie in the foundations of the building and hold the remains of early Christian martyrs—the lineage to which the dictatorship lays claim—are reached only at the end of scene 6, but all that is found is a body covered by a sheet, the sight of which so enrages the guide that he begins stomping on it and must be replaced. Thus murder is revealed as the foundation of "Argentine, Christian, and Western" culture, referencing both Videla's quote and the guide's opening lines.

The guide who replaces him, Guide 2, apologizes for his predecessor's behavior with the typical language of the dictatorship, which disclaims responsibility for the violence of its rule by blaming it on the uncontrolled excesses of a few marginal subordinates. As he relieves Guide 1, he says, "Sorry. We have a few like machines without an off-button. If you would be so kind as to follow me." As with the other incidents in the play where violent or potentially violent actions occur that seem "unplanned" and are witnessed by the audience, such as the moments when actors posing as audience members are killed, taken away, or commit murder, the guide makes passing reference to the incident in a way that minimizes its significance and then continues with the tour as though it has not happened.

The introductory lines in the extract above also emphasize the rigid regulation of the dictatorship, which worked to define adult/child and family structures as absolute and impermissible—"no one under eighteen"—and to maintain absolute social regulations even to the point of near impossibility. The narrow field of what constitutes an acceptable audience member—no one under thirty-five or over thirty-six—symbolizes the narrow restrictiveness of the dictatorship's insistence on Western, Christian culture and the guides' insistence on maintaining it—"no obscenity or strong words." The audience is then further admonished to stay together and remain silent, reminding them of the "proper" role of the spectator, which will be increasingly called into question as the play proceeds. The directly following and solicitous "careful on the stairs" takes on a sinister tone when placed in context of the restrictive instructions that have preceded it, which imply through their very restrictiveness that to exceed their bounds is to invite some unspecified "trouble."

The unease and threat that underlie these seemingly polite and helpful instructions are embodied by words such as "repent" and "incur," which carry the appearance of jest but, like the absurdist spectacle of the scenes, also have a sinister undertone. The guide, who is in control of the audience and responsible for them throughout the course of the play, endows these words with threat because of his position of power and control. By the second sentence he speaks, audience members have already been informed that they have made an irrevocable decision and, since they cannot change their minds and leave, they might as well enjoy themselves. By placing such overt restrictions upon the audience, the play invites rebellion but is relatively secure in the knowledge that it will not happen. Thus the introductory lines construct the exercise in social control and group behavior that is demonstrated throughout the play by the spectators' own participation in its strictures.

The first five scenes of the play set up the progression that the rest will follow along with the scenarios they will engage. Scene 1 consists of the guide entering a dark room from which has emerged a babble of voices and exposing with his flashlight a man sitting alone on a chair in his underwear, surprised, frightened, and humiliated at their intrusion. Already, in this scene, the cohesiveness of the audience group is attacked, as the guide reminds them to "guard their pocketbooks" from thieves among them taking advantage of the dark. Finding a man in a position of fear and humiliation is unsettling, as the audience must wonder how he got there and what has been done to him. The inability of the guide to make the electric light work and his fumbling attempt to find his flashlight are also unsettling, making the space seem insecure and out of control. This is the beginning of the guide's insistence on exercising his authority over what the audience will and will not see as he quickly closes the door, explaining that it is the wrong room.

The scene that follows finds the guide rudely told not to enter a room from which a "sweet voice" is singing the lines of a Lorca poem. Scene 3 introduces the recurring character of the "wet girl." Seated on a chair, soaking wet and shivering, with a guard solicitously attempting to warm her with his jacket and admonishing her for being so wet, she exemplifies a victimized woman. The very presence of the guard standing over her speaking of his gun implies the threat he poses to her. Throughout the scenes in which she appears, the threat of rape and sexual abuse hovers. Unlike the later scenarios that utilize ridiculous makeup, bad acting, and other distancing techniques, the scenes in which she appears are written as unstaged and realistic.

These two scenes play together to cement the audience's perception that the guide is not in control of his surroundings, while introducing the beginnings of the suspicion that he is not as innocent and objective an interpreter as he presents himself. Thus from its outset Gambaro's play begins to place its spectators in an untenable position. This is in keeping with the play as a vehicle to force people to think about ongoing issues of complicity, abuse, and intervention. While Delbo's *Who Will Carry the Word?* is about memory and memorializing as well as survival, Gambaro's play, like *The Little School*, is written from the position of a working interventionist document.

Confronting the audience directly with their willingness to follow authority unquestioningly, scene 4 dramatizes the Milgram experiments. Performed first at Yale in the 1960s and then at other U.S. universities and in Munich, Germany, the experiments placed one person in the role of teacher and the other in the role of pupil. The pupil was to receive an electric shock of increasing voltage for each wrong answer given in a series of recall exercises. Unknown to the teacher, the pupils were not actually receiving shocks and were acting as they screamed in pain at the increasing voltage. In the United States, 66 percent of the teachers shocked their pupils to death, while in Germany 85 percent did.[51] In Gambaro's play, as the pupil becomes increasingly agitated and in pain, he begins to confuse Argentina with Germany and nation with prison, enraging the "teacher," who then administers the lethal voltage.

Unlike many other scenes in the play, this one is written and staged in a very "realistic" fashion, inviting the audience into the narrative world of the scene and asking them to identify with one of its characters. When they do nothing to stop the death of the pupil, the spectators must either identify with the teacher and coordinator, who feel justified in their actions, or accept the horror of having watched the experiment without intervening. As the allusion to Argentina in the pupil's answers makes explicit, the scene asks the audience to recognize that if you play the game of unquestioningly following authority, you will become locked into the role of either murderer or victim.

Scene 5 then moves to caricature the role of the "traditional" family in supporting political oppression and terror. This scene employs two actors in the role of husband and wife. The wife is seated in a chair, wearing a long white dress and holding a baby (obviously a doll) in her arms. At her feet sits a man gazing up at her with an "enraptured" expression. The stage directions call for them to be "enveloped in a beam of rosy light" and for the acting to be "frankly crude." This is the first appearance of the guide's use of the "explanation for foreigners" dialogue as he interrupts the performance to report to the spectators, quoting from a contemporary news account, the kidnapping of Nestor Martins and Nildo Zenteno on December 16, 1970, by a group of armed men.

The dialogue that follows between the man and woman places this event in the form of a crudely told children's story about the "good guys" taking away the "bad guys" so that they are never heard from again. The woman speaks in a high, childish voice, calling the man "daddy" and begging for the story, clapping her hands and cheering when the bad guys are taken away. The man calls her "precious" and explains that the tall bad guy is one of the "dirty Bolivians" who pro-create a lot and send their children to Argentina to beg and steal in the streets. The disjunction between this vicious, farcical rendition of the "perfect" family and the story of the kidnapping of a prominent defense attorney and his client that has just been "explained" to the audience highlights the self-satisfied ignorance that supports such violence.

The structures of patriarchy on the level of the "private" family par-allel and support similar cultural structures that infuse the public sphere. The woman is an iconic but powerless and childlike presence who authorizes the violent racism and terror of the story the man tells. While the Bolivian/non-Argentine others procreate like "animals," she is a virgin/child dressed in white and carrying a doll. The man, mean-while, translates the violence of the story he tells into a story of good-versus-bad cartoon characters, robbing the story of its violence, political content, and human cost.

Representation, the Materiality of the Survivor's Body, and the Critic

The Little School and *Information for Foreigners* illuminate a trajectory of artistic and political response to the experience of military dictator-ship, the terror of state violence, and survival; as such, they are attempts to use performance and literary form to make political interventions into a wide cultural and political field. Like many works—especially by women—about the experience of torture and state violence, these works focus on issues of language, resistance, and community. They criticize the acceptance of violence through the refusal by the middle class and general public to acknowledge it, they expose traditional fam-ily and gender roles as localized sites of the violence that infuses the state structure of the dictatorship, and they focus on alternative family structures and forms of community through which resistance and sur-vival are possible. These are radical interventions that go beyond the universalized discourses of human rights—discourses that do not in themselves critique the foundations of cultural structures such as patri-archy—to critique the root of the cultural systems that engender such violence.

While the effectiveness of an organization such as the Mothers of the Plaza de Mayo lay in the women's turning of the Junta's rhetoric of the traditional family against itself so that they themselves became rhetori-cally sanctioned as "good mothers" within such rhetoric, their model

185

of the family was ultimately very similar to that of the dictatorship. In this way they gained a measure of protection from the state while mounting a strong challenge to its practices. The women of the Mothers, who organized to protest state terror by demanding information about their children who had been kidnapped and disappeared, were themselves targets of state terror and intimidation. But their positioning of themselves as virtuous mothers of the sort outlined by state discourses of the family allowed their very visible weekly protests to continue throughout the dictatorship, despite (and because of) the attention they drew from the international community.[52]

Like the texts of *The Little School* and *Information for Foreigners*, the structure of the Mothers' organization is nonhierarchical. As such, it opposes the monolithic hierarchy of the state with diffuseness and flexibility. Yet while the human rights discourse of the Mothers cuts across ideological and political lines, it does so through the reification of the traditional family as the foundational unit of state structure. As such, they use a very traditional model of human rights within which to position themselves as juridical, international—yet strongly national—subjects. Their work has been crucial in several ways, and I am not trying to suggest otherwise with this critique, but they stand as a paradigmatic example of both the promise and the difficulty of exactly what human rights documents such as the Universal Declaration strive for—a grassroots human rights organization arising organically within the country where the abuse is taking place. For many reasons, not least of which is the fraught and often impossible situation of international intervention into sovereign national affairs, organizations like the Mothers are crucial to the ability of international organizations to put pressure upon the state in question, to the community as bearers of memory and the power of resistance, and to the representation of national citizens as also international citizens who have rights and responsibilities that go beyond those of the nation.

The Mothers expand the definition of family to include the nonbiological daughters and sons who have been adopted into their ranks, but their success depends in large part on their search for the individual sons, daughters, granddaughters, and grandsons who have been lost. Partnoy and Gambaro, on the other hand, are much more suspicious of the family as a foundational site of the very culture that has produced the violent structures that climaxed in the dictatorship. In Gambaro's play this family, with the grotesquely acted wife/baby and husband/daddy, is the authorizing force behind the violence of the dictatorship.

Although she strongly identifies as a wife and mother, Partnoy also retains no nostalgia for the traditional "family." She and her husband are on equal terms in her formulations in *The Little School*. She neither valorizes her cultural position as "mother" and the right to suffering this could accord her—in fact, this attachment to the daughter is addressed most directly in the chapter "Ruth's Father," where it is accorded to her husband—nor acknowledges being in a secondary position to her husband, according him more importance with less value given to her suffering. Instead she posits the violence of the state as evidenced most in its attack on the independently chosen relationships into which people enter. It is not that the state is destroying the "natural" bonds that form biological relationships, but that the state is deliberately attacking the bonds and alliances forged between people as they form their own communities—of students, political or cultural groups, and so on—that are alternatives to those offered by totalitarianism.

Partnoy and Gambaro offer us an alternative to the spectacles and spectatorship of terror through the invitation to engage in performative relationships of witnessing. *The Little School* and *Information for Foreigners* provide us with opportunities to make conscious choices about our relationship to these texts and performances; we can choose to engage with the witnessing project or not, but either way, we must acknowledge the ethical demand of the text to witness to the dead and to the survivors. Distanced spectatorship is not allowed to remain the "unmarked" default position but is marked as the position that refuses the full humanity of the dead and of the survivors of atrocity. As Taylor notes, "The tortured bodies of the victims were necessary. They *made a difference* in that they made 'difference' visible."[53]

For us to engage as witnesses with these "bodies of difference" can be frightening, as we must recognize the ways in which totalitarian violence absolutely disrupts boundaries between private and public, zones of safety, and juridical and cultural fields. But through such recognition we also contribute to the building of ties to the human. Such violently disappeared and damaged bodies become people with histories, voices, and communities. The call of Partnoy, Gambaro, and other survivors and witnesses is not to elide difference, to "read over the gaps," but to acknowledge it and to witness with it through ethical, performative acts.

5

Testimonial, Trauma, and the Crises of Discourse in Bosnia

In this chapter I suggest a broadening of the category of testimonial literature to include a much greater range of texts than is generally considered as part of the genre. I have noted that testimonial literature draws attention to the inadequacy of two discourses—the purely literary and the purely legal—to address issues of violence and human rights abuse. For literary studies, testimonial literature blurs the ground between aesthetic form and personal experience, positing an "authentic" voice of experience and memory while also claiming the impossibility of a truth of authentic experience. For legal discourse, testimonial literature claims the position of the witness who was there and knows what happened because she or he experienced it with her or his own body. I argue, however, that such literature resists the fixing of any knowledge into one truth; the testimonial voice remains suspicious of the urge toward immobility, fixed boundaries, and the closing down of interpretations that are also the gestures toward consolidation and violence taken by repressive state regimes.

Testimonial works such as Elma Softic's *Sarajevo Days, Sarajevo Nights* and Slavenka Drakulič's *The Balkan Express* embody a shift of testimonial as a genre from the writings of Holocaust survivors to those written by survivors of state terror and oppression in Latin America in the 1970s and 1980s, to the writings published by survivors of the warfare that overtook the former Yugoslavia. Increasingly, such testimonials both participate in a historically aware dialogue with the genre itself—the authors are aware of women from previous moments of state-sponsored abuse who have produced testimonials—and is in dialogue with human rights bodies and international (especially Western) opinion that might be swayed to intervene politically into the (then) ongoing situation in Yugoslavia.

Softic and Drakuliç stress the importance of "cosmopolitanism," the primary characteristic of which they identify as tolerance for and enjoyment of differences, as an important identity formation through which to resist the essentializing ethnic and nationalist discourses by which the warfare is justified. They combine this with self-conscious examinations of the ways in which, under the intense pressures of refugee status and living under siege, their own affiliations with cosmopolitan identity become fragmented under the hegemonic expansion of such ethnic and nationalist discourses. However, they continue throughout their narratives to tell stories of the many ways in which community affiliations are formed that resist such pressures. Such critiques—of the ways identities are both shaped in violence and resist violence and the structures that authorize it—embedded in a testimonial form are radical interventions that go beyond the universalized discourses of human rights (which do not in themselves critique the foundations of cultural structures such as patriarchy or ethnicity), to critique the root of the cultural systems that engender such violence. In their position of writing both with and against the assumptions of the UN Universal Declaration of Human Rights (UDHR), these women's testimonials provide a necessary critique of the Declaration's underlying humanism.

Over the past several decades, testimonial literature has begun to develop as a distinct genre of literature, neither memoir nor autobiography, that addresses the specifically located moments of violence directed toward isolatable groups of people that have periodically occurred across the globe. As a form, testimonial is the voice of one survivor of mass violence who tells her or his own story while at the same time claiming not only that she or he speaks for those who did not survive but that any of these other persons would tell the same story. Thus, unlike traditional autobiography or memoir, which relies on the "I" of authorial experience, testimonial by its very act undermines the distinct claim of individualism. Instead, testimonial replaces the absolute, authorial "I" with an authorial voice that retains the individuality of the author's experience while also disclaiming the singularity of that experience, claiming that the story the author tells is the same story that could be told by any of the other people who shared the same experience. Embodied within the testimonial text is the same crisis of language, signified through this tension between individuality and communal experience, that the survivor must acknowledge in order to witness both for her- or himself and for/to others. In this gap between the specific authorial identity of experience and consciousness and the communal voice/experience of suffering and abuse and the imperative to witness lie the overlapping political, literary, and personal tensions of the genre.

Human rights discourses, which rely upon universalist assumptions about the basic sameness of human bodies, are in tension with the individual experiences of trauma that victims of human rights abuse experience. This tension rehearses one of the central problematics of the testimonial text, politicizing the gap between the communal and the individual experience of suffering. Just as witnessing is one of the primary imperatives of the testimonial, the testimonial itself is crucial to much human rights work. But while human rights work moves to stabilize the testimonial discourse at all times, insisting on the transparent authenticity of the singular experience of suffering, testimonial literature itself refuses such easy moves toward the naturalizing of experience. Instead, it performs the complexities of categories—drawing attention to the fragmentary nature of memory, experience, identity, and the literary—out of which a witnessing voice can be sutured together.

A common understanding many of us share about the retelling of the experience of trauma is that only by talking about it can the survivor understand and overcome its effects; it must be confronted and "worked through" in order to get beyond it. But what this narrative understanding of memory does not take into account is the necessity of silences and what happens outside the frame of the narrative to the life of the survivor. If trauma is an experience that happens outside the normative temporal narrative of history for the individual, then it is exactly what is outside the frame, in the shadows and cracks that haunt the conscious ordering of one's place in the world, that is integral to the experience of testimony. Witnessing, for the authors of these testimonial texts, is as much about the exploration of difference as it is about the cohesion of identity.

To recuperate bodies that have gone from being full citizens of civil and political life to being illegally removed from it, as difficult as this might be, is easier than granting such full citizenship to bodies that for specific structural reasons, such as the relationships of power and domination often inherent between different sexes and races, have never fully enjoyed it. As is clear from the UDHR, human rights as they are constituted today, although always in a process of change, have dealt with this by rhetorically enacting the universal individual and then attempting to provide some guidelines on the structure of social and cultural life through which the playing field will be made more equal. This is only half a solution, however, as the obfuscating veils of privacy serve the same function in supporting the state through terror (sites of mass murder and torture are usually "hidden" from public view) as they do in supporting the vast structures of economic and social power that oppositionally constitute themselves against women as the space of privacy and family.

Women and other bodies feminized by totalitarian violence must be disenfranchised as juridical subjects by violent regimes in order to justify not only the "random" outbreaks of violence against them but the systematic internment and murder of individuals who as universal humanist subjects have the right to human rights and considerations.[1] Thus, by excluding certain bodies from the juridical discourse of human rights, violent states can maintain the facade of civilization while enacting mass murder. As it has developed an increasingly sophisticated discourse both with past historical events, such as the Holocaust, and with interventionist human rights groups and structures, testimony increasingly plays a role in reappearing those bodies and voices that have been disappeared from the juridical fields of states and international law.

It is in the tension between the assumption of the always already private and juridically recognizable body of humanism and the inability of humanist, rights-based discourses to protect so many bodies around the globe that one of the great problems of a rights-based juridical theory surfaces. Torture and abuse happen within the confines of private spaces of the home as well as the state and in public spectacles involving actions by the police and the military, but in all instances they happen because the bodies that are being acted upon are not fully subjects and are therefore not fully human bodies. They are not the (universal individual) body that is juridically recognizable.

As an act that functions far more as an exploration of difference than as a solidifying of identity, testimony is a continually shifting ground of memory and present experience that refuses easy categorization or assimilation. It is exactly here that its resistant possibilities are strongest as it counters the totalitarian imaginary, which denies certain persons their subjecthood, with a fluid construct of performed memory. The self-conscious theatricality of memory and narrative performed in these texts creates not the universal subject/narrator, but a gendered subject/narrator who is aware of the necessity of her own instability. The paradox inherent in the act of using language to witness one's banishment from a juridical field comprised by the same language is overridden by the need for visibility and subjecthood.

John Beverley has defined testimonial (testimonio) as a new "antiliterary" form that is necessarily about class struggle and cultural revolution, but he does not address the importance of gender and the experience of extreme trauma in creating this form.[2] Adding an awareness of gender difference to testimonial theory suggests the necessity of broadening the category of testimonial to include a much greater range of texts. The issues raised by the authors in these texts cut across the lines of authorial class, ethnicity, and experience. As with Beverley's definition, it is antiliterary, speaks in the voice of all survivors/members of the community, and undercuts the traditional single author's voice.

These texts, however, through their insistence on formations of authorship and text that deny the unifying voice of humanism/juridical culture, create grounds for broad cultural critique. Although they are generated from experiences of extreme bodily and psychic trauma, these texts are not caught in a language of private individuality. Instead, they stress the collectivity of experience and fragmentary nature of identity and speak to a broad criticism of cultures of racist, patriarchal, economic systems of oppression that allow (and are founded on) genocide, violence, and "human rights" abuse. As such, gender is an imperative category for analysis in emergent discourses of testimonial and their political exigency. In its very position of writing both with and against the assumptions of the Universal Declaration, women's testimonial provides a necessary critique of the Declaration's underlying universal humanism.

Testimonial Resistance to Terror

As an important site of resistance, language is also, as with the testimonial discussed in previous chapters, a focus of these accounts of survival and witnessing from the former Yugoslavia. To be one's own witness is fundamental in perceiving oneself as a subject within the juridical field. Since to bear witness implies an audience to and for whom the story is told, for the authors of testimonials, the person to whom they bear witness is the imagined reader of the text who is called forth by the act of writing itself. The ability to speak and to act for oneself, which is so important and contested a position for the narrators of these testimonials, is a resistant act necessary to their survival. These moments are not constant, but as they punctuate the totalitarian concentrationary universe, they become important and remembered links in the attempt to rebuild a history and narrative within which the individual-as-subject, and therefore as person, can begin to exist again.[3]

From these kernels of memory comes the narrative of the testimonial, performed as oral or written event for the witness/survivor as well as the witness/audience—crucial to the rebuilding of the survivor's "internal witness."[4] This performative act of memory—the placing of oneself inside historical narrative and rebuilding of one's internal witness—does not construct a unified narrative of the historical event but instead functions as the truth of witnessing experiences whose truths can never be known.

The texts by Softic and Drakulič rehearse this difficulty by calling attention to the ways in which the authors themselves are increasingly implicated within ethnic and nationalist discourses and often take refuge in universalism in response. This universalism, however, is consistently destabilized within the texts as the narrators embrace ways in which identity is discontinuous and fragmented rather than cohesive as the best ground from which to speak and understand their situation. Their texts rehearse their concern that only by acknowledging and recognizing our own investments in fundamental inequalities and differences can we begin to bridge this paradoxical relationship between difference and universality.

Like many women Holocaust testimonial authors, women authors who are survivors of more recent moments of state-sponsored abuse betray a suspicion of the juridical language of state cultures from which they have been so effortlessly disappeared and fight for a voice that will encompass the fragmentation of their experience rather than simply trying to replicate the voice of coherent, seamless identity required for full visibility within humanist, juridical systems. There are differences, however, between Holocaust texts and the texts of more recent events such as the Argentinean dictatorship and the war in the former Yugoslavia that can be accounted for, I believe, in the way that the event is not "over" in the same way for the survivors of torture and state terror as it is for survivors of the Holocaust.

Aside from historical differences between the instability of Latin-American states such as Argentina and the reconstitution of the European nations as monolithically "stable" following the end of World War II and the beginning of the Cold War, the state terror and violent repression that happened in Argentina in the 1970s has been an ongoing problem in Latin-American countries in general. Even if the "event" is over for the speakers of these texts, it is not "over" in any way for many millions of other people in South and Central America. Thus the temporal differences embodied in these texts—the Holocaust texts are memorial in tone while the Argentinean texts are combative and interventionist—is symptomatic of the historically different situations in which these survivors find themselves. This is decidedly true, as well, of the Bosnian testimonial texts under consideration in this paper.

Although the women writing these texts were victims of the most vicious and murderous sort of attack by the State, they discuss their experiences not as individuals operating within a universal field of standards but as members of distinct and various communities that both overlap and require constant efforts of communication. In texts such as *Who Will Carry The Word?* and *The Little School* the systems of oppression that have combined to do violent damage to people like Charlotte Delbo and Alicia Partnoy cannot be separated and ranked as to their viciousness. In other words, the (hysterical) sexism that constituted part of the rhetoric of both the Nazi and the Argentinean fascist regimes was as important an element in those governments' murderous actions as was racism or nationalism. In the war in the former Yugoslavia, likewise, women's gender is specifically used against them in violent attacks (mass rape, torture, etc.), and women's bodies become the ground through which shifting ethnic and state discourses are constructed.

As I have discussed in previous chapters, the conflation of public and private during torture, the attack on the markers of domestic life, and the extreme destruction that the isolation and humiliation of torture effects are all aimed at heightening the pain, trauma, and terror of the torture. In Bosnia-Herzegovina and Croatia, this is an even more complex formulation. The well-organized campaign of rape and torture was orchestrated by Serbian and other forces against targeted populations, but the state itself was a contested ground, and it was in the service of solidifying one fundamentalist form of nation-state that these genocidal acts were being committed.[5] Thus the formulation of "cosmopolitanism" that both Softic and Drakulič deploy is in important opposition to the developing discourse of Serbian nationalism that created such massive violence.[6]

Women usually do not enjoy the same protection by the law in their daily lives as do men, and as victims of state oppression they often encounter violence aimed directly at their gender and sex, as Bunster-Burotto painstakingly illustrates in her article detailing the ways military

regimes have increasingly attacked women through patterns of punishment that attempt to coerce and dominate them through their gender
and position as women.[7] That this is not simply a Latin-American phenomenon was made very public through the systematic campaign of
rape and torture carried out against Bosnian women in the former Yugoslavia. Human Rights Watch states:

> In Bosnia, all parties to the conflict have raped civilian women of
> the "enemy" ethnic group, but the use of rape by Bosnian Serb
> forces has been particularly widespread and designed to further
> the policy of ethnic-cleansing. By attacking and terrorizing indi-
> vidual women, Serb soldiers and paramilitary forces send the mes-
> sage to the entire community that no one is or will be safe from
> violence. As a result, entire families and villages have fled.[8]

In addition, Serb soldiers engaged in the practice of forcibly impreg-
nating Bosnian and Croatian women—holding them prisoner until
their pregnancy is too advanced for abortion—in the attempt to inten-
sify the trauma of the rape. The children born of such violence are not
only a living reminder of the torture of their mother but are, within
the fantasy of ethnic categories underlying the Serbian aggression, half-
Serbian themselves. Such forced impregnation is pervasive enough that
Human Rights Watch considers that "the forcible impregnation of
women, or the intention to so impregnate them, constitutes an abuse
separate from the rape itself and should be denounced and investigated
as such."[9] The result of such torture is to reduce the women from conscious beings with individuality to body-vessels distinguishable only by
their having been marked as non-Serb, bodily representatives of the
enemy territory to be conquered, and thus subject to whatever abuse
the aggressors wish to subject them to in order to solidify their conquest.

Building on the argument Elaine Scarry makes, that the destructive
qualities of torture are enhanced through the use of everyday, domestic
objects to inflict pain, I believe that the fact that many of these women
know their rapists as former coworkers, neighbors, and so on and that
the rapists themselves often do little or nothing to hide their identity
works in a similar fashion to heighten the trauma of the rape and to
solidify further the ethnic and national categories that are being fought
out and constructed over and through these women's bodies.

To recognize the gendered nature of rape as a war crime, and to
address it as such, provides the possibility for intervening into the uni-

versalist assumptions upon which juridical human rights discourses are founded. Rhonda Copelan states:

> the international attention focused on Bosnia challenges the world to squarely recognize sexual violence against women in war as torture. Moreover, it is not enough for rape to be viewed as a crime against humanity when it is the vehicle of some other form of persecution; it must also be recognized as a crime against humanity because it is invariably a persecution based on gender. This is essential if the women of Bosnia are to be understood as full subjects as well as objects in this terrible victimization and if the international attention focused on Bosnia is to have meaning for women subjected to rape in other parts of the world.[10]

For the women of Bosnia to be "understood as full subjects" as well as the objects of human rights abuse, they must be understood to be subjects who are entitled to protection because of, not despite, their differences from men. Otherwise, they are the objects of protection only insofar as the crimes committed against them are crimes which could be committed against any body, regardless of its gendered, ethnic, or other statuses. Likewise, one cannot make rape a crime of violence that occurs outside of gendered discourses. Rape is a persecution based on gender because, like torture and many other forms of abuse, the person being raped, who is put in the position of the passive object who is penetrated and acted upon, is invariably feminized even if he is a man.

Softic and Drakulić engage these crucial distinctions in their texts. Unlike Holocaust survivors, they are writing from a post-UDHR global positionality and are aware of the existence of human rights as a juridical discourse, administered through the United Nations and other bodies, that attempts to formulate international guidelines for the behaviors of states toward their subjects/citizens. As such, their projects bear with them from the outset the imperative not just to bear witness to past murders but to intervene into ongoing situations of abuse and to stop it from happening again. While Holocaust survivors were writing into a void—the Holocaust itself was one of the imperatives out of which the Universal Declaration was written—more contemporary survivors of torture and human rights abuse know the crucial political role their testimonies can play for international human rights organizations.

Throughout the course of the war in Yugoslavia, the response by the European and American political community, both at the level of the

state and internationally (through the North Atlantic Treaty Organization [NATO] and the UN) was one of paralysis, appeasement, and reluctant engagement. Any commitment to an international community
of shared ideals and common interests was discarded at the first hint
that armed engagement might be a necessity to end the genocide and
ethnic partitioning of former Yugoslavia. News media reflected this
same paralysis of ethical engagement. Despite the fact that the war and
genocide were extremely well covered by world news media from the
beginning, including visual footage of concentration camps, starving
inmates, and piles of bodies that deliberately recall the Holocaust, public opinion was never mobilized to such an extent that governments
would feel compelled to commit large numbers of troops to potentially
life-threatening situations.

The discourse of international "cosmopolitanism" versus the discourse of "primitive, bloodthirsty fundamentalist ethnic division" was
engaged in both by the European and American media and by war
resisters within former Yugoslavia, and is exemplified by the iconic role
played by Sarajevo during the war. Sarajevo, with its diverse, multieth-
nic, and multireligious communities living as neighbors and intermarry-
ing, came to signify in the mass-media portrayals of the war an idealized
vision of the potential democratic communities of the future. As the
city was besieged, this vision of Sarajevo also became an important tool
for the activists trying to encourage relief efforts and military intervention by governments and citizens that would help to save lives, stop the
war, and restore order to the region. However, as it became clear that
nothing would be done to stop the war and that instead we had all
become front-row spectators to the massive destruction and murder,
this vision of Sarajevo as all that was ideal in "civilized" culture came
to be represented as a downfall that was not inevitable and had not yet
occurred.

The ethical paralysis brought on in the mass media and European
and American governments by such spectatorship to a relentless destruction that was resistant to any form of pressure besides military force
took the form of a voyeuristic fascination with what came to be seen as
an example of the inevitable march of the destructiveness of "human
nature." Such fatalism, of course, is an excellent excuse for noninvolvement, but what is also disheartening is the way that exhaustive media
coverage of the destruction—including death camps, complicity by UN
troops, the persistent shelling of Sarajevo—failed to fulfill the promise
that documentary witnessing seems to have held since the Holocaust.

Being witness to such violences—and bearing the slogan "never again" in mind—was to provide, it was hoped, the key to preventing or intervening into such events. What the mass documentary witnessing by the media and other observers proved instead was that witnessing such violence was not enough to mobilize an empathic response from the massed citizens of Europe and the United States that would cause them to feel the vital necessity of intervening to stop the warfare.

The various media and organizations that work to prevent and contain such radical violences have, therefore, increasingly relied on eyewitness accounts and testimonial as avenues of intervention. The personalized account of trauma, with its claims to a truth of individual experience, is a powerful and difficult document to deny. In contrast to the faceless unaccountability of governments and state agencies, testimonial provides the voice of the individual survivor/witness. However, testimony itself is not separate from this historical moment. To the extent that testimony as a personal and political act is imbricated within the panoptical systems of national and multinational state and corporate control, it faces the same untenable paradox as the authorial "I" in much testimonial literature. By using language as the mode of entry and intervention into the social and juridical fields from which they have been excised, survivors must accept implication within the totalitarian cultural field responsible in part for their abuse.

These survivors are also painfully aware of the role that torture and disappearances play in reinforcing state oppression through terror and fear. Their writings, therefore, must address this terror as an ongoing attack against the peoples of the nations in which it is being experienced. Such writing serves partly as a resistance to this terror. Yugoslavian writers such as Softic and Drakuliç, whose work was being published while the war was still underway, were aware that their work could play an important role in organizing international opinion against the war. These are not works of propaganda in any way; instead they are intellectual and artistic interventions into the vast, universalizing field of discourses about the war that speak in terms of troop movements, attack and defense, and groups of people defined only through a collective attribute such as ethnicity, gender, or death. Unlike the writings of women who were imprisoned in concentration camps or have been victims of a debilitating trauma such as torture, Softic's and Drakuliç's testimonial writing from within the event serves as a way for them to maintain during the event itself a (sometimes tenuous) voice and identity through which to resist oppressive state discourses.

Spectacles of Witnessing

Sarajevo Days, Sarajevo Nights is a collection of journal entries and letters to friends that Elma Softic wrote while living in Sarajevo from April 8, 1992 to June 23, 1995. Translated by Nada Conic and published in English in 1996, the writings combine to form a testimonial to Softic's experiences of living during the Serbian siege of Sarajevo. Having made friends through ham radio contact maintained between the Jewish community centers in Sarajevo and Zagreb during the siege, Softic wrote them letters that began to be published in Croatia and, along with her diary entries, were published in book form in Zagreb in 1994. As a teacher and an intellectual, Softic experiences the siege through the lens of continual self-critique and she documents the ways in which identity is shaped and altered by the changing affiliations, pressures, and discourses of the war.

Similarly, Slavenka Drakulić's *The Balkan Express* was written between April 1991 and May 1992 and concerns the author's experiences of the way in which the war changed or put pressure on her various identities as a journalist, a Yugoslavian, a Croatian, a woman, and an exile. Several of her chapters were originally published in various magazines and newspapers before she determined to gather them together and produce a book.

These texts function as testimonials not just because of the material conditions through which they were produced but because they speak to the pressures placed on individuality through the experience of trauma and to the ways in which community affiliations can be formed to resist such hegemonic pressures. Like many of the testimonials written by survivors of previous events of genocide and mass murder, these texts also focus on witnessing not just the authors' experiences but the lives and deaths of other people who have not survived, and by giving voice to the memories of these other people, Softic and Drakulić find a powerful ground from which to resist and to rebuild their own identities as particular individuals.

The Holocaust serves as a foundational event for both authors. While neither make claims for the commensurability of the events of the war they are experiencing with the events of the Holocaust, both Softic and Drakulić reflect upon the irony of the spatial and temporal proximity of the two events. And both authors reflect upon the importance of the filmic and the televisual in shaping both their own identities as they are caught up in the war and of the response to the war by the rest of the world. The understanding that we have of the Holocaust is mediated through numerous films and documentaries, and the ghosts of the many fictional accounts of World War II haunt the present writings of Drakulič and Softic as much as do the Holocaust documentaries.

In its opening and final chapters, Drakulič's book is structured through the lens of the Holocaust. She begins the book with a quotation from the Holocaust documentary film *Shoah* and ends it with five chapters that work as a final series, the first of which returns to the opening quotation. From this first chapter of the final series, she moves in the next chapter to a consideration of the Holocaust as an event that marks the ways in which genocide will always—rather than never—happen again while the cultural and social grounds that produce it remain intact. The following two chapters weave events of the war—the sniper murder of two lovers from different ethnic groups (one Muslim and one Serbian) trying to escape Sarajevo, and the destruction of the Old Bridge of Mostar—into metaphors that represent the massive destruction of war as it destroys the mythic foundations upon which cultures and identities depend. From this, Drakulič moves to her final chapter, which is a complex consideration of the way Sarajevo has become for observers the central metaphor of the destructiveness of the war and of the fight between cosmopolitan diversity and murderous fundamentalism. Observer witnessing, finally, is not enough for Drakulič, and in fact can be the worst form of collaboration with murder if it is not combined with action. Thus her testimony ends with a crisis of witnessing not just for herself but for all of the observers, well intentioned or not, of the war in the former Yugoslavia.

The quote from *Shoah* that provides the epigraph to her book is taken from a dialogue between the filmmaker, Claude Lanzmann, and a villager from present-day Treblinka about what it was like to work an agricultural field that bordered the death camp. In response to Lanzmann's question about whether he had been bothered by working within hearing of the screams from the camp, the villager replies, "At first it was unbearable. Then you got used to it." In chapter eighteen, Drakulič returns to this quote and responds: "What had a Pole to do with the fact that Germans were killing Jews? So we all get used to it. I understand now that nothing but this 'otherness' killed Jews, and it began with naming them, by reducing them to the other. Then everything became possible. . . . For Serbians, as for Germans, they are all others, not-us." She goes on to name a continuum of othering and collaboration—for herself, refugees are others, for Europe, it is the Balkans, for the United States, it is a European problem, and so on. She then declares:

> I don't think our responsibility is the same, . . . all I'm saying is that it exists, this complicity: that out of opportunism and fear we are all becoming collaborators or accomplices in the perpetuation of war. For by closing our eyes . . . we are betraying those "others"—and I don't know if there is a way out of it. What we fail to realize is that by such divisions we deceive ourselves too, exposing ourselves to the same possibility of becoming the "others" in a different situation.[11]

The problem for Drakulič is that "our defense is weak" in the face of this "othering" because it is caused by a central crisis of identity formation. How can we constitute ourselves as individuals without recourse to perceiving other people as "other," as separate from ourselves? Yet for her this seems to be the beginning of the slippage that leads to violence. Her answer lies in the form of the book itself: in her embrace of identity and voice as fragmentary and constituted through a diversity of affiliations and experiences and in her call for a continual self-awareness and critique of the ways we are all, as witnesses, implicated in violent acts, even while witnessing is an important first step in resistance.

In the next chapter, she critiques the ways in which witnessing has come to provide the illusion of action when in reality it is the excuse for nonaction. The post-Holocaust credo, "never again," has become perverted through the very mechanisms that were meant to prevent the recurrence of such events. Witnessing is a complex political position, and while for survivors to tell their stories after their return from a death camp or torture chamber is a powerful intervention into the totalitarian discourses that have sought to erase them from the field of discourse as well as the human community, documentary witnessing of an ongoing genocide is not, in and of itself, an interventionist act. Witnessing must be an engaged performative act, rather than a relationship between spectator and object. Drakulič states:

> Day after day, death in Bosnia has been well documented. . . . Fifty years ago this is how the Jews suffered; now it's the Muslims' turn. We remember it all, and because of that memory we have the idea that everything has to be carefully documented . . . generations whose parents swear it could never happen again, at least

not in Europe, precisely because of the living memory of the recent past. What, then, has all the documentation changed? . . .
The biggest change has happened within ourselves: the audience,
spectators. We started to believe this is our role, that it is possible
to play the public, as if war is theater. . . . To watch war from so
near and in its most macabre details makes sense only if we do
so to change things for the better. But today, nothing changes.
Documentation has become a perversion, a pornography of
dying.[12]

The line between spectatorship and voyeurism is very fine, and both
contain an erotic attachment to the object being viewed. Neither the
spectatorial nor the voyeuristic position is one of equitable exchange
between the viewer and the viewed object, and the power of the active
gaze rests with the viewer. Mediated through the technology of the
camera, the murdered, dying, broken bodies become objects of spectatorial interest but they have no power within themselves to demand an
active response from the viewer that would change their status to that
of a person who also holds power and can make demands for equal
footing as an individual with rights. Drakulić calls for a spectatorial position that is self-critical, that can "change things for the better"; otherwise such documentation is a form of complicity that engages the
erotics of murder and warfare and authorizes it to continue in order to
continue the voyeuristic pleasure of the viewer.

Such self-critique, however, is not enough to stop the war. For the
witness to be aware of the perils of witnessing as well as the continuing
imperative to witness leads Drakulić in her final chapter into the danger
of a nihilistic impasse. As a journalist as well as a refugee, she herself is
implicated in complex ways within the discourse of documentation
which she critiques. Recognizing that "[m]y words—any words—have
no real meaning," she confronts the crisis of language that all testimonial must ultimately confront. Faced with silence as the only other option when recognizing the inadequacy of language, witnessing must
necessarily perform this crisis and inadequacy as part of the testimonial
process. With her statement that "[f]inally, all we have achieved with
words is to establish Sarajevo as a metaphor for tragedy," the impo-
tence of language to effect change overwhelms the end of her text.

Language and witnessing are bound up in her text with the position
of Sarajevo as the metaphor for cosmopolitan culture, and ultimately all
are lost in the face of the relentless onslaught of nature. Winter, with

the specter of death brought on by starvation and cold, defeats her words and is itself a metaphor for the triumph of the "primitive" erotics of warfare and genocide over the "civilized" cosmopolitanism of language and culture. She is herself caught between positions of guilt and shame and cannot engage with the witnesses her text presents in an ethical performance. Instead she maintains a journalistic distance, which views the human body as an "authentic" ground of a truth that cannot be conveyed and mistakes critique for engagement. Such an ending to her testimony performs the crisis of witnessing, but her text also remains resistant to the extent that it has been written and published. It remains an act of memorial and of witnessing that contains in its form as well as its content possibilities for resistance to hegemonic discourses of otherness and violence.

Softic's testimony contains very similar concerns over language, witnessing, and the documenting of the war. In reflecting upon her reasons for becoming a teacher when she was drawn to becoming a war correspondent, she states that teaching held for her the promise of creation as opposed to the ethically compromised position of the war correspondent who searches out and documents slaughters to which she or he has no connection. The crisis of language is just as present for Softic as it is for Drakulić and other testimonial authors. Her text embraces the paradox of the inadequacy of language to convey such trauma while recognizing it as the only vehicle for doing so. She writes:

> I'm sharing with you all these wearisome and perhaps unedifying reflections in order to convince you that this is not the materialization of my despair or my bitterness. This is my need to recapitulate my wartime experience, and for that I require a listener, not a conversational partner, just a listener. For you and I cannot discuss this war. Nowadays we inhabit different worlds, you and I. We do not understand each other and in certain matters we will not only never understand each other, but there will also be times when we won't be able to communicate at all because we will be speaking different languages. Nevertheless, that does not diminish my need and my duty to tell you something about this war.[13]

Softic recognizes both the importance of language and witnessing and the inability of someone outside her experience to understand what she is saying. This incommensurability of experience between herself and the reader who is "outside" is both unbridgeable and yet necessary to cross for the act of witnessing—a need and a duty—to occur. Witnessing needs an engaged spectator, a "listener," for the act to occur, and as much as Drakulić is skeptical of the spectatorial position, Softic acknowledges its importance to the performance of witnessing. The understanding is by necessity fragmentary and incomplete, but this is itself integral to the act of testimony, as it refutes the possibility of building complete narratives and solid truths through which readers can integrate such traumatic experiences into their own historical narratives.

Both Softic and Drakulić are aware of the ways in which they themselves are prey to hegemonic ethnic and nationalist discourses and sometimes take refuge in the very universalism they critique. This universalism, however, moves quickly toward an embrace of the ways in which identity is discontinuous and fragmented, rather than consistent, as the best ground from which to speak and understand their situation. Thus Drakulić mourns the loss of coherent identity—of the fiction of the cohesive self—in a chapter that moves from her feelings of separation as an exile in Paris in December of 1991, to her retreat into the most basic recognition of all bodies of persons as human, to a loss of recognition of a familiarity with her own body.

The passage begins with Drakulić's recognition of the vast gulf of present experience that separates her from the people outside the war zone—in the normative world—who have not experienced the physical and psychic traumas enacted by the war; traumas that she does not recognize herself until she is confronted with the normative world:

> It seemed to me I was almost floating, not touching the pavement, not touching reality; as if between me and Paris there stretched an invisible wire fence through which I could see everything but touch and taste nothing—the wire that could not be removed from my field of vision and that kept me imprisoned in the world from which I had just arrived. And in that world things, words and time are arranged in a different way. Anything at all would take me back: the bitterness of my coffee, a sort of reluctance to move, a glimpse of shoes in a shop window and then instantly a feeling of futility, remoteness, not belonging. In a Europe ablaze with bright lights getting ready for Christmas I was separated from Paris by a thin line of blood: that and the fact that I could see it, while Paris stubbornly refused to.[14]

The experience of war is carried within her beyond the war zone. It enacts an alienation from the facades and rituals of cosmopolitan and intellectual life. Because in the world of war, "things, words and time are arranged in a different way," Drakulić cannot bring with her into the normative world the language of her experience. A gap exists between the memory of her experiences and the language through which she can express those experiences. Instead it is sensory experience that keeps her trapped in the alienating loop of memory. The experience of her body overrides that of her intellect; she cannot bridge the gap, but in recognizing it, she can attempt to suture over the chasm—recognizing in herself the role of witness. It is not just the fact of her alienation that is important—her separation from the normative world "by a thin line of blood"—but the fact that she sees and recognizes the importance of her role as witness as the cause of her alienation, while the other potential witnesses and actors around her "stubbornly" refuse to do so. As with so much testimonial literature, a central crisis of Drakulić's experience is the crisis of language to convey what seems so unreal, even to her. As Delbo, Buber-Neumann, and Partnoy all articulate, there is a profound silence that structures their testimonial witnessing. Despite the need to speak, to remember, and to witness, they are paradoxically aware always of the ways language and representation fail them—even in their memories of their own experiences.

It is the visual that crystallizes this crises over language and, by extension, over identity for Drakulić. Seeing a picture of a dead family beside a destroyed house in the newspaper, she represses it, only to have it return to her memory, floating up through her consciousness, when a cut on her finger she had thought closed comes open again, spilling blood into her bath water. It is not just the return of the repressed, the fear of death, that this moment enacts for her, but the destruction of her own fiction of coherent identity. This is the wound that comes unsutured, bleeding into the present reality of her physical comfort and safety in Paris. In the face of the terror of such a wound, such fragmentation, the imperative to witness, to give voice to the dead and to the "blood" that Paris "stubbornly refuses to see," becomes crucial. Remembering the picture, she realizes:

> Their smashed skulls canceled out my own effort to live. The naked brain on the grass is no longer death, horror, war—it eludes any explanation or justification, it makes no sense at all. You ask yourself how it is possible to live in a place where things like that are happening. I know I should have asked myself at this point whether the murdered people were Croats or Serbs and who killed them; perhaps I should have felt rage or a desire for re-

venge. But as I gazed at the dark gaping hole, at the blood-caked pulp, I only felt an unspeakable revulsion towards humankind. The naked brain is stronger than such questions, it is the evidence that we are all potential criminals, that we don't know each other really and that from now on, if we survive at all, we shall have to live in mortal fear of each other, forever and ever. The naked brain crushes, obliterates us, pulls us down into the darkness, takes away our right to speak about love, morality, ideas, politics, to speak at all. In the face of the picture of a naked brain all human values are simply reduced to nothing.[15]

It is not revulsion at the sight of a head split open with brains spilling out that appalls Drakulič. What she experiences is the death of "human values" at the sight of the violent death marked by the bodies of this couple. She is unable to take recourse in the national and ethnic identity constitutions that would enable her to distance herself from these bodies by labeling them as "like herself" or "other/enemy," thus allowing her to participate in discourses of "rage, or the desire for revenge." Her language here reads as slightly disingenuous precisely because she takes refuge in the universalist identity of human as an alternative to the identities that are proffered by the material conditions of her life and the context of the photograph. The materiality of the brain, as the basic substance that weds the body and the self to make a person, disrupts all other identity formations for Drakulič. This overly "civilized" response by Drakulič to the "naked brain" is, however, symptomatic of the trauma to her own identity that has been enacted by her experiences of the war and that has surfaced at the sight of the photograph.

Following on from this passage, Drakulič herself becomes aware of the rupture this has enacted on her identity. Overcome with a feeling that her body has suddenly become alien to her, she states:

It must have been a momentary death of sorts, a revulsion, a recoiling from the body I could no longer feel as mine. . . . I squeezed the cut on my finger as if trying to prove to myself I was still alive. . . . This body was no longer mine. It had been taken over by something else, taken over by the war. I had thought that the death of the body was the worst thing that could happen in war; I didn't know that worse was the separation of self from the body, the numbness of the inner being, extinction before death, pain before pain.[16]

This moment of misrecognition, of the recognition that the body one sees in the mirror or in front of one's eyes in the bath is not the body one had always assumed one saw and has taken for granted but is instead alien, seemingly an other even to the self contained within the body, is a crisis of identity enacted in most testimonial literature by survivors of trauma. It is both a moment that crystallizes for the survivor the absolute separation between the world of the war/concentration camp/torture chamber and the world of normative society and a moment that enacts the crisis of language that is the crisis at the heart of testimonial literature.

Language will never be able to bridge the separation represented through the incommensurability of these two bodies that must—to maintain the fiction of coherent identity crucial for the construction of the self—occupy the same space at the same time and yet can never do so. This realization is the "momentary death," the "extinction before death, pain before pain" that Drakulić experiences. Like Delbo and Partnoy, Drakulić sutures over the wound exposed through this moment with the imperative to witness. As she states in her introduction, "as the war came closer the urge to write about it and nothing else grew stronger and stronger. I ended up writing a book because, in spite of everything, I still believe in the power of words, in the necessity of communication. This is the only thing I know I believe in now." Although her text compulsively documents the way in which the experiences of war overtake "the inner self until one can scarcely recognize oneself any longer,"[17] this loss of recognition results for Drakulić in the need to witness both the process itself and the lives and deaths of others with whom she has come into contact. Her double remove in these passages enhances her sense of spectatorship and distance. She is neither within the war nor outside of it, viewing photos in Paris yet reliving her own memories. And, indeed, the chapter "Paris-Vukovar," from which I quote extensively above, occurs toward the beginning of her text as the seventh of twenty-two chapters.

Elma Softic also writes of experiencing such a disruption of identity, except that hers, unlike Drakulić's, occurs while she is still an "inmate" of Sarajevo. She writes of watching the television and seeing:

Beneath the azure sky of Barcelona—the Olympics. The twenty-fifth in the series began the twenty-fifth of July, 1992. I don't know how it came about, but we had electricity and we managed to watch the opening ceremonies. All those people in the audience seemed to me to come from another planet. The first reaction I had, when I saw the packed stadium, was dread, because it occurred to me—what if a shell lands! And once this ghastly anxiety lodged itself within me at the first sight of the stadium, there was no longer anything that could drive it out of me. Not the whole beautiful, fashionable, joyous and contented crowd. Not the overjoyed participants in their colourful uniforms, not the glamorous performance, not the spectacular divas singing arias from popular operas.

And here: death, starvation, horror. Yes, once upon a time there were Olympics in Sarajevo.[18]

One of the things that marks the horror of this war for Softic is not just the yawning gulf that separates her within the war from the normative world of nonwar but also the bizarre proximity of these two worlds. Through the technology of telecommunications—satellites, CNN, the Internet, and so on—not only does the outside world have unprecedented access to the intimate daily details of the carnage, but the people trapped within the war have the possibility of viewing both the gross detail of the destruction as they themselves are experiencing it and the simultaneous world of experience outside the boundaries of the war zone, where life is continuing on in the most normative way as though the horrors and traumas suffered by the people within the war were indeed happening on another planet. The fabric that separates her world from that of the Olympics is so thin to Softic that she is unable to believe emotionally that those people she sees on television are not in danger of a shell falling on them.

At this moment, as she forcefully realizes the absolute incommensurability of experience that separates her from the world in which the Olympics is taking place, the similarities, not the differences between the two worlds, cause a break with her identity to occur. Such a tactic recalls Drakulič's use of the metaphor of the "thin line of blood" as all that separates her from Paris, as well as echoing the profound feeling of unreality occasioned by Drakulič's realization that the normative world is both always within sight and yet completely unattainable. While toward the end of her text Softic will state that "I myself have changed so much that in the autobiographical film which was playing in my mind I had the greatest difficulty recognizing myself,"[19] here she already feels that "all those people in the audience seemed to me to come from another planet."

It is not Softic who is the alien, but all of us, the inhabitants of the world outside the circle of traumatic experience. Our world is built on fictions of stability, boundaries, and narrative coherence, the promise of which has so disastrously been proved false for Softic. By the end of her text she has become almost unrecognizable even to herself when she attempts to see herself within a narrative spectrum, the "autobiographical film." Mediated by the televisual, with her witnessing memory stretched across a media simulacrum, she writes her experiences, choosing written and published materiality over digital or filmic representation.

The Holocaust also haunts Softic's text, as it does Drakulić's. For Softic, the Holocaust is composed of memories, documentary knowledge, and the media representations that resonate through European and American culture. The experiences she has of Sarajevo under siege—a "giant concentration camp"—are haunted by the images she has seen of World War II. Thus she writes that, "In the Jewish Community Centre, bedlam. People have been coming to see whether they're on the departure list. It's a scene out of a movie: Paris, World War II, the Germans at the city gates, shadowy corridors and stairways packed with desperate people waiting for a visa to Lisbon or to who knows what more fortunate destination. That's how it was in the centre."[20]

The difficult conjunction of her perceived reality and the reality that is presented through media such as news broadcasts and film permeates Softic's text and provides opportunities for her to destabilize and reread seemingly fixed or coherent narratives. Thus the powerful image of bombs falling over the Olympic stadium at Barcelona and the lines of desperate people in Sarajevo seen as the desperate and doomed Jewish populations of World War II are powerful metaphors for the inability of narrative temporally to contain moments of history. At the same time as satellite hookups provide the possibility for the citizens of Sarajevo simultaneously to watch the siege that they are experiencing on their televisions sets (when the electricity is working), media representations of past events such as the Holocaust provide powerful moments of cultural déjà vu. The testimonial of Softic's text becomes not just a testimonial of her experiences in Sarajevo but a fragmentary witnessing to visions of past and possible future wars and genocides. This widens the spectrum of implication for the readers of her text, as they are witness not just to her testimony but to past genocide and the threat of future violences that could engulf them.

Both Softic and Drakulić figure their testimony as a form of resistance to the "normalization" of war, which is also the retreat into nationalism exemplified by this war. They oppose the totalitarian discourses of nationalism with a discourse of cosmopolitanism, exemplified by the metaphor of Sarajevo, which values diversity and difference as hallmarks of humanity and civilization over the "primitive" and "regressive" consolidations of nationalism. Softic writes: "Nationalism is the most serious form of disturbance of the consciousness of values. The person who is happy and content only when he lives in a ghetto where everyone is the same, . . . that person is definitively lost to culture and civilization, to the world and the future—in a word, to humanity. . . . What's happened to my, *my* Sarajevo?"[21] She opposes not just the nationalism of the Serbs but the nationalisms that the people within Sarajevo are falling into as well under the pressure of the war. For Softic, to participate in nationalist discourse is to stop participating in the human race. While she opposes the consolidation of sameness constructed through nationalism, she offers a universal sameness of humanity founded on the recognition and enjoyment of differences.

Drakuliç also writes against the sameness of nationalism. She declares:

the war is . . . reducing us to one dimension: the Nation. The trouble with this nationhood, however, is that whereas before, I was defined by my education, my job, my ideas, my character—and, yes, my nationality too—now I feel stripped of all that. I am nobody because I am not a person any more. I am one of 4.5 million Croats. . . . Just as in the days of brotherhood-unity, there is now another ideology holding people together, the ideology of nationhood.[22]

For Drakuliç, to lose one's differences from other people is to no longer be a person or, as Softic figures it, a member of "humanity." By writing her testimony, Drakuliç asserts her own individuality in the face of this hegemonic nationalism while at the same time speaking for those other people who can no longer speak for themselves. Although it is impossible for her to place herself outside the ideology of nationalism that has engulfed her, she can resist it through her text, especially in her embrace of fragmentary as opposed to cohesive formations of identity.

Toward a Testimonial of Instability

Softic and Drakuliç, like Delbo, Buber-Neumann, Partnoy, and Gambaro, refuse the stabilizing (authenticating) moves both that autobiography claims and that international agencies such as Amnesty International rely on when they use testimonial as an interventionist tool. These authors posit survival as much in accepting and balancing discontinuity as in rebuilding a continuous identity and narrative history.[23] The survivors insist again and again on the actuality of their experience while at the same time insisting upon its phantasmic nature, so that they themselves are no longer sure what was real and what was not. For these women, however, this very inability to tell the difference is somehow the essence of their experience. But rather than erasing the experience from history (as fascism hopes to do) they reclaim this instability as the "truth" of their experience.

As John Beverley notes in his work to define testimonial as an emergent, antiliterary form of textual communication, the testimonial dislodges the "I" of the narrator from that of the traditional author, so that, rather than the individual, "unique" voice of autobiography, the testimonial posits the narrator's experience and story as not unique but instead one that stands in for the experiences of all members of the community for whom she or he is speaking.[24] Works like Partnoy's *The Little School* and Gambaro's *Information for Foreigners* embody this within their textual/performative form.

This refusal of the authenticating "I," although they recognize the importance of its juridical usage for the furthering of human rights (for example, Partnoy's testifying before the Argentina Commission for the Investigation of Disappearance, the United Nations, and other international bodies), is a radical move that is due in part to their "already Other" gender positioning as women. They recognize that the urge toward continuity and fixed histories is also always an urge toward consolidation that can and has lead to the oppressive structures of nationalism, patriarchy, and fascist totalitarianism as well as human rights and interventionist discourses. As such, like Holocaust authors Charlotte Delbo and Margarete Buber-Neumann, they focus on the collectivity of experience, and their texts embody fragmentation, multiple narrative voices, and a collage of genres to resist the monolithic "official story" of the state.

While testimonials call on the carpet the ethical bankruptcy of humanist ideals and the engines of international enforcement of human rights law, at the same time they refuse to let go of the belief in the necessity for just such an international, cosmopolitan community that has let them down. Thus these testimonials, like the testimonials from other genocides and armed struggles in the past, both resist the totalizing, dehumanizing, authoritarian discourses through which the abuse suffered by the authors occurred while at the same time recognizing the need for a voice and presence within the very systems of the law and culture that have let them down. Unlike previous testimonials, however, testimonials such as Elma Softic's and Slavenka Drakulič's can take place from "within the event itself," as Dori Laub constructs it. As well as the difference in scope (which is obviously the overriding factor) between the Holocaust and the war in former Yugoslavia, mass-media technology makes possible an unprecedented perspective for the people trapped and trying to survive within the event. They can theoretically witness their own destruction over CNN on a television monitor as it occurs. This duality of perspective both breaks and reinforces the field of the "concentrationary" perspective.

Testimonial literature is both a contested term and an emerging genre. Softic and Drakulič are not survivors of the most immediate and extreme attack on their bodies that internment in a death camp or torture signifies. Nor are they writing as representatives of an indigenous community, telling a transcribed story of resistance through a "First World" translator, as is Rigoberta Menchú. Instead they are writing both from within the war and from a position where their writings are read by outsiders to the event while they themselves are still experiencing it. This creates the opportunity for them, as it did for Menchú, possibly to help to intervene into the ongoing event by organizing resistance to it in the countries where people will be reading their work. Their work is testimonial not just to the extent that it testifies to and translates experiences of collective suffering but also in the way that it resists the fixing of experience and identity into one narrative truth. By employing a discourse of "cosmopolitanism" to oppose discourses of nationalism and by telling stories of the many ways community affiliations are formed that resist such monolithic formations of identity, they open up possibilities for interventions into the universalizing discourses of human rights.

In dialogue with their audience and readers, these works bring a critique of the modern political field along with their vision of individual survival, spectatorship, and aesthetic forms. Following on this (already laid) groundwork, the testimonial form chosen by Softic and Drakulič is relentlessly self-critical and suspicious of any recourse to discourses of community that rely on cohesive-seeming formations of ethnic, national, or religious identity. Instead they employ a discourse of cosmopolitanism that lays claim to a human universality that paradoxically resides in the appreciation for and acceptance of differences. Such a conception of universality could provide the possibility for a different and perhaps more effective form of human rights discourse that is not founded on the universal sameness of all bodies.

6

Grounded Ethics: Testimonial Witnessing from Rural Afghanistan to the United States

> [T]he task is to operationalise cosmopolitan democracy. This is the idea which at the present stage of history is best calculated to produce a politics of true universalism—an inclusive multicommunity "multilogue," aimed as standard-setting in ways that will reduce human wrongs, and balance a tolerance of diversity with a diversity of tolerance.[1]

Center Field

I spent the academic year of 2000 to 2001 in Pakistan and Afghanistan doing initial research for a project on Afghan women and the international aid industry, returning to Washington, D.C., two weeks before the terrorist attacks of September 11, 2001. During that time, I also worked on several projects for the United Nations as a consultant specializing in gender, education, and human rights abuse. As part of one project, I conducted one hundred detailed interviews with displaced Afghan women and their families in the isolated northern province of Badakhshan on the subjects of both human rights abuses and war crimes they had suffered and witnessed during the recent fighting and the general human rights deficit they suffer as a result of over twenty years of ongoing warfare in their country. In undertaking such projects, I participated in the structure of international aid and engagement—an uneasy and impossible combination of vast sums of money, political maneuvering by self-interested governments, and activities by some committed humanitarian and human rights workers and many careerist bureaucrats.

The information and research under consideration in this chapter are based largely on the extensive research I conducted into the basic infrastructure of women's and girls' health, education, and development in the country, as well as the testimonials I collected during my trip to Badakhshan in October 2000. The multiple demands of conducting interviews such as these—from issues such as translation and cultural difference to the difficulties of collecting factually solid testimony under conditions of extreme duress for the witnesses—are crucial to the human rights and witnessing project of testimonial. What follows in this chapter is a reading of the complications that these various demands on the production of testimonial create both for the practice of ethical witnessing and for the terms "human" and "human rights" as I have developed them in the previous chapters.

From the center to the field, a movement many Americans would associate more with the terms of baseball than the trajectory of an international aid worker, denotes in both cases the basic structure in and through which certain forms of work and play take place. This discourse and figuration of a center from which players move across and through a field, carrying with it the whiff of the trained expert and anthropology—the scientific study of the other—increasingly describes the movement of well-educated and trained elites, based in New York or major European cities, into zones of almost indescribable devastation. This is generally an orderly enterprise, one played by an elaborate set of rules, guarded by massive bureaucracy, and of both crucial and highly questionable value. One of the questions I want to pose, then, has to do with the different arrangements for thinking of these relationships that may have occurred following this extended moment, beginning on September 11 of 2001 (or maybe a few days before) when the center literally became the field and the two overlapped (for Americans) for an extended period of weeks.

The "sport" of war, increasingly in the twentieth century and following us into the twenty-first, involves targeting groups of civilians for terror, mutilation, mass murder, and genocide. Over and over, we experience the most "civilized" of countries willing to engage in activities that undermine civil society and the rule of law—from genocide to the disregard of basic human rights and the Geneva conventions—when mobs or the state judge it to be in their best interests. The spectatorship of this sport of war—for example, from our watching the violence of mobs of Rwandan genocide perpetrators, to the mobs themselves that formed from listening to the exculpatory and inflammatory radio broadcasts, to the power-hungry officials who instigated the genocide—is a source of complex fascination for those of us who can watch from a distance as well as a site of amplification and even validation for perpetrators.

Communitarian identities, like those forming from the horrific footage of carnage in Palestine and terrorist attacks against civilians in countries such as Israel and the United States, are facilitated and mobilized partly through spectacles of massive violence that we, as global viewers with singularly local physicalities and communities, feel hyperaware of yet powerless to intervene into. Such disenfranchised yet emotively overattached spectatorship is crucial to the way the cannibalistic sport of war and atrocity is increasingly played as it mobilizes audiences and actors.

The meaning of such spectatorship and the hyperviolent actions it calls forth on the part of players facilitated through a converse amount of disengaged passivity on the part of viewers call into question our shared understanding of terms such as "civilized," "human," "responsibility," and "resistance." Civilization—to be civilized, to act with civility toward others—is dramatically undermined by the murderous incivility of atrocities committed by both state and individual actors around the globe as well as by the unwillingness of people both locally and globally to intervene into them. The voices of survivors throughout this book and in this chapter, however, suggest a redefinition of these terms in ways that demand we counter such spectatorial pleasures in ourselves and others. Through the ground of their own very particular experiences, these survivors suggest reconfigurations of these terms that counter the prevailing discourses.

Resistance is sometimes as basic and unglamorous as sharing a scarce resource, thus facilitating another's survival, and to be human is to facilitate actively the living rather than the dying of others. Civilization, many of these testimonials suggest, is not just the political and social frameworks that have lead us to the current impasse between state sovereignty and mass atrocity and death but is also the responsibility of engaged individuals who recognize that responsibility is defined by a set of behaviors that facilitate the always already state of becoming human.

Following these survivors, I want to suggest that we have an ethical obligation to the witnessing of violence that directly countermands the easy spectatorial engagements of mass media. When we consider the ethics of witnessing, we must move from the ground of the theoretical to the ground of the material—and the body of the survivor of atrocity bridges this movement. Ground Zero, as the September 11, 2001, site of the destruction of the World Trade Center in New York has come to be called, was shocking largely for its lack of survivors, but even events of atrocity that leave many survivors are shocking for the way in which the survivors quickly become living ghosts—disenfranchised—the over-determined mark of the traumatic event whose voice and body speak a moment of history that has been left behind and superseded.

The performative act of witnessing is itself an ethical endeavor and requires accountability from not just the witness/survivor but also the witness/spectator. Spectatorship, with its echoes of theatrical meta-phors (theater of war, fourth-wall realism, actors) may engage our emo-tions, even our guilt, but as Brecht and many before and after him have illustrated, it does not impel us toward intervention. News broadcasts, for example the video sound bites of CNN, do not encourage specta-tors to feel implicated in the various acts of violence being presented from around the globe; instead they encourage the spectator to feel overwhelmed by the volume of events happening far beyond one's sphere of living and experience and thus impotent to intervene into situations that seem so massive and so removed, as though they are happening in another world.[2] While we might feel guilt over our inac-tion in the face of atrocity, the guilt itself amplifies and reinforces our inaction. Testimony, however, requiring a difficult and more active en-gagement—witnessing rather than spectatorship—works to (re)build structures of responsibility and ethics.

As I collected the testimony under consideration in this chapter, my roles moved between those of spectator, "objective" collector, and wit-ness, depending on the fluctuating circumstances of my context. In meetings with local authorities and with internally displaced people I was interviewing, I was aware of the ways in which my position shifted between spectator and witness in a complex dynamic based not only on my own reactions to the situation but also on theirs to me. One proba-bly cannot and should not always claim or try to witness. But the major-ity of us happily live our lives as largely disenfranchised spectators who are very rarely mobilized as witnesses. For those of us living in the United States, this spectatorial position is aided and encouraged by the local social and political ideologies we live within as well as by our par-ticipation in consumer media culture.

We will not occupy an ethical position in relationship to others until we are able to recognize the other and engage with them even when they most terrify us—as reminders of the atrocity, mass death, and violence with which we are surrounded, within which many of us live, for which we are all partially responsible, and from which many of us will die. Witnessing the witness to atrocity is one avenue through which we can begin to build the ethical communities that are likely necessary to our global survival.

Ethics in the Field?

> An address is always singular, idiomatic, and justice as law (droit), seems always to suppose the generality of a rule, a norm or a universal imperative.[3]

In trying to puzzle out some of the problems and connections raised by my previous distinction between center, field, and ground, I want to move from talking about our role as spectators and participants at the "center" to talking about the "field" with a consideration of conditions in Afghanistan during the time the testimony I am considering was collected. Written testimony published for an international audience as a literary form to be read or a dramatic form to be produced is surely the elite strata of testimonial practice. The vast majority of survivors who have suffered human rights abuses, war crimes, or other forms of massive violence never have an opportunity to testify—beyond perhaps the confines of their family, social group, or local rehabilitation programs through storytelling. Especially women and men who have suffered the sexual violence that is endemic in situations of mass violence are often unable to speak of the experience for fear of social or community ostracization or even death. The oral testimonies collected by human rights workers, therapists, oral historians, and others, then, occupy an important intermediary position in this hierarchy.

Unpublished, often confidential, and sometimes given in transcribed written form to the survivor, such testimony makes small but important inroads into the communities of people who have survived mass violence. The written testimony discussed in previous chapters does give an important voice to some of these communities, but it is often a single voice standing in for tens, if not hundreds, of thousands. As an example, during the fall of 2000, when I was collecting the testimony under consideration in this chapter, there were an estimated eighty thousand internally displaced people in the province of Badakhshan, at least 80 percent of whom were illiterate. I was the only person in the province collecting testimonies at this time, and I spoke to just over one hundred people. There were no trauma recovery programs being run, either in Afghanistan or in the neighboring countries, by the international community (or the local nongovernmental organizations [NGOs] that I could find evidence of) and no plans to begin any.

The problem of trauma from such an entrenched conflict after twenty-five years of ongoing warfare was, as one World Health Organization (WHO) official explained to me, seen by the international organizations as such a massive task as to be insurmountable. Therefore, except for some limited trauma counseling for victims of land mines, there were no plans to begin what is surely a crucial aspect of the development of the civil society necessary for the rehabilitation of the country. In this chapter, then, I want to consider the voices of survivors who have been multiply disenfranchised of their living witnessing and the difficulties for testimony and witnessing that such testimonial collection raises. Because the testimonials I collected were confidential and because the various stages of their translation make the written English text of the testimonials a document that should make no claims to final authority, I do not quote from the testimonials directly in this chapter.

As suggested by the survivor testimonial considered in the previous chapters, witnessing carries within the act itself an ethical imperative. It is a performative act that requires care and self-consciousness on the part of the interviewer—an awareness of his or her own role in the testimonial process—and a humane engagement with the act of testimony itself. Testimony and witnessing are foundationally communal acts, taking place within and an integral aspect of communal situations, but they are also juridical acts, requiring the assumption of a distinct individual subject who can swear, under oath perhaps, that the witnessing story he or she tells is a true and authentic history. As I have argued, many written testimonial texts by survivors of mass atrocities (such as the Holocaust, state torture in Latin America, and the genocide in former Yugoslavia) employ a fractured testimonial voice that insists both on the distinct individuality of the witnessing voice and at the same time on the always already fragmented identity of the survivor, thus complicating the notion of the universal subject of human rights upon which juridical categories depend.

Oral testimony such as I collected in Badakhshan, however, carries with it an even higher burden of "authenticity." Such testimony is both the rawest material from which human rights abuse allegations are formulated and the least regarded aspect of the process. The various pathways though which the story of the experience is told—from the possible trauma of the experience itself and the meandering ways of memory to the interaction between the translator, the interviewer, and the other community members present—result in a wholly fragmented text that is then reassembled in narrative form for transcription. This produces both a stable and "authentic" record of testimony and a text that is always considered tainted, unstable, and incomplete from the juridical and sometimes the historical standpoint. The witnesses both to the acts themselves and to the testimony thus become crucial links in the reformulation of the universalized subject of human rights.

All subjects engaged in the act of witnessing are altered through its dynamic. However, to what extent can and should our understanding of categories such as "human" and "rights" be understood to be altered by the accretion of acts of testimonial upon the authentic historical structures of knowing foundational to our cultures?

Authors such as Charlotte Delbo and Alicia Partnoy suggest that through the memory of the survivor of extreme violence, the humanity of the victims and survivors of such violence can be reconstituted through ethically engaged witnessing. This memorial process, understood as a testimonial act, takes many forms—drama, poetry, written narrative, videotaped testimony, filmic documentary, and many others. But in the current proliferation of academic work addressing the areas of trauma, testimony, and witnessing, one assumption that goes largely unremarked is that of the transparency of the translation of the witnessing, whether from author to text, from text to reader, or from speaker to receiver. The assumption of trauma within testimonial witnessing directs us toward the unstable and unknowable aspects of the experience and historical knowledge being relayed, as I myself have argued in the previous chapters. But nonetheless, the nature of language itself, whether written or spoken/performed, lulls us into the promise of knowability. By acknowledging the unknowable, offstage, unseen, we stabilize the knowability of the testimonial narrative itself. And while the authors and speakers themselves might call attention to this very function of (un)knowability—that their own witnessing is predicated on a survivor's memory that is always both sure and unsure of the specificities of experience and the paradox of surviving the unsurvivable—the process of translation itself is not called into question.

As producers of testimonial texts, authors must struggle with the process of translating experience into written language. But while the experience of translation itself is sometimes addressed—for example, in Holocaust testimonies that address the babel of languages in the camps and their relation to people's experiences of the camps—the authors do not and probably cannot address the translation of their written text into other languages or into the readers' worlds. Filmic texts such as *Shoah* perform translation on screen, staging it for the audience without directly addressing its complexities; academic work on testimony applies critical reading practices to written texts, and the theoretical literature on trauma, often based on the oral exchanges of the therapeutic encounter, relies on exchanges between speakers with fluency in the same language. Oral historians, on the other hand, attempt to mark each moment of verbal exchange—including the pauses and verbal mannerisms that frame and compose speech—in the written transcripts of their interviews. Fixing the gaps and mistakes of speech into legibility in this way both insures as much as possible the veracity of the written transcription and elides any continuing anxiety that might be present on anybody's part as to the deviation of the written from the spoken testimony.

These various approaches to collecting, analyzing, and performing testimony all rely on the "knowability," if not transparency, of what is being said: plain language conveying "the truth" of horrific experience is one of the authenticating aspects of testimonial in whatever form. Largely for this reason, the literary devices of written testimony (metaphor, allusion, dialogue, etc.), testimony's performative elements, and the elisions of trauma make many spectators and witnesses to testimony uncomfortable. These literary devices seem to contravene and destabilize the authenticity of the bodily experience being recounted through the embodied vehicles of text and speech. Our investments in the authenticity of the experiences being recounted rest in the authenticity of the bodily experience of abuse, and the bridge between the historical experience of abuse (which, as trauma studies show us, is never fully historical) and the current testimony to the abuse is the survivor's body.

That this body might not be an open avenue to the past but instead a winding, overgrown path full of many branches and turnings—that memory changes over time, individuals (both speaker and listener) are self-interested no matter what their intentions, or language is always an imprecise means of communication—is both a fundamental element of academic and practitioner work with testimony and what our very means of addressing it tends to elide. Translation, then, in all the avenues through which it takes place, is one of the central problematics for testimony and, by extension, for the study of trauma, human rights abuse, and the development of civil society.

For human rights work especially, the veracity of testimony must be as unimpeachable as possible. The "truth" of the human rights violation resides not just in the testimony of survivors but in evidence, such as actual bodies/corpses/wounds, other witnesses' accounts, material evidence in the form of perpetrator documentation, "neutral" third-party accounts (journalists, doctors, aid workers, etc.), and other corroborating sources. Testimony alone is not enough, although it often serves as the initial evidence of the abuse to be investigated. Not just culturally, then, as I have outlined in previous chapters, but also juridically, the body of the victim/survivor becomes the overdetermined "proof" of the truth of the testimony.

This connection between testimony and an absolute truth of bodily experience bears an unfortunate connection to the traditional logic of torture. As Page duBois has rigorously documented, in ancient Greek culture torture itself originated in and constructed the idea that a fundamental, pure "truth" resides in the body and can be accessed if enough pressure (in the form of intense pain) is placed on the body—and by extension the consciousness—of the person believed to be in possession of this truth.[4] The embodied witness of testimony thus risks reproducing the same logic if the testimony emphasizes truth as it resides in the body.

However, the testimony under consideration in this book instead emphasizes the truth of a witnessing that arises from a dynamic interplay of sight, bodily experience, memory, and consciousness; "filtered" through the demand of the recognition of the human (which both the survivor witness and the spectator witness must accept for the witnessing to become testimony), these survivors testify to the embodied experience that truth does not reside in the body but in the interplay of consciousness and communal networks. The emphasis on networks of support and responsibility that provide locations for "the human" even under conditions of extreme physical and emotional distress is more than what might be understood as a survivor's attempt to recuperate in memory some aspect of an annihilating experience of atrocity or to overcome "survivor guilt." Such emphasis is a crucial aspect of building an ethical human community defined not by sentimentality and guilt but by empathy and by responsibility for violence and toward those affected by it.

Although I locate this move in testimony from a range of cultures and historical experiences from the Holocaust to rural Afghanistan, I do not claim that these survivors are making any conscious attempt to build a universal ethical community of experience. But what they are doing is to reach out through their witness beyond the boundaries of the communities and identities within which they exist toward a more global community of witness, responsibility, and intervention.

In this chapter, I consider the ways that the Afghan women and men interviewed clearly understand themselves to be humans with rights— the "universal" concept—yet also very particularized subjects with a specific localized cultural embeddedness. Such particularized understandings of human rights allow us to consider ways these rights, as a universal discourse, might be applicable to all humans while retaining the flexibility to encompass difference. As Ken Booth has argued, universality of rights does not necessarily entail sameness and can encompass global ethical communities of individuals who share particular affiliational bonds. Noting that "universal human rights are supposed to be invalid because there is no universal ethical community," Booth argues that there is "the ethical community of oppressed women; the ethical community of under-classes; the ethical community of those suffering from racial prejudice; the ethical community of prisoners of conscience; the universal ethical community of the hungry . . . and on and on. Universal human rights are solidly embedded in multiple networks of cross-cutting universal ethical communities."[5]

The Afghans I interviewed consistently articulated themselves to be members of a human community that entitled them to protection. Their appeal seemed to be largely in the context of an "ethics of care," although they themselves did not articulate the concept in this way. Because of their limited (if only apocryphal) contact with the international community—in the form of aid workers, tourists (in the past), merchants, journalists, and even soldiers—they had a perspective of the world as a global community whose members had responsibilities toward each other. The people I was interviewing were almost entirely rural, and most were women. They did not live with electricity (hence had no television), most were illiterate, and they did not have access to elite circles of politics or business, yet they knew and understood that there were states and world bodies (the United Nations) whose responsibility was to protect them as much as possible when they became disenfranchised by war or other disasters.

I am not claiming that the people I interviewed were idealistic (they were the opposite), but they were clearly articulating themselves as humans in the sense that I am deploying the term here. They defined themselves as part of a global community of members who maintain an ethical responsibility toward each other while respecting the rights of the other's cultural and other differences. For the most destitute of people in one of the world's most isolated areas to understand themselves in this fashion is surely of tremendous importance to the emerging understanding and struggle over the definition and role of human rights in global culture.

Rather than viewing human rights as a discourse of elites (and even "Western" elites, as the charge is sometimes leveled) and echoing a similarity of articulation to the characters in the Holocaust testimonies considered in chapter three, these people deployed a definition of human defined partly by their experiences of violence and atrocity. In a certain basic way, they were articulating that to be human is to care for others; to be inhuman is to violate them. As Booth notes, "What finally binds all this together and gives a firm anchorage for universal human rights is the universality of human wrongs."[6]

I am absolutely not suggesting that there is a universality of human response to suffering or that such suffering results in an amorphous "ethics" born from desperation. However, there is a commonality among certain survivors of articulation of an ethical relationship to others that is understood partly in response to their own experiences of violent disenfranchisement as well as their own cultural and social circumstances. Booth states that "development of a human rights culture is crucial, because it is one of the ways by which physical humans can try and invent social humans in ways appropriate for our dislocated, statist, industrialized and globalising age."[7] While Booth's theory places concern for victims as central to the development of workable human rights discourse, giving them voice by assuming that they all want to better their current situation, survivors themselves articulate this voice in a clear, uncompromising fashion. By giving witness to their experiences of atrocity, they move from victim to survivor while also shifting our relations to the dead. And their demand for an ethical witness to their witness, articulating and performing a universal but not undifferentiated human who has both rights and responsibilities and who recognizes them as human and thereby reinforces the witness/spectator's own humanity, is core to the development of a working, globalized discourse that can resist atrocity.

Afghanistan: Background

Some basic indicators on the social sectors of Afghanistan during the time this research was conducted:

225

- The last estimation of per capita income was made by the World Bank in 1997 and estimated at $280.
- Life expectancy rates are estimated at forty-four years for women and forty-three for men.
- Maternal mortality rates are the second highest in the world. Every day about forty-five women die of pregnancy-related causes, resulting in over sixteen thousand maternal deaths annually.
- Only 9 percent of deliveries in Afghanistan are attended by trained birth attendants.
- One quarter of all children die before the age of five, largely from acute respiratory infection, diarrheal diseases, and malnutrition.
- Health services reach less than one fourth of the total population and only 17 percent of the rural population.
- Tuberculosis rates for women aged fifteen to forty-five are among the highest in the world.
- There is less than one physician per ten thousand of the population.
- Literacy rates are estimated at 30 percent, but only 13 percent for women.
- The gross enrollment ratio for girls in primary education is estimated between 3 percent and 6 percent.
- Safe drinking water reaches only 20 percent of the population.
- The gender disparity index (a composite index based on the measurement of women's life expectancy, educational attainment, and income) ranks Afghanistan the lowest in the world.[8]

There had been devastating warfare in Afghanistan for more than twenty-five years, leaving the country heavily land-mined, with almost no infrastructure, and with a refugee population of over 2.5 million in addition to estimates of 1 million internally displaced people. The war waged by the United States and the Northern Alliance in 2001 and 2002, in the face of which the Taliban quickly disintegrated, brought an end to the current warfare. However, the extent to which the country will be able to replace an entrenched culture of local warlords, tribal chiefs, and drug runners and smugglers, all with their own militia, with a stable centralized government that will actually be able to exercise some control over these various local strongmen and build and rebuild the largely nonexistent infrastructure of the country is still very unclear.

It is a country of great diversity with several major ethnic groups—the Pashtuns, Tajiks, Uzbeks, Hazaras, Turkmen, Baluchi, and Nooristani—and two main languages, Pashtun and Dari. There are also various nomadic and seminomadic peoples and numerous languages, including the local language of each ethnic group. Within a population of approximately 25.8 million (nobody knows for sure, since there has been no credible census for so many years) there are Sunni, Shia, and Ismaili Muslims, along with small populations of Hindus and Christians, and one last Jewish man still living in Kabul.

With backing from Pakistan, the Taliban invaded Kandahar in 1994, two years later captured Kabul, and from 1996 until the fall of 2001 were engaged in a civil war to gain control of the rest of the country. Many of the Taliban came from poor rural or refugee families, grew up in the refugee camps in Pakistan in the 1980s, and were sent to religious schools called madrassas. One large problem is many of the madrassas do not provide what is by international consensus generally considered to be a functioning education. They are run by mullahs who do not themselves have to have any educational qualifications and who teach as they see fit. Often this consists of religious indoctrination into an ultraconservative interpretation of Islamic texts taught in tandem with a reactionary view of all aspects of culture that deviate from conservative rural and tribal codes and norms of conduct. Although the Taliban were Muslims and often claimed to be instituting Islam in its purest form, in reality they had merged this idiosyncratic and reactionary version of Islam with extremely conservative rural Pashtun mores and traditions.[9]

While both the Taliban and the Northern Alliance have been responsible for human rights abuses and war crimes, it is increasingly clear that the majority of atrocities in the last couple of years of their regime were committed by the Taliban. This included massacres of civilian populations—mainly men between the ages of sixteen and forty—the indiscriminate aerial bombing of civilian populations, forced conscription (in which both sides openly engaged), the burning of towns and fields, summary execution, and rape. The most prominent abuses by the Taliban that managed to make it into the American media, such as banning women from education and work, requiring women to wear the burqa, public executions in the Kabul and Kandahar sports stadiums, outlawing television, movies, and all music that was not religious, and destroying the millennia-old Buddha statues in Bamiyan, were only the most spectacular (media-friendly) of the widespread, systematic, ongoing abuses of civilians throughout the country.

Gender abuse and the systematic mistreatment and violent disenfranchisement of women under the Taliban did receive some attention by the international community prior to and during the American-led war but ceased to be of interest to the media and its American spectators after the war's end. However, the situation for women in Afghanistan was abysmal long before the advent of the Taliban (who took what was already a horrible situation and made it far worse) and continues to be so. The human rights deficit in Afghanistan for men as well as women—but especially for women—is very grave.[10] For example, a study of girls' education in 1979, when more girls were enrolled in school than at any other time, found that 99.2 percent of rural women and 88.2 percent of urban women had no schooling at all.[11]

The Northern Alliance, which was the United States' ally in Afghanistan and is extremely powerful and prominent in the emerging new government, is made up of the remnants of the reactionary, extremely religiously conservative Mujahideen who fought the Soviets with American aid in the 1980s. They only looked "good" to the American media because the Taliban were even worse. The new generation of Northern Alliance leaders holding prominent positions in the new government is less conservative and religiously ideological than the older generation (such as Burrahudin Rabbani, the former president), but these leaders must maintain their alliances with these older warlords and have no strong incentive for including women's enfranchisement in their programs.

Very few of the local or international NGOs, the UN agencies, or the donor countries whose money funds them have done more than provide basic lip service to the problem of the situation of women in Afghanistan and their relationship to development, civil society, and human rights. The unstated policy in these agencies, which are themselves bastions of male privilege, has been to concern themselves with gender issues only insofar as they impinge on other programming issues. For example, in an effort to fight malnutrition among women and children, the World Food Programme has created distribution guidelines that seek to insure that women will have access to the food staple being distributed. However, with the exception of programming initiatives that are undertaken by particular individuals within agencies rather than as agencywide initiatives, none of the major NGOs or UN agencies has been concerned with gender enfranchisement beyond the bounds of the most conservative cultural norms. Indeed, many humanitarian workers will use the excuse of "cultural difference"—not wanting to interfere with the supposed traditional cultural norms of Afghanistan as they have been emplaced and promoted through the successive policies of Mujahideen commanders, Islamist ideologues, and the Taliban over the past thirty years—as the reason for their lack of action in addressing the vast gender inequities in their own programming as well as in local areas of the country itself.

One key aspect of what the Taliban did that made them so much worse from a gender perspective from their predecessors was to take a set of reactionary conservative cultural norms and make them into juridical policies. This means that whereas before, a woman might have been able to find ways within her family and her social strata to resist cultural norms such as the wearing of the burqa in urban areas or restrictions on women's education and work, under the Taliban it was illegal for women to work and to appear in public without the burqa, and all girls' schools were closed. Domestically, by making the wearing of the burqa a legal imperative, the Taliban shifted the grounds of freedom and resistance for women. While cultural norms can be more or less flexible at the local level, allowing for differences of local culture, individual strategies of resistance, and change over time, state law allows no room for deviation from official policy. Because Taliban control did not extend equally over all parts of the country claimed as their domain, women especially in rural areas had and have greater flexibility in adhering to such laws, but the fact remains that they could, through a legal mechanism of the state, be violently punished for any infraction.

Institutionalizing certain cultural norms as state policy is integral to the process of nation-building and consolidating power during times of political upheaval. In the case of discriminatory cultural norms, for example the wearing of the burqa, control over women's bodies is made a foundational aspect of this process. By turning such a cultural norm into a juridical policy, the authorities also engage the international legal arena, which insists upon certain baseline juridical agreements between countries in order for states to engage at the international level. Thus the Taliban, in seeking to consolidate their domestic control over the country by institutionalizing as state policy a cultural norm that fundamentally represents their ideology, entered themselves into dialogue with international laws and agreements.

The international agencies have been very poor at recognizing this distinction between cultural norms and juridical policies as well as the different possibilities for resistance that they entail. This is partly due to the set of conditions within which many international aid workers operate. They move from country to country every few years, often do not have more than a cursory knowledge of the country within which they are operating, are under tremendous pressure, given the dire situation of the vast number of people in the country and on its fringes, to provide basic, short-term, emergency subsistence for large numbers of people with budgets that are both small and uncertain—which discourages long-term programming initiatives—and do not have training or education in the studies of gender, human rights, cultural or critical studies, and conflict.

In Afghanistan, the state has historically been largely a fiction of borders and central authority that has little reach beyond urban centers, especially in terms of the infrastructure of civil society. Afghanistan currently faces large infrastructural and historical obstacles to building the foundational structures of a developing country, especially functioning education and health systems that will serve a majority of the people. Strong infrastructures for health and education are key to development and civil society and along with the "hardware" infrastructure of roads, bridges, and buildings are some of the most necessary structures for a working society.

Historically, Afghanistan's health and educational facilities were located in urban centers and served primarily urban populations. Prior to the war, both sectors had been significantly expanded and had begun to reach more of the rural population. The educational sector, for instance, is reported to have enrolled 580,499 students in primary education in 1985, of whom 179,027 or 30.8% were women. This is despite the fact that more students were enrolled in school at this time than ever before. By 2001, it was estimated that assistance agencies were reaching about 350,000 (or 8 percent) of primary-school-aged children.[12]

The majority of Afghanistan is rural, and for women the problems of education and health are exacerbated by cultural norms that do not generally allow women freedom of movement beyond the immediate vicinity of the house—this may extend to the village and the fields, but not beyond. Thus, if educational and health facilities are not within the zone of women's immediate sphere of movement, their ability to utilize the facilities drops dramatically. Once girls reach the age of purdah, their movement becomes limited, so even if they had been traveling with some greater freedom to attend primary schooling, secondary and tertiary education are generally unattainable.[13]

Most women in Afghanistan do not have access to necessary health care. The acute shortage of trained female health workers contributes to the many problems of access that women encounter. Women face problems of nutrition because they usually have less access to food than male members of the household, have large numbers of children usually beginning from a young age, and work very hard both in the home and in the fields. These factors, combined with the lack of reproductive health services in general and the difficulty of receiving care even where it is available due to cultural and legal injunctions against seeing male practitioners and restrictions on travel, mean that women suffer greatly and die from easily treatable conditions.

The seclusion of women and girls also means that many parents prefer their daughters to be taught by female teachers. The historical problems of women attaining secondary and tertiary education, coupled with the Taliban's ban on women's employment and the current almost complete breakdown of secondary and tertiary education in the country for both boys and girls and especially for girls during the Taliban's rule, mean that finding even marginally qualified women teachers is very difficult for the agencies involved in educational projects. Although half of all primary school teachers in the mid-eighties were women, their numbers have since suffered a precipitous drop due to the Taliban ban on women's employment and restrictions on women's freedom of movement. In 2000, the largest NGO providing educational support in Afghanistan reported that only 14 percent of its primary teachers were women. Material problems such as the almost complete lack of supplies from books to writing instruments, the disrepair of schools, and lack of adequate supervision and monitoring of educational staff were additional burdens in an ongoing crisis.

This lack of qualified women professionals and restrictions on women's freedom of movement were equally problems for the health sector. Not only did the Taliban ban women from receiving medical attention from male doctors, but even without the ban, many women cannot seek medical attention from men due to social constraints. Thus village health posts staffed with women health practitioners are a necessity for the provision of basic women's health care to the majority of women in the country. The difficulties in building and maintaining such a network, especially given the current conditions in the country, are enormous despite the fact that the health sector of Afghanistan is the best-functioning sector left in the country.

Afghanistan is also a country of massive, institutionalized, and social discrimination, and the Taliban refusal to allow girls to be educated has created a problem with massive structural ramifications for the entire culture. This was not simply a momentary lapse in the forms of civil society by a fundamentalist regime but instead threatens the most basic developmental requirements of a country emerging from decades of destructive warfare. Education has a direct influence on the health of individuals, with development reports clearly indicating that people with basic education also exhibit higher basic levels of health. In addition, good curriculums reflect the needs of the local communities and in Afghanistan could (indeed some already do) contain sections on issues such as land-mine awareness, conflict resolution, sanitation, and basic health. People with basic education also do better economically, and communities and states where the level of basic education has risen have also seen rises in economic viability.[14]

Women's education in particular is linked with the health and development of the entire family through their role as caretakers of children. Learning to recognize the link between sanitation and health, the symptoms of common diseases, and how to provide a balanced, nutritious diet to their children are some of the important ways that women's education affects basic aspects of health and development. The strong links between women's secondary education and steep declines in infant mortality rates are associated with such factors.[15] In addition, some studies have found that men might directly benefit from "a significant association between women's education and male life expectancy."[16] The current severe constraints on women's education due to lack of resources, destruction during the Taliban regime, and continuing insecurity throughout the country thus pose serious long-term questions about Afghanistan's ability to recover in any meaningful fashion, even as the warfare ends.

As many have noted, the demand for education among ordinary Afghans is very high at this time and should be taken advantage of to build greater community involvement in education. Especially the rising demand for girls' education, in a country where girls often went unserved even when the infrastructure for providing modern education was much stronger, should be met with services. The demand for girls' schooling, which has traditionally come from urban centers responding to state policies and needs for trained personnel, has moved to the rural areas. Some people attribute this in part to a shift in the way education is being perceived in rural areas. Rather than seeing it as a state demand with little relevance to their own needs, parents are coming to see schooling as directly relevant to their needs and as providing tools for self-improvement that can help their children, including girls, to improve their position in society.

One NGO found that rural parents reported valuing education for its socializing aspects as well as its practical aspects, such as literacy and numeracy. They reportedly valued its ability to cultivate courtesy and respect for elders, knowledge of Islam, and self-discipline, among other positive results. An international NGO that is heavily involved in educational projects in Afghanistan and in Afghan refugee camps in Pakistan reported that the "bride price" in one camp where the NGO operates was higher for educated than for uneducated women.[17] While the bride price institution itself is an inherently discriminatory practice, this information does indicate a growing demand for women's education as a culturally desirable attribute.

Given the strong links between education, health, development, and the growth of civil society—including the fact that while most girls and many boys do not stay in school past grade three in Afghanistan, the completion of primary school has been shown to provide a marked improvement in quality of life—it is not hard to extrapolate these factors to the dire situation of the country. International aid and involvement are not even keeping up with the promised donations, despite the heavy involvement of the United States following the September 11, 2001, terrorist attacks.

Afghanistan is unfortunately a country that has very little educated population left with which to rebuild itself, despite the postwar return of some expatriates. Not only had almost everybody with any education already left the country by fall 2001—the doctors, nurses, teachers, engineers, and so on who are vital to a functioning modern society—but there is virtually no educational system left to produce more of them. This is not a promising situation from which to rebuild the country, should the United States actually undertake to begin such a process. To rebuild the infrastructure of Afghanistan—not just to return the country to where it was prior to the war with the Soviets but to correct the massive human rights deficit that already existed—will need a very unglamorous, frustrating, extended hands-on engagement by Afghans in tandem with many different members of the world community, which the United States is showing no signs of being willing to undertake. How, then, are we to even begin a consideration of theoretical conditions of ethical witnessing and testimony in conditions such as these? And what is our relationship and obligation to these people, bound as we suddenly are not just through the easily forgettable exploitations of history but through sudden, recent acts of massive violence?

In the Field

At the time I was there, Badakhshan was the last full province held by the Northern Alliance, a coalition of former Mujahideen commanders led by Ahmed Shah Masood and representing the government of former President Burnahudden Rabbani, who were engaged in a civil war with the Taliban. During late July 2000, Taliban forces began an attack on the province of Takhar, which borders Badakhshan to the west. During this offensive and especially during the extended battle over the provincial capital of Taloqan, over eighty thousand people fled their homes for Badakhshan province to escape the fighting.

In early July 2000, the Taliban had begun a major offensive in northern Afghanistan north of Kabul, in Shomali and around the Bagram Air Base. By the end of July, the Taliban had captured the Nahreen district in Baghlan province, which links the Panjsher valley with Takhar province, cutting off a vital supply line for the Northern Alliance. As the Taliban moved north toward Taloqan, the provincial capital and seat of the Rabbani government, the offensive was accompanied by aerial bombardment of towns and villages, heavy shelling and ground combat between the opposing forces, and use of land mines by both sides. On August 5, the Northern Alliance lost control of the Bangi district to the Taliban, who then began an aerial bombardment of Taloqan. Control of Taloqan changed from the Northern Alliance to the Taliban under heavy aerial bombardment, artillery shelling, and gunfire during the days of September 6 to 11. Fighting was sporadic but ongoing in Takhar province and on the borders of Badakhshan throughout the time I was there in October.

I was in Badakhshan to conduct a study at the request of the Human Rights Advisor, Office of the UN Coordinator for Afghanistan, assessing vulnerable internally displaced people (IDPs) who had newly arrived in Badakhshan. The information for this study as well as this chapter was gathered through interviews with IDPs in Faizabad and the districts of Argo and Bararak as well as with local and international NGOs and concerned UN agencies in Faizabad dealing with the IDP population of northern Afghanistan. I also arranged meetings with NGO and UN personnel to collect further information on the IDP situation as well as to verify information obtained during IDP interviews.

For this project I conducted extensive, structured interviews with 101 IDPs, representing a cross section of the IDP population. As a woman with a woman translator, I had access to both the men of the community and the women. The interviews almost always took place inside the living quarters of IDP families—usually a tent or a small area of a room shared with one or two other families in an abandoned building—and included several members of a family group and sometimes neighboring groups as well. In this way, I was able to see what material resources the family had been able to bring with them. Although I interviewed both women and men for this report, the majority of IDPs interviewed were women, leading to valuable insights about women's experience of displacement.

I will very quickly try to outline the situation into which I was arriving to assess these people's needs and conduct my interviews. Badakhshan, currently and at the time of these interviews, is one of the poorest and most inaccessible provinces in Afghanistan. It has tremendous food scarcity, high levels of tuberculosis and debilitating childhood diseases, a mountainous landscape with very poor roads that make much of the province virtually inaccessible, and at best access to only the most rudimentary forms of health care and education for most of the population. For example, Badakhshan exhibits some of the highest rates of tuberculosis (TB) infection in the country—and unique to Afghanistan is the fact that female rates of TB infection are almost twice that of males. Usually, male rates of infection are higher than those of women. A contributing factor to this unusually high rate of infection is the difficulty women encounter in leaving their homes and traveling to receive medical attention or even information. As one NGO doctor told me, TB is a disease of poor standards of living, and women who are confined indoors with poor ventilation, sanitation, and nutrition, working very hard on farms, and without access to basic health care are at high risk.

An NGO that conducted a survey on TB in 1998 found that in 50 percent of households surveyed, the rooms were not exposed to sunlight and were overcrowded and unhygienic. The survey also found that women had less access to education and food intake, were exposed to other negative factors related to impaired reproductive health, and were often unable to distinguish between TB and other diseases, routes of transmission, and how to protect themselves from TB.[18] Lack of adequate health care and education for women, poverty, and the seclusion of women greatly contribute to the high TB infection rates in Badakhshan. The influx of eighty thousand displaced people with virtually no resources was a disaster for a province without enough resources for its own population and with an international aid presence that was already overstretched and resource-poor.

Internally Displace People's Experiences of the Conflict

My interviews with IDPs revealed a number of human rights abuses and abuses of civilians, especially reports of indiscriminate and heavy aerial bombardment, artillery shelling of civilian areas, and the mining of towns and villages. There were also clear trends of human rights abuse as the Taliban entered villages, such as the arbitrary arrest of civilian men, summary execution, the forced relocation of civilians out of their villages, and rape. A majority of the IDPs I interviewed had been repeatedly displaced, many of them up to four or five times. Each time these IDPs are displaced, they lose all of their belongings.

The violation most widely reported by a majority of respondents and which was greatly responsible for the large numbers of IDPs in the north was the indiscriminate bombing of villages and of Taloqan by the Taliban. Most of the people I interviewed did not leave their homes until well after the bombs had begun falling in their area. Of the people who stayed throughout the bombing campaign, most reported being forced to leave Taloqan or their villages when they became a site of direct conflict between the Taliban and Northern Alliance forces. At these times, both warring parties engaged in behavior that caused indiscriminate and excessive damage to the civilian population and property of the villages, including continual bombing and shelling of the village, using houses occupied by civilians as shields behind which firing positions were located, and, in the case of Northern Alliance forces, retreating amid groups of civilians fleeing their village, thereby drawing Taliban fire onto the civilians. There were also several accounts of Taliban shelling or bombing of the road they were using to evacuate their villages. Several people I interviewed stated that their villages and the surrounding areas had been mined by both the Taliban and the Northern Alliance during the conflict.

Uniformly, the people who experienced the entry of the Taliban into their villages reported widespread arbitrary detention of village men, from young to elderly, who were sent away by truck, the searching of homes at gunpoint, demands for weapons and/or money, isolated rapes, and beatings. There were also accounts of looting, of village children being given money to show Taliban the homes of suspected Northern Alliance sympathizers, and of arbitrary murders and abductions. The failure by the Taliban to distinguish between civilians and military targets was repeatedly stated by IDPs as a primary reason for not returning to their homes.

Humanitarian Situation

A wide variety of NGOs and UN agencies were attempting to help this current group of IDPs. Due to the onset of winter, the extreme difficulty of the terrain, and the ongoing war, as well as the general shortage of aid, however, many of the IDPs were in an extremely vulnerable state. Many of the them had traveled to their destinations on foot and therefore were able to bring at best a change of clothes and a couple of blankets or other small items. In addition, since most of the IDPs had left their homes in August or early September, they did not have any warm winter clothing with them.

Among the people I interviewed, the majority of households had both parents, but there was a significant minority of female-headed households, and they were visibly less well-off than the two-parent households—in terms of both material possessions and food supply. Symptoms of trauma were also widespread among the IDPs, especially the children, and the absence of any program available to address these problems of trauma in the population will hamper long-term efforts at development and reconstruction.

People who had stayed in their villages during previous periods of Taliban control complained that when the Taliban entered villages they abused the people in the form of beatings, rapes, and arrests, did not let the people go about their daily lives, did not differentiate between soldiers and civilians, and engaged in summary execution and the burning and looting of homes. Even for the IDPs who did not directly experience abuses at the hands of the Taliban, the stories and rumors about atrocities clearly fed a terror of returning to their lands while the Taliban occupied them. Many IDPs also expressed the fear that returning while the Taliban held the area of their home would expose them to the charge of being government sympathizers and result in abuse. Thus most of these people, despite their wounds, malnutrition, and current lack of shelter, health care, and education for their children, had no plans to return to their homes in the foreseeable future.

The high incidence of repeat displacement among them also made them much less likely, due to previous experiences of abuse and war crimes, to return quickly to their homes while combat was still ongoing in the province. Because of the high incidence of fear and trauma from previous loss and abuse as well as that suffered in this current displacement, these IDPs exhibited a willingness to live under extremely harsh conditions in Badakhshan rather than returning to homes and lands that were still in a state of high insecurity, as they perceived it.

237

Collecting Testimony

When I arrived in Faizabad, the provincial capital, I found several immediate difficulties. My most immediate problem was the lack of a fluent English-speaking female translator with whom I could work.
Finding a woman as a translator was a necessity, since otherwise in this
culture I would be able to interview only men. There are not many
English-speaking translators in Badakhshan, and only a few of them are
women. I worked with a woman named Marie, who spoke passable
English and fluent Arabic—of which I speak a little—and who was herself a teacher at the local pedagogy institute. She had almost no experience as a translator and no experience of translation at the level at which
I needed it.

Additional complications for me included the coercive aspect of collecting testimony from displaced people in a war zone, the development
of empathic relationships with people that could not be continued, and
the multiple goals of the testimonial collection itself. Collecting testimony in a war zone from people who have been badly disenfranchised
and often traumatized has a coercive aspect that needs to be mitigated
as much as possible. People feel they have no choice but to speak to
you because you represent the UN, upon which they are largely depen-
dent. Also, because I was collecting testimony for the human rights
advisor rather than for an aid agency such as the World Food Programme, I was unable to offer any possible material exchange for my
request that people speak to me at length and in irritating and often
repetitive detail about very horrifying and traumatic experiences. I
could not, for example, offer that in exchange for speaking with me,
they might receive additional shelter, blankets, or food. In addition to
representing the UN, Marie and I were also speaking to the IDPs with
the permission of the local commanders, and therefore our request for
peoples' testimony carried with it the demand by the authorities to
speak with us.

Gender roles were a complicating factor; although most of our testimonial collection occurred within the "domestic spaces" of tents or
living areas, where the women and children tend to remain during the
day while the men gather outside, some men were very eager to make
sure that we interviewed their wives. Although we were concerned that
this would make it particularly difficult to give women the option of
not speaking to us, in practice we found that the women were very
interested in having contact with us quite independently of their hus-

band's or other male family member's wishes. The procedure we followed was to begin with an introduction, explaining who we were, what we were doing, and what we were asking of people, then individually collect testimony beginning with name, age, village, size of family, and method of travel to their current location, and end by asking if there was anything they would like to ask of us. During the interview, we would first ask them to narrate their experience of displacement and the conflict and then return for as much detail as we needed or could gain about specific issues.

Although I was concerned by the coercive possibilities of this demand for testimony, the people I interviewed—and especially the women—were quite receptive to speaking with us. While I was concerned by issues such as triggering traumatic memories, the rhetorical violence of my demand, the unequal distribution of power in the interview situation, and interviewees' fears for their safety through possible lapses of confidentiality, the interviewees were eager to speak with us and have some contact with a person from outside the conflict. Many of the men, used to public space and stating their opinions, understood the ways in which such testimony might help to publicize their circumstances (possibly resulting in more aid) and were willing if not happy to tell the stories of what had happened to them. Some of the men who understood some of the international dimensions of the conflict and who knew something of politics also understood that such interviews were an aspect of international humanitarian engagement in conflict situations. Most of the women stated that it was the first time that they had been approached by anybody and asked to speak about their experiences. Even within their own families, in most cases they had not narrativized their experiences to each other in this way.

Because the majority of international workers in Badakhshan (the few that there were) were busy trying to manage a fast-growing IDP crisis, they did not have time to conduct personal interviews with many people and contacted IDP groups through the male elders of each group, who were expected to make decisions for and pass on information to the rest of the IDPs. And since all but a handful of the international workers were men, the women especially had almost no contact with international staff. These women were telling their stories not just to us but to the other women (and children and occasionally men) listening, and our questions gave them a "sanctioned" space recognized by the international community within which to talk about what they had seen, felt, and experienced. As we emphasized certain details, asked repetitive questions about things that the women glossed over, and tried to arrange timelines for events, the women engaged us in a dynamic process of testifying. They did not accede to our demands weakly. Instead, they engaged us as equals, with respect but skepticism. They both tried to give us what we asked for and laughed at or chided us for the seeming irrelevance, simplicity, and/or naïveté of some of our questioning. These women, uneducated, displaced, and often suffering from trauma and loss, were, through our presence, strongly claiming the place of witness and refusing to inhabit the site of the victim. They also often thanked us for providing them the opportunity for some version of a normative social visit in their current framework.

In gathering the testimony, we had to struggle with the communal setting, where there were anywhere from four to twenty-five people listening to the story being told. This is not the ideal setting for collecting testimony, since invariably there are interruptions, concerns about audience, and distractions, among other things, that interrupt the dialogue. This communal setting put ethical pressures on Marie and myself, as we negotiated the need for detailed testimonial collection with the needs of the women. In a situation where there has been ongoing warfare for over twenty years and where most of the people we interviewed had been displaced multiple times—each time losing all of their belongings—the levels of trauma among the population were quite high. Although I was not dealing directly with the trauma other than to note it when I found evidence of it, I found many indicators of traumatization, especially among the children.

While the gathering of testimonial, from our perspective, might have benefited from private interviews, the women themselves seemed to benefit from the communal participation in a form of storytelling. Although Afghan families and communities are very closely knit and supportive, which is the major reason for their survival in as intact a way as they are over the past decades of atrocity, it was clear that the women appreciated the ritualized way they were able to tell their stories. Rather than just being a story of personal pain told to friends in conversations during daily life, their stories were being asked for by outsiders, one of whom had traveled vast distances to reach them, and were being recorded. They thanked us and often told us it was the first time anybody had ever been interested in what had happened to them. The women themselves were using us to build new forms of historical memory in the dynamic setting of interviewer, translator, witness, and audience/participants.

Testimony

The women I interviewed came from a variety of backgrounds. They were Tajik, Uzbek, and Pashtun; some came from extremely isolated rural areas, and others were from the provincial capital of Taloqan. Some could read and write, and a few had held jobs outside of their homes, as teachers, for example, but most were largely uneducated and did not work outside the family. Most had lost immediate family members—children, parents, siblings, or spouses—during the years of conflict. Their different identities and backgrounds distinguished them quite clearly from each other. Although there were similarities in the way they expressed experiencing the events to which they were witnessing, there were also distinct differences. Some women expressed anger at their disenfranchisement by the Taliban. For example, several women complained about being unable to leave the house unaccompanied by a male relative, which made trips to the bazaar for basic provisions difficult, among other things, and therefore disrupted their abilities to care for their families. Other women expressed no anger, just fear and terror at having been in the middle of violent conflict. Many women did not hew to a particular political line (supporting the Northern Alliance, which was currently protecting them, in conversations with a stranger, for example) and instead gave witness to abuses committed not just by the Taliban but by local warlords and Northern Alliance troops. Men were much more likely publicly to support the Northern Alliance.

In a culture that strongly emphasizes distinct gender roles, which were even more polarized in many areas by the Islamist Mujahideen and the Taliban, the women I spoke with were very self-conscious of themselves as women and of the limits within which they operated. Given that many of them were primary caretakers for sick and dying children, could not go to the toilet during daylight hours because of the proximity of so many strange men, and were acutely aware of the threat of sexual violence during the conflict, they nonetheless articulated clear positions in favor of reconciliation, an end to the conflict, and development, especially education—for their daughters as well as their sons. They largely emphasized the injury and disenfranchisement they had witnessed and experienced, rather than articulating a need for retaliation.

Repeatedly, women made reference to the Taliban actions as inhumane, claiming that their violence was opposed to the identity of Afghan and proper codes of behavior and was against religious teachings.

By doing this, the women were claiming an Afghan identity that is opposed to the kinds of violence they had witnessed and experienced,
performatively enacting this identity as they cast out the transgressors
through their discourse. To enact such a move for an international
(non-Afghan) visitor moves it into a wider public realm. Through their
witnessing, they were constructing a discourse of what constitutes
human and Afghan behavior and laying claim as witnesses to the right
to make this distinction.

This witnessing emphasized seeing ("I have seen with my own
eyes . . .") and bodily experience rather than bodily pain—women and
men described bodily pain, but emphasized the actions they took in
response to pain and what they had seen rather than felt. Although they
would use phases such as "it hurt very much" when describing beatings, or "I was sad" to describe an experience of imprisonment, they
then moved on to locate their testimony in the actions of those around
them (what they saw others doing along with themselves) or in the
actions they took (fleeing as soon as they were able, etc.) and did not
talk about their emotional responses to the situation except in the most
cursory way. Many, however—both men and women—cried.

One of the ways such witnessing works is to locate "truth" outside
the physical body and within the interplay of consciousness, memory,
and community. Their truth claims did not rest on what their own body
had experienced but on the interaction between the physical experiences they were relating, the things they had seen with their eyes, and
the actions they had taken as part of a larger group of people who were
also experiencing the same thing. Even people with exceptional stories
referred to the other witnesses to the event they were relating, the other
participants no matter who they were, or the others they had heard of
who had experienced the same thing. They resisted the way in which
group experiences, such as displacement, with a whole village fleeing
shelling, detracted from the particularity of their experience by emphasizing their own actions, what they had owned or lost, what they were
doing during the event, and so on. But they also always emphasized
the similarities between their own experiences and those of the others
people around them suffering similarly.

Stories that could have been told in self-aggrandizing ways were not.
Instead witnesses emphasized the ordinariness of their actions and the
fact that they were not alone in committing them. For example, several
men told of staying behind in their villages after the Taliban arrived,
hiding in the fields during the day in an attempt to retain some control

over their belongings. One man who saw a village girl kidnapped later went with several other men to search for her; finding her body, they carried it back to the village at great risk to themselves. However, this story was not told as an act of courage but as an act of obligation that the witness undertook as part of his role in staying behind. Others told of going as groups to attempt to discover information about where prisoners had been taken or trying to protect family members who were being assaulted.

In all of these recountings, the perpetrators were described as men who were persecuting people for no obvious reasons (they were not demonized), and the witnesses described themselves as doing what was necessary within the terms that they understood to be ethical behavior of responsibility toward others. Such constructions do not partake of communitarian identity formation and frictions nor participate in the violence of the discourse that they encountered. Instead they counter such discourse with a discourse of passivity, respect, and responsibility.

The people I was interviewing were not armed combatants and dissociated themselves from the armed men on both sides of the conflict. Although they had been more recently abused by and were afraid of the Taliban, they did not hesitate to employ the same formations of discourse toward members of other factions. In addition, quite a few of them asked me why other governments were not sending troops to stop the fighting and keep the peace. Rather than the antiforeigner hostility that Afghans are often portrayed as exhibiting, following their successful battles against the British, the Russians, and other invaders, these people were asking why the global community, which they clearly envisioned themselves to be a part of, had abandoned them to such ongoing conflict. The women as well as the men, despite having only the vaguest sense of world geography beyond the borders of the country, nonetheless envisioned a global community that had a responsibility to come to their aid—not in the form of food and shelter but in the form of putting an end to the violence that was repeatedly disenfranchising them.

Many of the similarities between the different testimonial accounts are due to the ways in which the testimonial collection itself tended to elide differences. My asking of the questions was oriented toward actions, not feelings, and then there were layers of translation—from Dari into English (with some difficulties) and sometimes first from Uzbek through a second translator from within the IDP community to Dari, then into written form. Once the testimonials were in written English, I then read them through the lens of several different discourses depending on my project: in reference to war crimes, human rights, trauma discourses, gender studies, and critical work on testimonial theory. In addition, the women's own local storytelling traditions and experiences, their past experiences of displacement, and any contacts with the international community would have influenced what they chose to tell and how they chose to tell it. Through these myriad translations, many differences could have been elided, as the pressures of creating a communal, understandable discourse about these experiences came to bear on the testimony from before it was ever told through my writing about it here.

The one testimonial I collected that was significantly different from the others was also the only testimonial I collected by an armed combatant. A woman who had fought for a period of months with a group of Mujahideen against the Russians showed no remorse at her claim of having killed seven men. She presented herself as being proud of her accomplishments and was clearly held in some esteem in the local community, since she was staying at the home of the local commander. In answer to my questions about how her family and fellow villagers as well as the men she was fighting beside reacted to her very nontraditional actions as a woman taking up arms alongside men, she replied that they were all extremely happy that she was fighting for them.

Ethically, her position is very different from that of the other displaced men and women I interviewed. She articulated a firm position on using violence as a means of resistance and of killing as many of the enemy as possible. However, she was uninterested in talking about her current situation as an IDP within the terms of armed resistance. She answered our questions briefly and factually, but did not advocate taking up arms for either side. Instead, she articulated irritation—but not grief or panic—over the loss of her belongings and a stoic acceptance of her current circumstances, which would probably end with her living once again as a refugee in Pakistan. Clearly, she had access to more resources than most of the other IDPs with whom I had contact; she also occupied a privileged woman's role—that of the older woman who has earned the equal respect of the men and can behave largely as she likes. She also did not currently place herself within a community of IDPs sharing extreme hardships, as did many of the other women and some of the men whose testimony we collected.

Justice in the Breech

Law is the element of calculation, and it is just that there be law, but justice is incalculable, it requires us to calculate with the incalculable; and aporetic experiences are the experiences, as improbable as they are necessary, of justice, that is to say of moments in which the decision between just and unjust is never insured by a rule.[19]

As a form, testimonial is the voice of one survivor of mass violence who tells her or his own story while at the same time claiming that not only does she or he speak for those who did not survive, but that any of these other persons would tell a story both fundamentally the same and different according to their particular experiences. One of the paradoxical difficulties of testimony is its inherent claim to encompass both a universalism of experience and a distinct particularity. Many written testimonials make regular use of dialogue as part of their text, thus emphasizing the individuality of the people portrayed within the text. Nonetheless, in published form, unlike traditional autobiography or memoir, which relies on the "I" of authorial experience, testimonial by its very act undermines the distinct claim of individualism through claiming that the story the author tells is the same story that could be told by any of the other people who were present during the atrocity experience.

Such a dynamic is maintained in this collection of oral testimonies. The IDPs I interviewed emphasized both their own distinct experiences of suffering and displacement and also the communal aspect of the experience. Not only did they often verbally state that others would tell the same story, they also verbally worked this in to the testimony they gave, speaking of the masses of people who shared their experiences.

Discussing the materialist positioning of testimony, Derrida states, "In testimony, truth is promised beyond all proof, all perception, all intuitive demonstration. . . . It is involved/engaged in every address to the other. From the first instant it is coextensive with this other and thus conditions every "social bond." . . . The act of faith demanded in bearing witness exceeds, through its structure, all intuition and all proof, all knowledge."[20] The body, as the site within which truth resides, is not the location of the "truth" of testimonial. This truth is a communal, dynamic understanding, performatively enacted by the witnessing survivor and the witness/spectator. Acts of atrocity make the body the totality of the world for the victim, working to cut off language and communal identity. By moving the "truth" of experience beyond the individual body, out of the embodied victimization of the atrocity experience, testimony, "engaged in every address to the other," engages the "human" on the level of address.

The atrocity experience is not a privileged site of witnessing. It would be the worst form of injustice to suggest that experiences of mass and massive pain and abuse are somehow formative of necessary configurations of witnessing. But such experiences, endemic to our current global circumstances, result in important possibilities for understanding the effects of mass violence on generations and on cultures. The opportunities witnesses to mass violence provide for us to become witnesses within a testimonial dynamic, to reconfigure terms of responsibility and ethics, will never in any way recuperate the atrocities, but testimony does suggest the opportunity to consider acts of justice, incommensurate as they may be, with the victims and with future victims.

Incommensurability of experience and language is inherent in all addresses to the other, and the other who has experienced atrocity occupies an especially overdetermined site of incommensurability in global discourses. Derrida, writing about Levinas's work on "infinite right," notes: "Here equity is not equality, calculated proportion, equitable distribution or distributive justice but rather absolute dissymmetry."[21] Equity and the ethics of the address of the other who is the embodied survivor of atrocity must acknowledge incommensurability as being fundamental to address, yet the dynamics of testimony—that secular "act of faith" upon which bearing witness depends—demands a justice that resides in this interstitial, incommensurable space. The particularity and difference of survivors, our recognition of their call to the human, and their claim to a communal experience of atrocity are the beginning point for a performative ethics of testimony that locates human rights in a universal human who is always already the site of difference.

The Role of the Translator

> To address oneself to the other in the language of the other is, it seems, the condition of all possible justice, but apparently, in all rigor, it is not only impossible (since I cannot speak the language of the other except to the extent that I appropriate it and assimilate it according to the law of an implicit third) but even excluded by justice as law [*droit*], inasmuch as justice as right seems to imply an element of universality, the appeal to a third party who suspends the unilaterality or singularity of the idioms.[22]

The translator of these testimonies I collected in Badakhshan, then, is at the crux of the difficulty. Occupying a borderline position both inside and outside the events, she is the joint upon which these various stresses rest and through with they pass. Her position as a middle-class, educated, Afghan woman who returned to the country from Pakistan out of a sense of desire to help, her lack of fluency both in English and in Uzbek, one of the other languages that many of the IDPs spoke, and her relative independence in the context of local women's roles marked her as both an outsider and an insider in profound ways. Having a translator who did not speak fluent English and some interviewees who did not speak Dari, but Uzbek, presented profound difficulties for the accuracy of the testimonial collection. Ultimately such problems of translation highlight the central problem of all testimony, which is the profound problem of translation and language. Translation, as Derrida notes, is "an always possible but always imperfect compromise between two idioms."[23]

Marie and I carried on an ongoing dialogue during the interviews, discussing various English words she might use to translate particular sentences, negotiating over turns of phrase, and teaching each other the languages we were using to communicate. Thus the interviews were a dynamic process not just of exchange between me, through Marie, and the interviewee, and between us and the larger gathering of witnesses, but also between Marie and myself.

Marie had to translate me to the interviewees not just linguistically but culturally. Most of the people we interviewed had almost no knowledge of the larger world outside of their region, and while they were extremely hospitable and open to talking about their experiences, they had little understanding of the reason their stories might be necessary or even of interest to the larger world. Thus part of our job necessitated trying to explain such things as the transportation aspects of aid delivery and the role of the international agencies, the importance of distinguishing between eyewitness, secondary, and tertiary testimony, and the realistic prospects for immediate relief. Again, the ethical responsibilities inherent in these exchanges—these logistical acts of determining language and explaining positions, which must formulate a recorded testimony that has political consequences—must be kept in balance with the ethical responsibility toward the witnesses and the dynamic process of testimony itself. A process whereby through the telling of their story in recontextualized form, these women create the possibility for a new sense of authority and of communal sharing of the experience is an aspect of the "equity" to which Derrida's reading of Levinas's work on ethics addresses itself.

As well as the theoretical problems of translation, exemplified through this testimonial collection are serious concerns with physical safety. Marie is and was in a very vulnerable position in the culture as a divorced woman with two small children, and I needed to be very careful not to place her at undue risk in the local community. Although working for a period of time for the UN gained her certain social and political status and opportunities as well as much-needed cash, it also carried with it risks that could have repercussions far beyond her weeks of work with me. Any local with access to the international community is an object of struggle between the local factions that hold power—the corrupt officials, the local commanders, and the different factions of the government. And very few women participate in these structures (including international women, who make up only a fraction of the international staff in Afghanistan).

It was dangerous for Marie to come to the UN compound, where men not of her family work and live, to ride alone in a UN car without me present, since all the drivers are local men, or to leave the city of Faizabad without a male relative accompanying her. All of these were complications that Marie and I had to negotiate with her family and with the UN in order to get our work done. Still, despite our precautions, there were dangerous ways we could all fail to foresee possible threats. For example, I had been told, by the notoriously corrupt local director of the International Committee of the Red Crescent (ICRC) that the IDPs had free access to the health care facilities of the hospital, but I was later told by IDPs that they were turned away when they went for treatment. I went to the director in a friendly manner to ask for clarification, and he assured me that the problems were mistakes and would be resolved. However, that evening, he called Marie at home—they both happened to have two of the only phone lines in the city—and threatened her, telling her that she had no right translating complaints to me that made him look bad. Marie is a strong woman and stood up to him, but it was a frightening experience for her, and one that I did not foresee properly.

Such physical dangers—and the ongoing dynamics of the local situation long after I had left—are hard to foresee and mitigate but provide difficult ethical terrain. Marie, who was at first reluctant to sit on the blankets or pillows offered us by the IDPs for fear of fleas, developed deep empathic relationships with them and continued to visit with the Faizabad IDPs and to serve as their liaison to local and international authorities long after I had left. I continue to feel strong responsibilities toward people I interviewed, who still live vividly in my memory. That some of the men we interviewed had almost certainly at various times taken up arms or were actively repressive toward the women in their families and that some of the women used advantages of class and status to the detriment of other women makes the testimonials a site of ongoing, engaged, ethical conflict. The verbal and structural enactments of "human" community from experiences of atrocity do not make the testimonials ethically even and transparent texts to be valorized. They are the result of and embody vast conflicts of the physical, the linguistic, and the theoretical from which the witnesses themselves—us as well as the survivors—are not exempt.

Conclusion: How Well Do We Act?

> This responsibility toward memory is a responsibility before the very concept of responsibility that regulates the justice and appropriateness [*justesse*] of our behavior, of our theoretical, practical, ethico-political decisions.[24]

As a performative act that requires an ethical engagement different from that of spectatorship and other forms of viewing, witnessing entails, as one of the ethical considerations necessary for such witnessing to occur, the recognition of the survivor as more than just the overdetermined trace of a traumatic event. The witness must recognize the survivor both as bearing the trace of the atrocity event and as a human with a particularity and historical location in the present moment they both occupy. In testimonial, paradox is perhaps the articulated manifestation of the traumatic event, a balancing of impossibilities that mirrors the interstitial existence of the atrocity in memory. Thus for these women to tell their stories in the context of my detail-oriented and repetitive questions brought to the fore both their lack of knowledge of the very events they were relating—for example, the specifics of date and time, or the lapses of memory that blanked out certain elements of events they had witnessed—and their authority to speak as witnesses to crimes and events that had affected them.

Such testifying results in the doubled role of testimony as the political and ethical act of witnessing an event that has been radically denied—through silence, inattention, and the practices of the authorities—and the individual necessity to rebuild one's historical link to the experience by recounting one's memories of it in front of a witness— language and representation serve to give substance and "reality" to an experience that no longer materially exists or seems real.[25] Or, as Peter Van Der Veer has formulated it, "There is no true story of violence. Violence is a total phenomenon, but it comes to us totally as a fragment. . . . the fragment shows the limits of historical knowledge."[26]

Because of their cultural positions, the extreme exigencies of survival, and lack of interest by outsiders, these women seemed not to have previously parsed out the extremity of the violence they had witnessed from the possibilities for different ways of remembering and living—the fragmentary nature of the total phenomenon, in Van Der Veer's words. I am not suggesting that they did not understand their rights to live in a conflict-free environment—despite their rural isolation and lack of education, they clearly articulated themselves to be humans with a solid understanding of their basic rights, including education. But in contrast to some of the men I interviewed, who clearly at the time of violent events had a sense that they might later be called upon to witness them, these women had never thought of themselves as witnessing in the way it is articulated as a public dynamic—whether in a local level gathering of elders, a juridical setting, or a therapeutic setting.

Just as extreme violence blurs the boundaries of the public and the private for the people who experience it, so survivors of extreme violence blur the boundaries of culturally sanctioned historical narrative and the narratives of extreme atrocity that the present moment "forgets." From the most private of acts that a person is forced to perform for others during torture, to the extreme lack of privacy experienced by the inmate of the concentration camp, to the total violation of bodies by war crimes, the body of the person who experiences atrocity becomes "public" in a way that violates their deepest cultural norms. Likewise the body and person of the survivor of such atrocity becomes the overdetermined marker of cultural trauma; visually indistinguishable at first glance from nonsurvivors, perhaps, they nonetheless become the trace or ghost of the event itself.

While cultures in various ways memorialize and mark moments of massive atrocity, these actions also serve to seal the events in a historical past. Thus the survivor's very bodily existence is a mark of the event that the cultural "suture" forgets. Even the act of valorizing the survivors is an act of setting them apart as survivors; one does not need to hear their stories over and over again, as one already "knows" the story. In the situation of Afghanistan, where the crimes and atrocities are ongoing and have been so for decades, these people are still within the frame of the atrocity event. They do not yet have a normative culture to attempt to return to, and their stories of atrocity and violence are part of an ongoing process of trauma that is largely invisible—both to those inside the event, because of their proximity, and to those outside the event, us, the potential witnesses who do not care to know. The most important possibility that testimonial suggests is that the performative enactment of witnessing produces an effect exceeding that of the individuals involved in the witnessing itself. Although testimony might be a project deeply rooted in the internal faith-act of testifying, it is exactly the acknowledgment of the impossibility of this act while at the same time performing it that marks testimonial as the expressive genre inextricably bound with the totalitarian violences of the current and past century. The recognition of the scar, the trace of the sutured wound, marks the site of instability where the performative act of testimony occurs, where the witnessing to the trauma is acknowledged as an always impossible act yet still insists on action. It denies both the universal identification of the modernist "I" of the narrator and the particularity of "authentic" individualism, rejecting the compassion of the liberal subject for the victim. Instead, among other things, it demands a traumatic identification—an identification that occurs partly outside the discursive realm—with the delusional ideology of the event that, as Laub notes, prevents one from witnessing from within the event itself. Although, as Derrida states, "the act of faith demanded in bearing witness exceeds, through its structure, all intuition and all proof, all knowledge,"[27] the witnessing engaged in through the testimonial of survivors thoroughly destabilizes this very act of faith upon which bearing witness depends.

But the failed ability to witness from within the event has been made powerfully apparent recently by the very public genocides in Rwanda and Bosnia. Despite the fact of extensive news coverage of atrocities being committed, which in Bosnia was often almost simultaneous, no greater intervention was apparent on the part of the world community that watched. The axiom of "never again" took on a hypocritical and hollow resonance as publics across the globe watched the failure of the world community to intervene into ongoing events of mass death. Witnessing occurred through the iconic journalistic representations of atrocity and was unable to call forth an active, ethical engagement with either past atrocities or the current atrocities being represented.[28] While well-known survivors such as Elie Wiesel spoke out strongly of the need for active response, their arguments were met with a blank and uncomprehending inaction.

As the various testimonial texts and performances under consideration in this book suggest, testimony is itself a performative process necessitating witnessing as opposed to spectatorship. Witnessing necessarily happens in a performative dynamic, and it is in this performative dynamic that a space for justice, as Derrida terms it, might be created. This is just as crucial for the wartime gathering of testimony in conflict zones as it is for more academic considerations of literary testimony. To conduct testimonial interviews in conflict zones is a politically as well as ethically weighted act: as a form of intervention with possible juridical consequences, as a form of "capacity-building" within the local community as women speak their stories in narrativized ways, and as a form of academic analysis.

Spectatorship is not enough; it is in active *witnessing* that the ethical demand occurs. The survivor who is marked as a survivor does not by her or his very existence compel an ethical engagement with atrocity. But there might be an ethical position to witnessing as a performative act between the historical dead, the survivor and the witness to the survivor, which resists both the cultural forgetting implied by iconic journalistic representations (the men behind barbed wire, the woman holding a baby, etc.) and the depletion of the self effected by the pervasive possibility of extinction within which we all now exist—by nuclear explosion, biological warfare, genocide, terrorism.

We exhibit a tremendous refusal to engage with the actual survivors among us—the "ghosts" of the mass atrocities of our century who travel among us unremarked-upon and who carry with them the double burden of their own excessive materiality as survivors and the many ghosts of the murdered dead for whom they witness. These are the mute witnesses who haunt our present moment and cannot provide us with a solution to the dilemmas they pose. We are left at best to feel our position as always one of untenable fascination, repulsion, and exploitation in the face of their demands. We look to biological explanations of behavior or irresolvable "ethnic" or "religious" hatreds that transcend history to provide the distance we need from perpetrators and victims. But perhaps what we must build with this ghost is what we most resist: an ethical relationship that engages the survivor through all the facets of her humanness so that witnessing can take place within a mutually constructed frame.

Ethical witnessing can take place only through such an engagement rather than one disciplined by the demands of the spectator, the representative of the normative culture that fears the contamination of atrocity through its survivor. To become a ghost who is always marked by the scars of atrocity is the violent burden placed by normative culture upon the survivor of atrocity, whose excessive materiality carries the burden of the numerous dead for whom the survivor witnesses. To witness the survivors is to acknowledge the ethical demand of the dead, and to refuse to acknowledge them leaves us not just with the burden of their silence but with the seeping violence of our history. We are all living in the field and in the center—and this center should not and will not hold in its current configuration. We must resist the siren call of ideologies and nationalisms, instead seeking out the difficult engagements with difference that mark both the ethical relationship between individuals and the ground on which dynamic and humane civil societies are built.

NOTES

Preface

1. See Wyschogrod, *Spirit in Ashes,* for a strong philosophical analysis of this terror in structures of modernity.

2. I argue that survivors' stories function very similarly to the way that Zelizer, *Remembering to Forget,* argues photos of atrocity have increasingly come to function. It is not that there is not an immense and wide range of stories and photos available to us but that the ones we care to look at—reprinted in magazines and journals, for example—increasingly follow a stock structure that signifies "atrocity." Two additional books on photography and trauma are Cadava, *Words of Light;* and Baer, *Spectral Evidence.*

3. The burqa is an enveloping garment falling to the ground, with no arms and with a small mesh screen in front of the eyes.

4. Genet's self-identification as gay "outlaw" and Fornes's as a feminist Cuban American mark ways in which they both, as authors, have had an awareness of and negotiated difference and cultural violence.

5. While this book does not undertake an analysis of American slave narratives, they are another crucial form of testimonial. Current works on the subject include S. Hartman, *Scenes of Subjection;* and McBride, *Impossible Witnesses.*

1. Witness and Testimony: Ethics, Trauma, Speech, and Paradox

1. Agamben, *Remnants of Auschwitz,* 60.
2. Ibid., 39.
3. Derrida, *Specters of Marx,* xix.
4. Agamben, *Remnants of Auschwitz,* 164.
5. Lyotard, *Différend.*
6. Derrida, "Force of Law," 16.

7. Kristeva, *Powers of Horror*. Kristeva formulates the abject in a way that is reminiscent of Agamben's formulation of the Muselman. This formulation of the death camps of the Third Reich as the chiasmatic site of abjection that structures post–World War II European and American culture, politics, and thought is a major interest for many of the theorists, political as well as philosophical, who have emerged in the past fifty years. See Derrida, *Specters of Marx*, for an extended elaboration on the ghost as it relates to issues of justice, responsibility, and political culture.

8. Derrida, "Force of Law," 17.

9. Ibid., 20.

10. Ibid., 47, 41.

11. Ibid., 64.

12. Critchley, *Ethics-Politics-Subjectivity*, 280.

13. Ibid., 281.

14. Caldwell, "Bio-Sovereignty."

15. Caldwell, "Bio-Sovereignty," 47.

16. Norris, "Giorgio Agamben," 53.

17. Caldwell, "Bio-Sovereignty," 52.

18. Derrida, "Force of Law," 60. The "order of representation" Derrida references is not just that of the Third Reich but recalls his earlier statement that "the concept of violence belongs to the symbolic order of law, politics and morals" (31). Following from his reading of Benjamin's essay "Critique of Violence," Derrida suggests that "the final solution" was a project that attempted "to annihilate . . . the other of representation: destiny, divine justice and that which can bear witness to it, in other words man."—to eliminate, as he has termed it elsewhere, *différance*, which cannot be apprehended or heard within the logocentric order. If the radical violence experienced by the women whose testimony is under consideration in this book has as its goal the elimination of *différance* and difference, then to speak or write testimony from within the violence of logocentrism is to be always engaged in a crisis of witnessing.

19. Felman and Laub, *Testimony*.

20. Ibid., 63–64.

21. See Young, *Writing and Rewriting*.

22. Felman and Laub, *Testimony*, 65.

23. Ibid., 65.

24. My sense of the terms justice and reconciliation are influenced by, among others, Jacques Derrida, Martha Minow, Jean-François Lyotard, and the survivor testimony under consideration in this book. For a detailed and careful parsing of Derrida's notion of justice as it is developed in *Specters of Marx* along with its relation to his notion of "democracy to come" (*la démocratie à venir*), Benjamin's notion of messianic time, and Levinas's notion of ethical time, see Critchley, *Ethics-Politics-Subjectivity*.

25. Felman and Laub, *Testimony*, 62.

26. Trauma studies, a growing field of intellectual and psychological inquiry, encompasses a number of contested theories, and there is no good single definition. For the purposes of this book, I am employing the term to reference the psychic state described by psychoanalytic theorists who understand trauma as a descriptive term whose development can be traced from Freud and early analysts through to Kristeva and Lacan, and by practitioners, such as Dori Laub, Jack Saul, and Bessel van der Kolk, who trace the lineage of the term from "shell shock" to "posttraumatic stress disorder." I also understand the psychoanalytic notion of trauma to be integral to Levinas's development of the ethical subject and hence to Derrida's.

27. Minow, *Between Vengeance and Forgiveness.*

28. Ibid.

29. He writes, "Unlike the guilty, who wallow in the mire of their own guilt, weighed down by their urge to talk, to be listened to and to confess, those who are ashamed often will to recover or to improve themselves, and even to bond or interact with the violated. The experience of guilt always has a cut-and-dried threshold: an individual or group has either done wrong or not. Shame is by contrast a standard admitting of degrees of realization: the ashamed feel that they have failed to live up fully to a standard towards which they nevertheless still strive. The ashamed accordingly seek to decipher what has happened—sometimes for the purpose of rebuilding both themselves and the world in which they and their offspring have to live their future lives." Keene, *Reflections on Violence,* 184–185.

30. For an extended engagement with the term responsibility and its relationship to deconstructive ethical thinking see Keenan, *Fables of Responsibility.*

31. Lehtinen, "How Does One Know," 56–77.

32. My thinking on performance, as I employ the term in this book, is primarily influenced by the work of performance theorists such as Peggy Phelan, Lynda Hart, Elin Diamond, Richard Schechner, Freddie Rokem, Michael Taussig, and Joseph Roach.

33. Caruth, *Unclaimed Experience,* 91–92.

34. Felman and Laub, *Testimony,* 67.

35. Minow, *Between Vengeance and Forgiveness,* 63.

36. Ibid., 119.

37. Press briefing by Mr. Nigel Fisher, Deputy Special Representative of the Secretary-General for Afghanistan, July 14, 2002.

38. Norah Niland, United Nations Office for the Coordination of Humanitarian Affairs, private conversation.

39. Jerome Shestack, *Understanding International Human Rights: A Primer,* Monograph.

40. See Goodhart, "Origins and Universality," 935–64. Goodhart argues that the preoccupation with the cultural-relativism-versus-universalism debate in human rights theory has kept scholars from recognizing the crucial influence

of globalization on human rights and argues for a critical reevaluation of contemporary approaches and for an alternative framework to cultural relativism as the lens through which to consider human rights.

41. See, e.g., Bunch, "Women's Rights." She argues that the Mothers of the Plaza de Mayo in Argentina played an important role in the UN's recognition of disappearances as a human rights abuse.

42. See, e.g., Sieghart, *Lawful Rights of Mankind,* 64. He states that "it is . . . now strongly arguable that the Universal Declaration is becoming, if it has not already become, part of customary international law, and so binding on all states, regardless of any treaty obligations."

43. Henkin, "International Bill of Rights," 1–19.

44. Ibid., 14.

45. Rodley, "Collective Intervention."

46. Ibid., 17.

47. Ibid., 20.

48. Ibid., 18.

49. Ibid., 21–23.

50. Ibid., 25–26.

51. Ibid., 29.

52. Ibid., 30.

53. Ibid., 31.

54. Ibid.

55. The United States' refusal to include human rights as an issue in foreign trade with countries like Indonesia and China is a good example of the double standard that is regularly employed by the United States, France, and Britain.

56. Monshipouri and Welch, "Search for International Human Rights," 399.

57. Ibid., 400.

58. Henkin, "International Bill of Rights," 18.

59. Sieghart, *Lawful Rights of Mankind,* 83.

60. See, e.g., Nickel, *Making Sense of Human Rights.*

61. Ibid., 9.

62. For a careful parsing of the European philosophic thought underlying human rights as well as a strong refutation of cultural relativism as an argument against human rights, see Shestack, "Philosophic Foundations of Human Rights," 201–34.

63. Minogue, "History of the Idea," 4.

64. Nickel, *Making Sense of Human Rights,* 75–76.

65. See Verdirame, "Testing the Effectiveness," 733–68, for an detailed analysis of the UN's difficulties in applying international legal norms prohibiting discrimination against women to its relations with the Taliban and other authorities in Afghanistan post-1996. While Verdirame provides a strong cri-

tique of the timidity of the UN in applying its own legal and ethical policies to its programming in Afghanistan, he does not address the solution to the UN's crisis of continuing to deliver humanitarian aid to vulnerable populations while upholding standards that most probably would have seen it banned from the country.

66. Article 8. Everyone has the right to an effective remedy by the competent national tribunals for acts violating the fundamental rights granted him by the constitution or by law.

Article 9. No one shall be subjected to arbitrary arrest, detention or exile.

Article 10. Everyone is entitled to full equality to a fair and public hearing by an independent and impartial tribunal, in the determination of his rights and obligations and of any criminal charge against him.

Article 11. (1) Everyone charged with a penal offense has the right to be presumed innocent until proved guilty according to law in a public trial at which he has had all the guarantees necessary for his defense. (2) No one shall be held guilty of any penal offense on account of any act or omission which did not constitute a penal offense, under national or international law, at the time when it was committed. Nor shall a heavier penalty be imposed than the one that was applicable at the time the penal offense was committed.

Article 13. (1) Everyone has the right to freedom of movement and residence within the borders of each state. (2) Everyone has the right to leave any country, including his own, and to return to his country.

Article 14. (1) Everyone has the right to seek and to enjoy in other countries asylum from persecution. (2) This right may not be invoked in the case of prosecutions genuinely arising from non-political crimes or from acts contrary to the purposes and principles of the United Nations.

Article 15. (1) Everyone has the right to a nationality. (2) No one shall be arbitrarily deprived of his nationality nor denied the right to change his nationality.

67. Parsons, "Conclusions and Recommendations," 227.

68. Scoble and Wiseberg, "Problems of Comparative Research," 149.

69. Ibid., 149.

70. Pateman, *Disorder of Women*, 47.

2. "The Erotics of Violence": Performing Violence in *The Balcony* and *The Conduct of Life*

1. Genet, *Balcony;* and Fornes, *Conduct of Life.*

2. Genet, *Balcony,* 1, 2.

3. The brothel in *The Balcony* is also named The Balcony.

4. Chaudhuri, *No Man's Stage,* 42.

5. Ibid., 52.

6. Schechner, *Between Theater and Anthropology,* 272.

7. Mulvey, "Visual Pleasure."
8. Chaudhuri, *No Man's Stage*, 72.
9. Ibid., 74–75.
10. Derrida, *Specters of Marx*.
11. Genet, *Balcony*, 10.
12. Ibid., 10.
13. Bataille, *Erotism*, 16–18.
14. Bataille, *Literature and Evil*, 25.
15. Genet, *Balcony*, 10.
16. See Copjec, *Radical Evil*, for an excellent collection of essays on the relationship of totalitarian violence to the Kantian concept of evil and its relationship to social order.
17. Bersani, "Is the Rectum a Grave?"
18. Bataille, *Literature and Evil*, 20, 22.
19. Ibid., 29.
20. Felman and Laub, *Testimony*, 78.
21. The plot of the play involves four major characters, Orlando, Nena, Olympia, and Léticia, and a minor character, Alejo, to whom Orlando is subordinate at work. Orlando works as a torturer for the dictatorship and has kidnapped a young girl, Nena, whom he secretly holds in the basement of the house he shares with his wife, Léticia, and their maid, Olympia. During the play, he proceeds to torture Nena sexually through rape and psychological abuse until she becomes mute and believes that the torture is her own fault. She is discovered by Olympia and Léticia, who bring her up into the main part of the house and help her to recover her language and her story (which includes her family) by integrating her into the domestic routines of the house. When Orlando discovers them, he attempts to discipline the women, but is shot dead by Léticia, who places the gun in Nena's hand as the play ends.
22. My reading of the dynamics of torture and its relationship to domesticity, theatricality, language, and everyday objects is based largely on the work of Scarry, *Body in Pain*.
23. Wilden, *Man and Woman*.
24. Ibid., 42.
25. Ibid.
26. Ibid., 70.
27. Theweleit, *Male Fantasies*, 432.
28. Ibid., 432.
29. Fornes, *Conduct of Life*, 13.
30. Theweleit, *Male Fantasies*, 196.
31. An alternate reading of the ending would be that Léticia hands the gun to Nena, saying "please," as a plea for Nena to kill her out of guilt for her, perhaps unconscious, collusion with Orlando as the wife who refuses to "know" what her husband does.

32. Žižek, *For They Know Not*.

33. I'm thinking, in particular, of Foucault, *Discipline and Punish*, and *Madness and Civilization*.

34. see Foucault, *Discipline and Punish;* and duBois, *Torture and Truth*.

35. Bunster-Burotto, "Surviving beyond Fear."

36. Bunch, "Women's Rights," 488.

37. Ibid., 491.

38. See, e.g., Bunster-Burotto, "Surviving beyond Fear"; Scarry, *Body in Pain;* and Franco, "Gender, Death and Resistance."

39. Foucault, *Discipline and Punish*, 33–34.

40. Foucault, *Discipline and Punish*, 34.

41. For further readings of the complex American cultural context of the Rodney King beating and subsequent riots, see Gooding-Williams, *Reading Rodney King*.

3. Testimonial and Surviving: Gender and the Crisis of Witnessing

1. Felman and Laub, *Testimony*, 67.

2. I say that testimony is considered always already flawed by many historians and legal practitioners because of the inaccuracies of memory even for people who have survived horrific and well-remembered atrocities.

3. When I speak of the necessary fiction of the unified and coherent speaking subject, I am thinking of identity as it is formulated by, e.g., Sigmund Freud, Jacques Lacan, and Louis Althusser.

4. Delbo, *Who Will Carry the Word?;* and Buber-Neumann, *Milena*.

5. In referring to these works as testimonials, I am taking for granted that they are eyewitness accounts of experience written after the fact and necessarily fictionalized to some extent because of deliberate authorial intent, the constraints of narrative, or the idiosyncrasies of memory. Nonetheless, they are both true—to the extent that they attempt to write the author's own experience from the perspective of a witness—and historical in that they describe historically specific events as they were witnessed and experienced by individuals. For an excellent account of the differences between and the difficulties of the various genres of Holocaust literature, see especially Young, *Writing and Rewriting*.

6. Felman and Laub, *Testimony*, 81.

7. Young, *Writing and Rewriting*, 38.

8. See, e.g., Felman and Laub, *Testimony;* Caruth, *Unclaimed Experience;* and Phelan, *Mourning Sex*. For a nice parsing of the connection between current work on psychic trauma and Holocaust testimony as Lawrence Langer and others define it, see M. Rothberg, *Traumatic Realism*.

9. Felman and Laub, *Testimony*, 81.

10. See the documentary *Shoah*, by Claude Lanzmann, for an excellent portrayal of these complex relationships.

11. Wyschogrod, *Spirit in Ashes,* 57.
12. Theweleit, *Male Fantasies.*
13. Young, *Writing and Rewriting,* 39.
14. Ibid., 192.
15. Some examples of this work, specifically in the context of Holocaust studies, are Horowitz, *Voicing the Void;* Ofer and Weitzman, *Women in the Holocaust;* Heinemann, *Gender and Destiny;* and Baumel, *Double Jeopardy.*
16. Langer, "Gendered Suffering?"
17. Until recently, gender studies in Holocaust studies was relegated to the sidelines in a field dominated by male scholars who largely considered the testimonies of male survivors to represent a universal experience of the Holocaust as an event that transcended gender difference in its enormity. See Ofer and Weitzman, *Women in the Holocaust,* among other works.
18. Millu, *Smoke over Birkenau,* 7.
19. Langer, "Gendered Suffering?" 360.
20. Ringelheim, "Split between Gender," 349–50.
21. Langer, "Gendered Suffering?" 361.
22. M. Rothberg, *Traumatic Realism,* engages Delbo's prose work to further his analysis of the category of "traumatic realism," noting that "she fashions an ethical-aesthetic practice that maintains the history-negating 'experience' of Auschwitz while insisting on historical specificity and difference, and on the overlap of the everyday and the extreme" (175). His reading of Delbo's work as it engages trauma, memory, and narrative is careful and largely in accord with my readings of her testimony, although his refusal to engage the difficulties of gender as a site of difference and to consider the larger historical sweep of testimony, atrocity, and trauma as categories and experiences that inform our current critical, cultural, and even political practices is unfortunate. For a nuanced reading of Delbo's play in the context of performance and Holocaust studies, see Patraka's excellent *Spectacular Suffering.*
23. See Scarry, *Body in Pain.*
24. Wyschogrod, *Spirit in Ashes,* 30.
25. Nomberg-Przytyk, *Auschwitz.*
26. Felman and Laub, *Testimony,* 81.
27. Ibid., chap. 3.
28. Ibid., 80 (emphasis in original).
29. Ibid., chap. 3.
30. Ibid., 82.
31. Scarry, *Body in Pain,* chaps. 1 and 2.
32. Felman and Laub, *Testimony,* 78.
33. For example, Agnès and Gina discuss this early in the play.

Agnès: If there is only one who returns, I don't want to be her. What can she do, that one who returns, to start life again? Do you think you could start life again, Gina?

Gina: I don't know. But if you think of the resources inside ourselves and each other, that we find to draw upon, to help each other come out alive, you realize that we will find other resources to live again if we return.

Delbo, *Who Will Carry,* 1, 4.
34. Ibid., 3, 2.
35. Copjec, "Introduction," xxiii–xxiv.
36. Wyschogrod, *Spirit in Ashes,* 21.
37. Lyotard, *Différend.*
38. Wyschogrod, *Spirit in Ashes,* 33.
39. Ibid., 93.
40. Derrida, *Specters of Marx.*
41. Delbo, *Who Will Carry,* 276.
42. Ibid., 278.
43. Ibid., 280.
44. Lyotard, *Différend,* 8.
45. Delbo, *Who Will Carry,* 279.
46. Felman and Laub, *Testimony,* 81 (emphasis in original).
47. De Lauretis, "Sexual Indifference," provides a detailed analysis of lesbian difference and heterosexual "indifference." See also, e.g., De Lauretis, *Practice of Love;* and Grosz and Probyn, *Sexy Bodies.*
48. Buber-Neumann, *Milena,* 151.
49. Ibid., 185.
50. Ibid., 186.
51. Ibid.
52. Ibid., 187.
53. Ibid.
54. Ibid., 188.
55. For further reading on the criminalization of lesbianism in modern culture, see Krafft-Ebing, *Psychopathia Sexualis;* Hart, *Fatal Women;* De Lauretis, "Sexual Indifference."
56. Buber-Neumann, *Milena,* 192.
57. Ibid., 192.
58. Ibid.
59. Ibid., 193.
60. Ibid., 11.
61. Ibid., 5.
62. Ibid.
63. Ibid.
64. Laub's formulation in Felman and Laub, *Testimony.*
65. Buber-Neumann, *Milena,* 156.
66. Ibid., 170.
67. Ibid., 172.
68. Ibid., 179–80.

69. Ibid., 30.
70. Ibid., 33.
71. Ibid., 66.
72. Ibid., 3.
73. Ibid., 40.
74. Ibid., 11.
75. Ibid., 39.
76. Ibid., 40.
77. Ibid., 153–54.
78. Tillion, *Ravensbrück,* xxii.
79. Young, *Writing and Rewriting,* 44.
80. Ibid., 46.
81. For an excellent and more detailed account of this, see Young, *Writing and Rewriting,* 43–50.
82. Nomberg-Przytyk, *Auschwitz,* 102.
83. Ibid., 106.

4. State Terror and the Ethical Witness

1. See in particular Beverley, *Against Literature;* Sommer, "Keeping Sacred Secrets"; Sommer, *Real Thing;* Yúdice, "Testimonio."
2. Yúdice, "Testimonio."
3. Ibid., 44.
4. Moreiras, "Aura of Testimonio," 195.
5. Ibid., 206.
6. See Beverley, *Against Literature;* and Sommer "Keeping Sacred Secrets."
7. Yúdice, "Testimonio," 49.
8. Taylor, *Disappearing Acts,* 151.
9. Partnoy, *Little School,* 18.
10. Yúdice, "Testimonio," 42.
11. See Caruth, *Unclaimed Experience.*
12. Taylor, *Disappearing Acts,* 160.
13. Ibid., 165 (emphasis in original).
14. Feitlowitz, *Lexicon of Terror.*
15. For this formulation of the workings of solidarity with the "secret" of *testimonio* I am following Alberto Moreiras's reading of Doris Sommer in "Aura of Testimonio."
16. Taylor, *Disappearing Acts.*
17. See Scarry, *Body in Pain.*
18. Feitlowitz, *Lexicon of Terror,* 62.
19. Saul, "Therapeutic Uses."
20. See Zelizer, *Remembering to Forget.*

21. Partnoy, *Little School;* Gambaro, *Information for Foreigners.*

22. Partnoy, *Little School,* 17.

23. See Feitlowitz, "Introduction."

24. Like all such numbers, this figure is contested but is the number of disappeared stated by the Mothers of the Plaza de Mayo and is widely accepted within Argentine human rights circles.

25. Scarry, *Body in Pain.*

26. Ibid., 53.

27. Filc, "Representations of Family."

28. Ibid.

29. Timerman, *Prisoner without a Name.*

30. I am not suggesting that language and problems of understanding were not crucial within the camps. Most Holocaust literature includes a discussion of the importance of understanding and adapting to the linguistic variations in the camps as an important element of survival. And while the eruptions of massive violence that attend war and other situations of broad social terror and upheaval certainly alter and do violence to language, they do not entail a complete breakdown of linguistic signifiers.

31. Partnoy, *Little School,* 18.

32. For a detailed analysis of this process, see Filc, "Representations of Family."

33. Partnoy, *Little School,* 25.

34. Ibid., 31.

35. Ibid., 42.

36. Ibid., 78.

37. Ibid., 68.

38. Ibid., 72.

39. Ibid., 73.

40. Feitlowitz, *Lexicon of Terror.*

41. Partnoy, *Little School,* 73.

42. Ibid., 32.

43. Ibid., 94–95 (emphasis in original).

44. Levi, *Survival in Auschwitz.*

45. Feitlowitz, interviewing Astelarra, *Lexicon of Terror,* 64.

46. For a detailed and informative study of the torture and abuse directed specifically against women in Argentina and other Latin-American countries, see Bunster-Burotto, "Surviving beyond Fear." See also Dworkin, *Nunca más,* the collection of witness testimony collected by the Argentine government at the end of the dictatorship.

47. This quotation is also included in the introduction to the English-language edition of Gambaro, *Information for Foreigners.*

48. Feitlowitz, *Lexicon of Terror,* 65.

49. Ibid., 107.

50. Taylor, *Disappearing Acts.*

51. These statistics are given in the footnotes to the introduction of Gambaro, *Information for Foreigners.*

52. For a good history of the organization, see Mellibovsky, *Circle of Love.*

53. Taylor, *Disappearing Acts,* 157 (emphasis in original).

5. Testimonial, Trauma, and the Crises of Discourse in Bosnia

1. As I noted in chapter four, not only is torture itself usually an act hidden by the perpetrators, but the relationship between the perpetrator and the person being tortured comes to be constructed as a gendered relationship between men and women, with the victim occupying the position of the woman whose body is controlled, penetrated, emasculated, and immobilized. See, e.g., Bunster-Burotto, "Surviving beyond Fear"; Scarry, *Body in Pain;* and Franco, "Gender, Death and Resistance."

2. Beverley, *Against Literature.*

3. I use the term "concentrationary" as it is often used in Holocaust studies to refer to the almost phantasmic nature of the experience of trying to survive within the event in a death camp, work camp, and so on, but I am also broadening its use to include the experience of living within any ongoing situation of traumatic physical and psychic abuse, such as imprisonment and torture, that occurs under pervasive structures of totalitarian violence.

4. Felman and Laub, *Testimony,* chap. 3.

5. Some books on the subject of the war and abuses in former Yugoslavia include: Campbell, *National Deconstruction;* Weine, *When History Is a Nightmare;* Nikolic-Ristanovic, *Women, Violence and War;* Gutman, *Witness to Genocide.*

6. See Brennan, *At Home in the World;* and Derrida, *On Cosmopolitanism.*

7. Bunster-Burotto, "Surviving beyond Fear."

8. Human Rights Watch, *Human Rights Watch Global Report.*

9. Ibid., 10.

10. Copelan, "Resurfacing Gender," 208.

11. Drakulic, *Balkan Express,* 144–45.

12. Ibid., 149–50.

13. Softic, *Sarajevo Days,* 90.

14. Drakulic, *Balkan Express,* 42–43.

15. Ibid., 47.

16. Ibid., 48.

17. Ibid., 4.

18. Softic, *Sarajevo Days,* 62.

19. Ibid., 168.

20. Ibid., 66.

21. Ibid., 50.

22. Drakulic, *Balkan Express,* 51.
23. Laub's chapters in *Testimony* also contain suggestions that some survivors perceive their identities as more a balancing of discontinuities than an unbroken narrative.
24. Beverley, *Against Literature.*

6. Grounded Ethics: Testimonial Witnessing from Rural Afghanistan to the United States

1. Booth, "Three Tyrannies," 57.
2. Zelizer, *Remembering to Forget,* has an excellent analysis of this mechanism in her final chapter.
3. Derrida, "Force of Law," 17.
4. duBois, *Torture and Truth.*
5. Booth, "Three Tyrannies," 61.
6. Ibid., 62.
7. Ibid., 65.
8. Data extracted from United Nations Development Program, *Human Development Report 1995* and *Human Development Report 1996,* and from the World Health Organization Afghanistan, 2000. The age of this data reflects the extreme difficulty of collecting even semireliable information in a situation of such ongoing chaos. Due to the worsening of the security situation from 2002 to 2004, over the past two years there are still no reliable, systematic, countrywide data, and the recent data that have been collected show little change.
9. For an excellent history of the Taliban Islamic Movement in Afghanistan, see Rashid, *Taliban.*
10. By human rights deficit, I refer to the deficit in basic development—such as access to clean drinking water, food, shelter, basic education, health care, and work as well as freedom from violence—that needs to be closed in the country to bring it up to the level where international human rights standards can begin to be broadly applied.
11. Le Duc, "Gender and Education," quoting from the UNESCO Statistical Yearbooks for 1977, 1988, and 1990.
12. World Bank, *Education for Afghans,* 26.
13. Purdah is the isolation of women from all men except near relatives once they have passed the age of puberty. Although in Islam there is no definite, unqualified requirement for purdah and the veil, in Afghanistan, as in many other places, it is such an entrenched cultural norm that it is often understood to be and portrayed as religious law.
14. See United Nations Development Program, *Human Development in South Asia 1998,* for more detailed discussion of these relationships.
15. Subbaro and Raney, *Social Gains.*

16. Stromquist, *Increasing Girls' and Women's Participation*, 18.

17. Save the Children, U.K., private conversation with author, April 2001.

18. Data from the Swedish Committee for Afghanistan, *Nutrition and Tuberculosis Baseline Survey*, 1998.

19. Derrida, "Force of Law," 16.

20. Derrida, ". . . and pomegranates," 341.

21. Derrida, "Force of Law," 22.

22. Ibid., 17.

23. Ibid., 5.

24. Ibid., 20.

25. I am particularly indebted to Dori Laub for this formulation.

26. Van Der Veer, "Victim's Tale," 199.

27. Derrida, "Force of Law," 22.

28. As has been nicely elaborated by Zelizer, *Remembering to Forget*.

SELECTED BIBLIOGRAPHY

Ackerly, Brooke. *Political Theory and Feminist Social Criticism*. London: Cambridge University Press, 2000.

Afary, Janet. "The Human Rights of Middle Eastern and Muslim Women: A Project for the 21st Century." *Human Rights Quarterly* 26.1 (2004): 106–25.

Agamben, Giorgio. *Remnants of Auschwitz: The Witness and the Archive*. Translated by Daniel Heller-Roazen. New York: Zone Books, 1999.

Agosin, Marjorie. "Notes on the Poetics of the Acevedo Movement against Torture." *Human Rights Quarterly* 10 (1988): 339–443.

———. "So We Will Not Forget: Literature and Human Rights in Latin America." *Human Rights Quarterly* 10 (1988): 177–92.

Alcoff, Linda, and Laura Grey. "Survivor Discourse: Transgression or Recuperation?" *Signs: The Journal of Women in Society* 18.2 (Winter 1993): 260–90.

Alston, Philip. *The United Nations and Human Rights: A Critical Appraisal*. Oxford: Clarendon Press, 1992.

Althusser, Louis. "Ideology and Ideological State Apparatuses." In *Lenin and Philosophy, and other essays*, translated by Ben Brewster. New York: Monthly Review Press, 1972.

Alves, Jose A. Lingren. "The Declaration of Human Rights in Postmodernity." *Human Rights Quarterly* 22.2 (2000): 478–500.

Agger, Inger. *The Blue Room: Trauma and Testimony among Refugee Women: A Psycho-Social Exploration*, translated by Mary Bille. London: Zed Books, 1994.

Agger, Inger, and Søren Buus Jensen. *Trauma and Healing under State Terrorism*. London: Zed Books, 1996.

Anzaldúa, Gloria, and Cherríe Moraga. *This Bridge Called My Back*. New York: Kitchen Table, Women of Color Press, 1981.

Arendt, Hannah. *On Violence*. New York: Harcourt Brace Jovanovich, 1970.

————. *The Origins of Totalitarianism*. New York: Harcourt Brace Jovanovich, 1951.

Avisar, Ilan. *Screening the Holocaust: Cinema's Images of the Unimaginable.* Bloomington: Indiana University Press, 1988.

Baer, Ulrich. *Spectral Evidence: The Photography of Trauma.* Cambridge, Mass.: MIT Press, 2002.

Balfour, Ian, and Eduardo Cadava. "The Claims of Human Rights." *South Atlantic Quarterly* 103.2/3 (2004): 277–96.

Bataille, George. *Erotism: Death and Sensuality.* San Francisco: City Lights Books, 1986.

————. *Literature and Evil.* New York: Marion Boyars, 1985.

Baumel, Judith Tydor. *Double Jeopardy: Gender and the Holocaust.* Portland, Ore.: Vallentine Mitchell, 1998.

Bell, Daniel A., and Joseph H. Carens. "The Ethical Dilemmas of International Human Rights and Humanitarian NGOs: Reflections on a Dialogue between Practitioners and Theorists." *Human Rights Quarterly* 26.2 (2004): 300–29.

Benthall, Jonathan. *Disasters, Relief and the Media.* New York: I.B. Tauris, 1993.

Berman, Russell. *Modern Culture and Critical Theory.* Madison: University of Wisconsin Press, 1989.

Bersani, Leo. "Is the Rectum a Grave?" In *AIDS: Cultural Analysis, Cultural Activism,* edited by Douglas Crimp. Cambridge, Mass.: MIT Press, 1988.

Bersani, Leo, and Ulysses Dutoit. *The Forms of Violence.* New York: Schocken Books, 1985.

Berting, Jan, ed. *Human Rights in a Pluralist World: Individuals and Collectivities.* London and Westport, Conn.: Meckler, 1990.

Beverley, John. *Against Literature.* Minneapolis: University of Minnesota Press, 1993.

Blanchot, Maurice. *The Unavowable Community,* translated by Pierre Joris. Barrytown, N.Y.: Station Hill Press, 1988.

————. *The Writing of the Disaster,* translated by Ann Smock. Lincoln: University of Nebraska Press, 1986.

Blanchot, Maurice, and Jacques Derrida. *The Instant of My Death: Demeure: Fiction and Testimony,* translated by Elizabeth Rottenberg, edited by Werner Hamacher and David E. Wellbery. Stanford, Calif.: Stanford University Press, 2000.

Booth, Ken. "Three Tyrannies." In *Human Rights in Global Politics,* edited by Tim Dunne and Nicholas J. Wheeler. Cambridge: Cambridge University Press, 1999.

Borradori, Giovanna. *Philosophy in a Time of Terror.* Chicago: University of Chicago Press, 2003.

Bosmajian, Hamida. *Metaphors of Evil: Contemporary German Literature and the Shadow of Nazism.* Iowa City: University of Iowa Press, 1979.

Brems, Eva. "Enemies or Allies? Feminism and Cultural Relativism as Dissident Voices in Human Rights Discourse." *Human Rights Quarterly* 19.1 (1997): 136–64.

Brennan, Timothy. *At Home in the World: Cosmopolitanism Now.* Cambridge, Mass.: Harvard University Press, 1997.

Bridenthal, Renate, Atina Grossman, and Marion Kaplan, eds. *When Biology Became Destiny: Women in Weimar and Nazi Germany.* New York: Monthly Review Press, 1984.

Brodzki, Bella, and Celeste Schenck, eds. *Life/Lines: Theorizing Women's Autobiography.* Foreword by Germaine Brée. Ithaca, N.Y.: Cornell University Press, 1988.

Buber-Neumann, Margarete. *Milena: The Story of a Remarkable Friendship,* translated by Ralph Manheim. New York: Schocken Books, 1977; New York: Seaver Books, 1988.

Bunch, Charlotte. "Women's Rights as Human Rights: Toward a Re-Vision of Human Rights." *Human Rights Quarterly* 12 (1990): 487–98.

Bunster-Burotto, Ximena. "Surviving beyond Fear: Women and Torture in Latin America." In *Women and Change in Latin America,* edited by June Nash and Helen Safa, 297–325. South Hadley, Mass.: Bergin and Garvey, 1985.

Burgin, Victor, James Donald, and Cora Kaplan. *Formations of Fantasy.* New York: Methuen, 1986.

Butler, Judith. *Gender Trouble: Feminism and the Subversion of Identity.* New York: Routledge, 1990.

Cadava, Eduardo. *Words of Light: Theses on the Photography of History.* Princeton, N.J.: Princeton University Press, 1997.

Caldwell, Anne. "Bio-Sovereignty and the Emergence of Humanity." *Theory & Event* 7.2 (2004).

Campbell, David. *National Deconstruction: Violence, Identity and Justice in Bosnia.* Minneapolis: University of Minnesota Press, 1998.

Card, Claudia. "Responsibility, Ethics, Shared Understandings and Moral Communities." *Hypatia* 17.1 (2002): 141–55.

Caruth, Cathy. *Unclaimed Experience: Trauma, Narrative, and History.* Baltimore, Md.: Johns Hopkins University Press, 1996.

Caruth, Cathy, and Deborah Esch, eds. *Critical Encounters: Reference and Responsibility in Deconstructive Writing.* New Brunswick, N.J.: Rutgers University Press, 1995.

Casy, Edward S. *Remembering: A Phenomenological Study.* Bloomington: Indiana University Press, 2000.

Chambers, Samuel A. "Ghostly Rights." *Cultural Critique* 54 (2003): 148–77.

Chaudhuri, Una. *No Man's Stage: A Semiotic Study of Jean Genet's Major Plays.* Ann Arbor, Mich.: UMI Research Press, 1986.

Chow, Rey. *Ethics after Idealism: Theory, Culture, Ethnicity, Reading.* Bloomington: University of Indiana Press, 1998.

Cook, Rebecca J. *Human Rights of Women*. Philadelphia: University of Pennsylvania Press, 1994.

Copelan, Rhonda. "Resurfacing Gender." In *Mass Rape: The War against Women in Bosnia-Herzegovina*, edited by Alexandra Stiglmayer. Lincoln: University of Nebraska Press, 1994.

Copjec, Joan. "Introduction: Evil in the Time of the Finite World." In *Radical Evil*, edited bu Joan Copjec. New York: Verso, 1996.

———, ed. *Radical Evil*. New York: Verso, 1996.

Cornell, Drucilla, Michel Rosenfeld, and David Gray Carlson, eds. *Deconstruction and the Possibility of Justice*. New York and London: Routledge, 1992.

Corradi, Juan E., Patricia Weiss Fagen, and Manuel Antonio Garretón, eds. *Fear at the Edge: State Terror and Resistance in Latin America*. Berkeley: University of California Press, 1992.

Critchley, Simon. *The Ethics of Deconstruction: Derrida and Levinas*. London: Blackwell, 1992.

———. *Ethics-Politics-Subjectivity: Essays on Derrida, Levinas and Contemporary French Thought*. New York: Verso, 1999.

Cvetkovich, Ann. *An Archive of Feelings: Trauma, Sexuality and Lesbian Public Cultures*. London and Durham, N.C.: Duke University Press, 2003.

———. "Sexual Trauma/Queer Memory: Incest, Lesbianism, and Therapeutic Culture." *GLQ: A Journal of Lesbian and Gay Studies* 2 (20 October 1995).

Dawidowicz, Lucy S. *The War against the Jews 1933–1945*. 2nd ed. New York: Seth Press, 1975.

Daws, James. "Atrocity and Interrogation." *Critical Inquiry* 30.2 (Winter 2004).

De Lauretis, Teresa. "Sexual Indifference and Lesbian Representation." In *Performing Feminisms: Feminist Critical Theory and Theater*, edited by Sue-Ellen Case. Baltimore, Md.: Johns Hopkins University Press, 1990.

———. *The Practice of Love: Lesbian Sexuality and Perverse Desire*. Bloomington: Indiana University Press, 1994.

Delbo, Charlotte. *Who Will Carry the Word?* In *The Theatre of the Holocaust*, edited by Robert Skloot. Madison: University of Wisconsin Press, 1982.

Deleuze, Gilles, and Félix Guattari. *Anti-Oedipus: Capitalism and Schizophrenia*, translated by Robert Hurley, Mark Seem, and Helen R. Lane. Minneapolis: University of Minnesota Press, 1983.

———. *A Thousand Plateaus: Capitalism and Schizophrenia*, translated by Brian Massumi. Minneapolis: University of Minnesota Press, 1987.

Derrida, Jacques. "Force of Law: The 'Mystical Foundation of Authority.'" In *Deconstruction and the Possibility of Justice*, edited by Drucilla Cornell, Michel Rosenfeld, and David Gray Carlson. New York: Routledge, 1992.

———. *Desiring Revolution: On Cosmopolitanism and Forgiveness*. New York: Routledge Press, 2001.

———. *Of Spirit: Heidegger and the Question*. Chicago: University of Chicago Press, 1989.

———. *On Cosmopolitanism and Forgiveness*, translated by Mark Dooley and Michael Hughes. New York: Routledge, 2001.

———. "Passages—From Traumatism to Promise." Interview with Elizabeth Weber. In *Points . . . Interviews, 1974–1994*, edited by Werner Hamacher & David E. Wellbery. Stanford, Calif.: Stanford University Press, 1995.

———. *Points . . . Interviews, 1974–1994*, edited by Werner Hamacher and David E. Wellbery. Stanford, Calif.: Stanford University Press, 1995.

———. *Specters of Marx: The State of the Debt, the Work of Mourning, and the New International*, translated by Peggy Kamuf. New York: Routledge, 1994.

———. ". . . and pomegranates." In *Violence, Identity and Self-Determination*, edited by Hent de Vries and Samuel Weber. Stanford, Calif.: Stanford University Press, 1997.

———. *Writing and Difference*. New York: Routledge, 1981.

Des Pres, Terrence. *The Survivor: An Anatomy of Life in the Death Camps*. New York: Oxford University Press, 1976.

de Vries, Hent, and Samuel Weber, eds. *Violence, Identity and Self-Determination*. Stanford, Calif.: Stanford University Press, 1997.

Diamond, Elin. *Unmaking Mimesis: Essays on Feminism and Theatre*. London and New York: Routledge, 1998.

Douglas, Mary. *Purity and Danger: An Analysis of the Concepts of Pollution and Taboo*. New York: Routledge, 1966.

Drakulić, Slavenka. *The Balkan Express: Fragments from the Other Side of War*, translated by Maja Soljan. New York: W. W. Norton, 1993.

duBois, Page. *Torture and Truth*. New York: Routledge, 1991.

Dunn, Tim, and Nicholas J. Wheeler, eds. *Human Rights in Global Politics*. London: Cambridge University Press, 1999.

Dworkin, Ronald. "Introduction." In *Nunca más: The Report of the Argentine National Commission on the Disappeared*. New York: Farrar, Straus and Giroux, 1986.

Eide, Asbjørn, et al. *The Universal Declaration of Human Rights: A Commentary*. New York: Scandinavian University Press; Oxford University Press, 1992.

Elam, Diane, and Robyn Wiegman, eds. *Feminism Beside Itself*. New York: Routledge Press, 1995.

Enns, Diane. "Bare Life and the Occupied Body." *Theory and Event* 7.3.

Ezrahi, Sidra DeKoven. *By Words Alone: The Holocaust in Literature*. Chicago: University of Chicago Press, 1980.

Fein, Helen. *Accounting for Genocide: National Responses and Jewish Victimization during the Holocaust*. Chicago: University of Chicago Press, 1979.

Feitlowitz, Marguerite. "Introduction." In *Information for Foreigners: Three Plays by Griselda Gambaro*, edited and translated by Marguerite Feitlowitz. Evanston, Ill.: Northwestern University Press, 1992.

————. *A Lexicon of Terror: Argentina and the Legacies of Torture.* New York: Oxford University Press, 1998.

Felman, Shosana. *What Does a Woman Want: Reading and Sexual Difference.* Baltimore: Johns Hopkins University Press, 1993.

Felman, Shoshona, and Dori Laub. *Testimony: Crises of Witnessing in Literature, Psychoanalysis, and History.* New York: Routledge, 1992.

Figley, Charles R., ed. *Trauma and Its Wake.* New York: Brunner/Mazel, 1985.

Filc, Judy. "Representations of Family and Practices of Resistance against Argentine Dictatorship, 1976–1983." Dissertation, University of Pennsylvania, 1994.

Filopovic, Zlata. *Zlata's Diary: A Child's Life in Sarajevo,* translated by Christina Pribichevich-Zoric, Introduction by Janine Di Giovanni. New York: Penguin Books, 1995.

Fornes, Marie Irene. *The Conduct of Life.* In *Plays.* New York: PAJ Publications, 1985.

Forsythe, David. *Human Rights and World Politics.* Lincoln: University of Nebraska Press, 1989.

————. *The Internationalization of Human Rights.* Lexington, Mass.: Lexington Books, 1991.

Foucault, Michel. *Discipline and Punish: The Birth of the Prison.* New York: Random House, 1977.

————. *The History of Sexuality: Volume 1, an Introduction.* New York: Random House, 1978.

————. *Madness and Civilization: A History of Insanity in the Age of Reason,* translated by Richard Howard. New York: Pantheon Books, 1965.

Franco, Jean. "Gender, Death, and Resistance." In *Fear at the Edge: State Terror and Resistance in Latin America,* edited by Juan E. Corradi, Patricia Weiss Fagen, and Manuel Antonio Garretón, 104–118. Berkeley: University of California Press, 1992.

Friedlander, Saul. *Memory, History, and the Extermination of the Jews of Europe.* Bloomington: Indiana University Press, 1993.

————, ed. *Probing the Limits of Representation: Nazism and the "Final Solution."* Cambridge, Mass.: Harvard University Press, 1992.

Gates, Henry Louis, Jr., ed. *"Race," Writing, and Difference.* Chicago: University of Chicago Press, 1986.

Gambaro, Griselda. *Information for Foreigners.* In *Information for Foreigners: Three Plays by Griselda Gambaro,* edited and translated by Marguerite Feitlowitz. Evanston, Ill.: Northwestern University Press, 1992.

Genet, Jean. *The Balcony.* New York: Grove Press, 1966.

Gerhard, Jean. *Desiring Revolution: Second-Wave Feminism and the Rewriting of America Sexual Thought, 1920 to 1982.* New York: Columbia University Press, 2001.

Gibson, Pamela Church, and Roma Gibson, ed. *Dirty Looks: Women, Pornography, Power.* London: British Film Institute, 1993.

Goodhart, Michael. "Origins and Universality in the Human Rights Debates: Cultural Essentialism and the Challenge of Globalization." *Human Rights Quarterly* 25.4 (2003): 935–64.

Gooding-Williams, Robert, ed. *Reading Rodney King/Reading Urban Uprising.* New York: Routledge, 1993.

Gordon, Avery F. *Ghostly Matters: Haunting and the Sociological Imagination.* Minneapolis: University of Minnesota Press, 1997.

Grosz, Elizabeth, and Elspeth Probyn, eds. *Sexy Bodies: The Strange Carnalities of Feminism.* New York: Routledge, 1995.

Guest, Iain. *Behind the Disappearances: Argentina's Dirty War against Human Rights.* Philadelphia: University of Pennsylvania Press, 1990.

Gugelberger, George M., ed. *The Real Thing: Testimonial Discourse and Latin America.* Durham, N.C.: Duke University Press, 1996.

Gutman, Roy. *A Witness to Genocide: The 1993 Pulitzer Prize-Winning Dispatches on the "Ethnic Cleansing" of Bosnia.* New York: Maxwell Macmillan International, 1993.

Hannum, Hurst, ed. *Guide to International Human Rights Practice.* 2nd ed. Philadelphia: University of Pennsylvania Press, 1992.

Harlow, Barbara. *Resistance Literature.* New York: Methuen, 1987.

Harpham, Geoffrey Galt. *Shadows of Ethics.* Durham, N.C., and London: Duke University Press, 1999.

Hart, Lynda. *Between the Body and the Flesh.* Princeton, N.J.: Princeton University Press, 1998.

———. *Fatal Women: Lesbian Women and the Mark of Aggression.* Princeton, N.J.: Princeton University Press, 1994.

Hartman, Geoffrey H., ed. *Holocaust Remembrance: The Shapes of Memory.* Cambridge, Mass.: Blackwell, 1994.

———. *The Longest Shadow: In the Aftermath of the Holocaust.* Bloomington: Indiana University Press, 1996.

Hartman, Saidiya V. *Scenes of Subjection: Terror, Slavery, and Self-Making in Nineteenth-Century America.* New York: Oxford University Press, 1997.

Harvey, David. "Cosmopolitan and Banality of Geographical Evils." *Public Culture* 12.2 (2000): 529–64.

Heinemann, Marlene. *Gender and Destiny: Women Writers and the Holocaust.* New York: Greenwood Press, 1986.

Henkin, Louis. *The Age of Rights.* New York: Columbia University Press, 1990.

———. "The International Bill of Rights: The Universal Declaration and the Covenants." In *International Enforcement of Human Rights,* edited by Rudolf Bernhardt and John Anthony Jolowicz, 1–19. New York: Springer-Verlag, 1985.

Hesse, Carla, and Robert Post. *Human Rights in Political Transitions: Gettysburg to Bosnia.* New York: Zone Books, 1999.

Holland, Sharon Patricia. *Raising the Dead: Readings of Death and (Black) Subjectivity*. Durham, N.C.: Duke University Press, 2000.

Horowitz, Sara. *Voicing the Void: Muteness and Memory in Holocaust Fiction*. Albany: State University of New York Press, 1997.

Huffer, Lynne. "'There Is No Gomorrah': Narrative Ethics in Feminist and Queer Theory." *differences: A Journal of Feminist Cultural Studies* 12.3 (2001): 1–32.

Human Rights Watch. *Human Rights Watch Global Report on Women's Human Rights*. Washington, D.C.: Human Rights Watch, 1995.

Ignatieff, Michael. *Human Rights as Politics and Idolatry*. Princeton, N.J.: Princeton University Press, 2001.

Insdorf, Annette. *Indelible Shadows: Film and the Holocaust*. New York: Vintage Books, 1983.

Keenan, Thomas. *Fables of Responsibility*. Stanford, Calif.: Stanford University Press, 1997.

Keene, John. *Reflections on Violence*. New York: Verso, 1996.

Kolk, Bessel A. van der. *Psychological Trauma*. Washington, D.C.: American Psychiatric Press, 1987.

Kolk, Bessel A. van der, Alexander C. McFarlane, and Lars Weisaeth, eds. *Traumatic Stress: The Overwhelming Experience on Mind, Body and Society*. New York and London: Guilford Press, 1996.

Krafft-Ebing, Richard von. *Psychopathia Sexualis: A Medico-Forensic Study*, translated by Franklin S. Klaf. 1886; repr., New York: Bell Publishing, 1965.

Kristeva, Julia. *Powers of Horror: An Essay on Abjection*. New York: Columbia University Press, 1982.

LaCapra, Dominick. *History and Memory after Auschwitz*. Ithaca, N.Y.: Cornell University Press, 1998.

Lacoue-Labarthe, Philippe. *Heidegger, Art, and Politics: The Fiction of the Political*. London: Blackwell, 1990.

———. *The Subject of Philosophy*. Minneapolis: University of Minnesota Press, 1993.

Langer, Lawrence L. *The Age of Atrocity*. Boston: Beacon Press, 1978.

———. "Gendered Suffering? Women in Holocaust Testimonies." In *Women in the Holocaust*, edited by Dalia Ofer and Lenore J. Weitzman. New Haven, Conn.: Yale University Press, 1998.

Le Duc, Carol A. "Gender and Education in Afghanistan: A Historical Perspective." Paper presented at the Education for Afghans Conference, World Bank, Washington D.C., 13 December 1999.

Lehtinen, Ullaliina. "How Does One Know What Shame Is? Epistemology, Emotions, and Forms of Life in Juxtaposition." *Hypatia* 13 (Winter 1998): 56–77.

Levi, Primo. *Survival in Auschwitz*. New York: Macmillan Publishing Company, 1961.

Leys, Ruth. *Trauma: A Genealogy*. Chicago: University of Chicago Press, 2000.

Lifton, Robert Jay. *The Nazi Doctors: Medical Killing and the Psychology of Genocide*. New York: Basic Books, 1986.

Losi, Natale, Luisa Passerini, and Silvia Salvatici, eds. *Archives of Memory: Supporting Traumatized Communities through Narration and Remembrance*, Psychosocial Notebook Vol. 2. Geneva: International Organization for Migration, 2001. Available at http://www.forcedmigration.org/psychosocial/papers/WiderPapers/iom_notebook2.pdf.

Ludden, David, ed. *Contesting the Nation: Religion, Community, and the Politics of Democracy in India*. Philadelphia: University of Pennsylvania Press, 1996.

Lyotard, Jean-François. *The Différend: Phrases in Dispute*, translated by Georges Van Den Abbeele. Minneapolis: University of Minnesota Press, 1988.

McBride, Dwight A. *Impossible Witnesses: Truth, Abolitionism, and Slave Testimony*. New York: New York University Press, 2001.

McClintock, Anne. *Imperial Leather: Race, Gender and Sexuality in the Colonial Contest*. New York: Routledge, 1995.

McLagan, Meg. "Human Rights, Testimony, and Transnational Publicity." *Scholar and Feminist Online* 2.1 (Summer 2003) issue on "Public Sentiments." Available at http://www.barnard.edu/sfonline/ps/.

Means, J. Jeffrey. *Trauma and Evil: Healing the Wounded Soul*, with contributions by Mary Ann Nelson. Minneapolis: Fortress Press, 2000.

Mellibovsky, Matilde. *Circle of Love over Death: Testimonies of the Mothers of the Plaza de Mayo*, translated by Maria Proser and Matthew Proser. Willimantic, Conn.: Curbstone Press, 1997.

Merry, Sally Engle. "Rights Talk and the Experience of Law: Implementing Women's Human Rights to Protection from Violence." *Human Rights Quarterly* 25.2 (2003): 343–81.

Miller, J. Hillis. *Speech Acts in Literature*. Stanford, Calif.: Stanford University Press, 2001.

Millu, Liana. *Smoke over Birkenau*, translated by Lynne Sharon Schwartz. New York: Jewish Publication Society, 1991.

Minogue, Kenneth. "The History of the Idea of Human Rights." In *The Human Rights Reader*, edited by Walter Laqueur and Barry Rubin. New York: Penguin, 1990.

Minow, Martha. *Between Vengeance and Forgiveness: Facing History after Genocide and Mass Murder*. Boston: Beacon Press, 1998.

Monshipouri, Mahmood, and Claude E. Welch, "The Search for International Human Rights and Justice: Coming to Terms with the New Global Realities." *Human Rights Quarterly* 23.2 (2001): 370–401.

Moreiras, Alberto. "The Aura of Testimonio." In *The Real Thing: Testimonial Discourse and Latin America*, edited by Georg M. Gugelberger. Durham, N.C.: Duke University Press, 1996.

Mulvey, Laura. "Visual Pleasure and Narrative Cinema." *Screen* 16.3 (1975): 6–18.

Nancy, Jean-Luc. *Being Singular Plural*. Stanford, Calif.: Stanford University Press, 2000.

———. *The Inoperative Community*. Vol. 76, Theory and History of Literature Series. Minneapolis: University of Minnesota Press, 1991.

Nickel, James W. *Making Sense of Human Rights: Philosophical Reflections on the Universal Declaration of Human Rights*. Berkeley: University of California Press, 1987.

Nikolic-Ristanovic,Vesna, ed. *Women, Violence and War: Wartime Victimization of Refugees in the Balkans*. Budapest: Central European University Press, 2000.

Nomberg-Przytyk, Sara. *Auschwitz: True Tales from a Grotesque Land*, translated by Roslyn Hirsch. Chapel Hill: University of North Carolina Press, 1985.

Norris, Andrew. "Giorgio Agamben and the Politics of the Living Dead." *Diacritics* 30.4 (2002): 38–58.

Novac, Ana. *J'avais 14 ans à Auschwitz*. Paris: Presses de la Renaissance, 1982.

Ofer, Dalia, and Lenore J. Weitzman, eds. *Women in the Holocaust*. New Haven, Conn.: Yale University Press, 1998.

Parsons, Anthony. "Conclusions and Recommendations." In *To Loose the Bands of Wickedness: International Intervention in Defense of Human Rights*, edited by Nigel S. Rodley. London: Brassey's, 1992.

Partnoy, Alicia. *The Little School: Tales of Disappearance and Survival in Argentina*. Pittsburgh: Cleis Press, 1986.

Pateman, Carole. *The Disorder of Women: Democracy, Feminism, and Political Theory*. Stanford, Calif.: Stanford University Press, 1989.

Patraka, Vivian M. *Spectacular Suffering: Theatre, Fascism and the Holocaust*. Bloomington: Indiana University Press, 1999.

Pepper, Thomas. *Singularities: Extremes of Theory in the Twentieth Century*. Cambridge: Cambridge University Press, 1997.

Peters, Edward. *Torture*. New York: Basil Blackwell, 1985.

Phelan, Peggy. *Mourning Sex: Performing Public Memories*. London and New York: Routledge, 1997.

Phelan, Peggy, and Lynda Hart, eds. *Acting Out: Feminist Performances*. Ann Arbor: University of Michigan Press, 1993.

Power, Samantha. *A Problem from Hell: America and the Age of Genocide*. New York: Basic Books, 2002.

Preis, Ann-Belinda S. "Human Rights as Cultural Practice: An Anthropological Critique." *Human Rights Quarterly* 18.2 (1996): 286–315.

Rainsford, Dominic, and Tim Woods, eds. *Critical Ethics: Text, Theory, and Responsibility*. New York: St. Martin's Press, 1999.

Ranciere, Jacques. "Who Is the Subject of the Rights of Man?" *South Atlantic Quarterly* 103.2/3 (2004): 297–310.

Rashid, Ahmed. *Taliban: Militant Islam, Oil, and Fundamentalism in Central Asia.* New Haven, Conn.: Yale University Press, 2000.

Renteln, Alison Dundes. *International Human Rights: Universalism versus Relativism.* Newbury Park: Sage Publications, 1990.

Ringelheim, Joan. "The Split between Gender and the Holocaust." In *Women in the Holocaust,* edited by Dalia Ofer and Lenore J. Weitzman. New Haven, Conn.: Yale University Press, 1998.

Rodley, Nigel S. "Collective Intervention to Protect Human Rights and Civilian Populations: The Legal Framework." In *To Loose the Bands of Wickedness: International Intervention in Defense of Human Rights,* edited by Nigel S. Rodley. London: Brassey's, 1992.

———, ed. *To Loose the Bands of Wickedness: International Intervention in Defense of Human Rights.* London: Brassey's, 1992.

Rokem, Freddie. *Performing History: Theatrical Representations of the Past in Contemporary Theatre,* edited by Thomas Postlewait. Iowa City: University of Iowa Press, 2000.

———. *Theatrical Space in Ibsen, Chekhov and Strindberg: Public Forms of Privacy.* Ann Arbor, Mich.: UMI Research Press, 1986.

Rosenfeld, Alvin H. *A Double Dying: Reflections on Holocaust Literature.* Bloomington: Indiana University Press, 1980.

Rothberg, Michael. *Traumatic Realism: The Demands of Holocaust Representation.* Minneapolis: University of Minnesota Press, 2000.

Rothchild, Sylvia, ed. *Voices from the Holocaust,* foreword by Elie Wiesel. New York: New American Library, 1981.

Saul, Jack. "Therapeutic Uses of Oral History Interviews in Clinical Practice." Workshop at the Oral History Association conference, St. Louis, Missouri, 2001.

Scarry, Elaine. *The Body in Pain: The Making and Unmaking of the World.* New York: Oxford University Press, 1985.

Schaffer, Kay, and Sidonie Smith. "Conjunctions: Life Narratives in the Field of Human Rights." *Biography* 27.1 (2004): 1–24.

Schechner, Richard. *Between Theater and Anthropology.* Philadelphia: University of Pennsylvania Press, 1985.

Schirmer, Jennifer. "Whose Truth? Where Are the Armed Actors in the Stoll-Menchú Controversy?" *Human Rights Quarterly* 25.1 (2003): 60–73.

Scoble, Harry M., and Laurie S. Wiseberg. "Problems of Comparative Research on Human Rights." In *Global Human Rights: Public Policies, Comparative Measures, and NGO Strategies,* edited by Ved P. Nanda, James R. Scarritt, and George W. Shepherd, Jr. Boulder, Colo.: Westview Press, 1981.

Shawcross, William. *The Quality of Mercy: Cambodia, Holocaust and Modern Conscience.* New York: Touchstone Books, 1984.

Shestack, Jerome J. "The Philosophic Foundations of Human Rights." *Human Rights Quarterly* 20.2 (1998): 201–34.

Shute, Stephen, and Susan Hurley, eds. *On Human Rights*. New York: Basic Books, 1993.

Sieghart, Paul. *The Lawful Rights of Mankind: An Introduction to the International Legal Code of Human Rights*. New York: Oxford University Press, 1985.

Skloot, Robert. *The Darkness We Carry: The Drama of the Holocaust*. Madison: University of Wisconsin Press, 1988.

———. *The Theatre of the Holocaust*. Madison: University of Wisconsin Press, 1982.

Smith, Paul. *Discerning the Subject*, foreword by John Mowitt. Minneapolis: University of Minnesota Press, 1988.

Softic, Elma. *Sarajevo Days, Sarajevo Nights*, translated by Nada Conic. Saint Paul, Minn: Hungry Mind Press, 1995.

Sommer, Doris. "Keeping Sacred Secrets." In *Life/Lines: Theorizing Women's Autobiography*, edited by Bella Brodzki and Celeste Schenck. Ithaca, N.Y.: Cornell University Press, 1988.

———. *The Real Thing: Testimonial Discourse and Latin America*, edited by Georg M. Gugelberger. Durham, N.C.: Duke University Press, 1996.

Spivak, Gayatri Chakravorty. *A Critique of Postcolonial Reason*. Cambridge, Mass., and London: Harvard University Press, 1999.

———. "Righting Wrongs." *South Atlantic Quarterly* 103.2/3 (2004): 523–81.

Sprinker, Michael, ed. *Ghostly Demarcations: A Symposium of Jacques Derrida's "Specters of Marx."* London and New York: Verso, 1999.

Stiglmayer, Alexandra, ed. *Mass Rape: The War against Women in Bosnia-Herzegovina*. Lincoln: University of Nebraska Press, 1994.

Stromquist, Nelly P. *Increasing Girls' and Women's Participation in Basic Education*. Paris: UNESCO, International Institute for Educational Planning, 1988.

Subbaro, K., and Laura Raney. *Social Gains from Female Education: A Cross-National Study*. World Bank Discussion Paper 194. Washington, D.C.: World Bank, 1993.

Tal, Kalí. *Worlds of Hurt: Reading the Literatures of Trauma*. Cambridge and New York: Cambridge University Press, 1996.

Taylor, Diana. *The Archive and the Repertoire*. London and Durham, N.C.: Duke University Press, 2003.

———. *Disappearing Acts: Spectacles of Gender and Nationalism in Argentina's "Dirty War."* Durham, N.C.: Duke University Press, 1997.

Theweleit, Klaus. *Male Fantasies*, Vol. 1. Minneapolis: University of Minnesota Press, 1987.

Tillion, Germaine. *Ravensbrück*, translated by Gerald Satterwhite. Garden City, N.Y.: Anchor Books, 1975.

Timerman, Jacobo. *Prisoner without a Name, Cell without a Number*. New York: Alfred A. Knopf, 1981.

Tumber, Howard, ed. *News: A Reader*. Oxford: Oxford University Press, 1999.

United Nations Development Program. *Human Development in South Asia 1998: The Education Challenge*. New York: United Nations Development Program, 1998.

———. *Human Development Report 1996: Economic Growth and Human Development*. New York: United Nations Development Program, 1996.

———. *Human Development Report 1995: Gender and Human Development*. New York: United Nations Development Program, 1995.

Universal Declaration of Human Rights. Adopted 10 December 1948, G.A. Res. 217A(III), U.N. Doc. A/810 (1948).

Van Der Veer, Peter. "The Victim's Tale: Memory and Forgetting in the Story of Violence." In *Violence, Identity and Self-Determination*, edited by Hent de Vries and Samuel Weber. Stanford, Calif.: Stanford University Press, 1997.

Veer, Guus van der. *Counselling and Therapy with Refugees and Victims of Trauma: Psychological Problems of Victims of War, Torture, and Repression*. 2nd ed. Chichester, U.K., and New York: John Wiley, 1998.

Verdirame, Guglielmo. "Testing the Effectiveness of International Norms: UN Humanitarian Assistance and Sexual Apartheid in Afghanistan." *Human Rights Quarterly* 23.3 (2001): 733–68.

Walzer, Michael. *On Toleration: The Castle Lectures in Ethics, Politics, and Economics*. New Haven, Conn.: Yale University Press, 1997.

Warner, Michael. *The Trouble with Normal: Sex, Politcs, and the Ethics of Queer Life*. Cambridge, Mass.: Harvard University Press, 1999.

Weine, Stevan M. *When History Is a Nightmare: Lives and Memories of Ethnic Cleansing in Bosnia-Herzegovina*. New Brunswick, N.J.: Rutgers University Press, 1999.

Wilden, Anthony. *Man and Woman, War and Peace: The Strategists Companion*. New York: Routledge, 1987.

Wilson, Richard A., ed. *Human Rights and Cultural Context: Anthropological Perspectives*. London: Pluto Press, 1997.

Wittig, Monique. *The Straight Mind and Other Essays*. Boston: Beacon Press, 1992.

World Bank. *Education for Afghans: World Bank Workshops, November 10, 1999, Islamabad, December 13, 1999, Washington D.C.* Conference Proceedings. Washington, D.C: World Bank, 1999. Available at http://lnweb18 .worldbank.org/SAR/sa.nsf/Attachments/98/$File/eduAfgh.pdf.

Wyschogrod, Edith. *An Ethics of Remembering: History, Heterology and the Nameless Others*. Chicago: University of Chicago Press, 1998.

———. *Spirit in Ashes: Hegel, Heidegger and Mass Death*. New Haven, Conn.: Yale University Press, 1985.

Young, James E. *The Texture of Memory: Holocaust Memorials and Meaning*. New Haven, Conn.: Yale University Press, 1993.

————. *Writing and Rewriting the Holocaust.* Bloomington: Indiana University Press, 1990.

Yúdice, George. "Testimonio and Postmodernism." In *The Real Thing: Testimonial Discourse and Latin America,* edited by Georg M. Gugelberger. Durham, N.C.: Duke University Press, 1996.

Zelizer, Barbie. *Remembering to Forget.* Chicago: University of Chicago Press, 1998.

Žižek, Slavoj. *For They Know Not What They Do: Enjoyment as a Political Factor.* New York: Verso, 1991.

INDEX

Absolute difference, 4, 92, 104–106, 118, 120–21, 129, 133–35, 144
Aesthetics, xii, 10, 143, 146
Aesthetic apparatus, 145
Abject, 5, 9, 108, 113, 119–21, 136, 141, 150–51, 256n7
Agamben, Giorgio, 2–16, 20, 70, 255n7
Afghanistan, ix, xiv, 18–19, 28, 32, 215–35, 248–50, 258n65, 276n13
Alienation, 118, 147, 149, 205–206
Amnesty International (AI), 16, 27, 35–41
Argentina, xiv, 29, 68–69, 150–85 passim, 194, 212, 258n41, 265n46
Atrocity, vii–xvi, 2–19, 75–80, 89–110, 118–26, 136–41, 143–54, 179–80, 217–19, 223–25, 245–53, 255n2, 262n22; as spectacle, 11; event, xiv, 12, 79, 99, 103, 110, 249–50; experience, 99, 146, 245–46; mass, xi, 15–16, 79, 100, 122, 144, 217; post-atrocity, xii, 79, 103
Authentic, 49, 75, 94–98, 143–48, 153–54, 191, 204, 211–12, 220–22

Biosovereignty, 7, 8, 20
"Blindness of seeing," 155
Bosnia, 66, 189, 195–97, 202, 251
Bricolage, 148, 161–62

Buber-Neumann, Margarete, xiv, 76–77, 94, 106, 111–41, 145, 152, 155, 160, 206, 211–12
Burqa, xii, 69, 227, 229, 255n3

Chaudhuri, Una, 45–48
Citizen, xi, 5, 18–20, 25–26, 40, 72, 156, 161, 191, 197; international citizen, 29, 35–36, 66, 186
Civil, 36, 41; and political life, 65, 69, 72, 191; civilization, 55, 59–61, 174, 211, 217; civilized, 176, 198, 204, 207, 216–17; society, xiv, 17, 216, 220–22, 230–33; war, 19, 227, 234
Community, xii–xvi, 8–26, 35–39, 70–71, 89, 93–8, 100–17, 130, 144–49, 163–64, 172, 193, 212, 235; ethical, xvi, 224; global, 224, 243; human, 85–89, 104, 107–108, 202, 249; international, 19, 190, 224, 239; of witness, 98, 127, 224
Complicity, xiv, 8, 56, 62, 104–105, 122, 137, 149, 153, 172, 181–83, 198, 202–203
Copjec, Joan, 105, 260n16
Cosmopolitanism, 190, 195, 198, 204, 211–14
Covenant on Civil and Political Rights: 22–24, 28–30, 38, 66, 72

283